POVERTY

AND

PROGRESS

REALITIES
AND MYTHS
ABOUT GLOBAL
POVERTY

POVERTY

AND

PROGRESS

WITHDRAWN

DEEPAK LAL

CATO
INSTITUTE
WASHINGTON, D.C.

Library of Congress Cataloging-in-Publication Data

Lal, Deepak.
    Poverty and progress : realities and myths about global poverty / Deepak Lal.
      p. cm.
    ISBN 978-1-938048-83-8 (cloth : alk. paper) -- ISBN 978-1-938048-84-5 (paper-
back : alk. paper) ISBN 978-1-938048-85-2 (ebook)
    1. Poverty. 2. Economic development. 3. Economic development--Africa.
4. Development economics. I. Title.

    HC79.P6L346 2013
    338.91—dc23

                               2013006655
Printed in the United States of America.

CATO INSTITUTE
1000 Massachusetts Ave., N.W.
Washington, D.C. 20001
www.cato.org

Contents

Contents

List of Tables, Figures, and Boxes

Tables

Figures

Boxes

Introduction

In the late 1980s, I codirected with Hla Myint a vast comparative study of the political economy of poverty, equity, and growth for the World Bank based on detailed in-depth studies of 21 developing countries, conducted by some of the leading development economists in the world.[1] The volume synthesizing these studies was finally completed in 1994 and published by the Clarendon Press in 1996—after the publications committee of the World Bank in its wisdom disowned it by not providing the subsidy normally given to World Bank publications. This was fortunate, as *The Political Economy of Poverty, Equity and Growth–A Comparative Study*,[2] besides meeting the market test, unlike most World Bank publications, was well received, being nominated as "an outstanding academic book" by *Choice* in 1997. And it is still selling well!

This ancient history is relevant to this book, as it reveals the dyspeptic response (only strengthened over the years) of the foreign-aid industry to anything that smacks of the classical-liberal viewpoint from which the book was written and which if adopted would lead to the euthanasia of these Lords of Poverty.

The central message of this book is that efficient economic growth is the only means to alleviate the ancient structural poverty[3] of the Third World, and that if countries grew rapidly, with per capita income growing above 3 percent per year, the much derided processes of "trickle down" would rapidly diminish structural poverty. This judgment has been resoundingly confirmed in the last two decades by the largest reduction in poverty seen in human history, as the two emerging giants—India and China—have increasingly adopted classical-liberal economic policies, which have led to large increases in their growth rates of per capita income. So when the Social Affairs Unit in London asked me if I would write this book as part of a research project funded by the

Templeton Foundation, I agreed, since I was curious to see how, if at all, views about alleviating Third World poverty had changed in the two decades since our comparative study was conducted. The Cato Institute, where I am a senior fellow, kindly agreed to publish the U.S. edition of the book. This is timely because of the torrent of writings and initiatives by the world's great and the good who seek to end poverty, particularly in Africa. This in turn has led to a burgeoning literature that seems both to support and criticize the continued desire to use tax money (both domestic and international) to eliminate this ancient scourge. Unlike my earlier book, this one is not based on any new primary research but is more a summing up and critique of the secondary literature that has evolved on the subject since the 1990s.

The first chapter summarizes the evidence I find most credible to assess the current state of Third World poverty according to the now conventional head-count index of those below a $1-per-day poverty line using 1993 purchasing power. It also summarizes the evidence on how the West ascended and the Rest are now slowly ascending from mass poverty. This has occurred through the creation of mineral- and energy-based economies, which can generate modern Promethean intensive growth, as opposed to the traditional extensive growth of organic land-based, energy-dependent economies. I show how the rapid growth generated since the 1980s, during the second period of globalization, has led to the greatest alleviation of mass structural poverty in human history.

The second chapter charts the rapid convergence of most developing countries with the West in other social indices of well-being relating to education, health, and life expectancy.

The third chapter looks at two other types of poverty—conjunctural and destitution—and examines how public (government) transfers compare with private ones in dealing with them. It also looks at international transfers: private (international remittances from migrants) and public (foreign aid).

The fourth chapter looks at the political economy of poverty alleviation. It also summarizes the novel features of the architecture of the Lal–Myint comparative study in terms of two classification schemes: one relating to the relative abundance of land and natural resources, the other to their polities. Welcome features of the academic research in the last two decades have been the recognition that "government failure" is more ubiquitous than purported "market failure" and the incorporation of the "precious bane" of natural resources—though these analyses use methods I do not find persuasive, for reasons outlined in Chapter 6.

This concludes the first part, providing the reality in the subtitle of this book. The following chapters of part two examine some of the myths.

Chapter 5 is concerned with exposing the numbers game still being played by the international organizations, which exaggerate the extent of world poverty and minimize the extent of poverty alleviation that has already taken place in the current second historical period of globalization since the late 1980s. It also points to the fragility of the international purchasing power parity (PPP) databases increasingly being used unthinkingly by young researchers in their burgeoning technocratic statistical analyzes.

My earlier book provided a methodological discussion of the comparative-study method based on analytical economic histories of different countries. With this method, Mill's[4] "method of agreement" and "method of difference" can be combined by using several positive cases along with suitable negative cases as contrasts for causal qualitative induction,[5] to make the pattern predictions that Hayek[6] emphasized are possible in sciences of "complex" phenomena (such as biology and economics). This contrasts with the specific predictions based on quantitative induction that use only Mill's Method of Difference, but which, per Hayek, is only possible in the sciences of "simple" orders like physics.

With the availability of various cross-country data sets of dubious quality, a whole new industry, attempting quantitative induction, claims to find all sorts of causal relationships explaining the development process, in particular the role of foreign aid. It seeks to encompass a whole host of variables, including amorphous ones like institutions and politics, based on cross-country regressions using the econometric technique of instrumental variables (IV). Some of these studies that in my view are purveying statistical snake oil are considered in Chapter 6.

That chapter also critically examines another method (increasingly popular among a younger generation of scholars) of providing "scientific" policy advice for alleviating poverty. This is the method of randomized trials, which the *randomistas*—as we may label them—claim provide the same robust conclusions about "treatments" as randomized medical trials to determine the efficacy and side effects of various drugs. I take a cool look at the "scientific" pretensions of this method and what, if anything, it provides for understanding Third World poverty and the policies for its alleviation.

One of the banes of "development economics" has been its attraction with theoretical curiosa. I discussed many of these in my 1983 critique, *The Poverty of Development Economics* (Lal 1983, 2002). A number of these—including vicious circles of poverty and the need for a Big Push—that were completely discredited by the early 1980s have recently been resurrected to provide various dirigiste panaceas to eliminate world poverty. These have been revived along with new-fangled theories being peddled by mathematical economists and some economic historians. These are discussed in Chapter 7.

One of the major change in emphasis from the early "development economics" has been a welcome shift towards understanding the microeconomics of development. Some of the insights from the more careful studies based on microeconomic household surveys are highlighted in Chapter 8. But there has also been the development by the pretentiously named Poverty Lab at MIT of randomized controlled experiments as a method for evaluating foreign-aid projects, of which I take a skeptical view. This chapter also critically examines the current fashion to see microfinance as the panacea for Third World poverty.

Chapter 9 examines the burgeoning literature on saving Africa. With a host of pop stars, sundry Western politicians, and celebrity-seeking economists advocating massive foreign aid for Africa on the lines of the postwar Marshall Plan for Europe, this chapter critically examines the desirability and feasibility of this latest plea for international public charity by the world's great and the good.

Chapter 10 critically examines the latest twist in promoting global dirigisme based on the global warming scare. It argues that the means advocated to mitigate this purported global catastrophe in fact represent the greatest potential threat to the world's poor.

A final chapter provides my conclusions.

This book has been written for the general reader, say, one who reads *The Economist*. Any unavoidable technical discussions to make my judgments credible to my professional peers have been put into boxes that the general reader can skip without losing the thread of the argument.

I am grateful to David Henderson, a long-time friend and former colleague at University College London, for comments on an earlier draft and for saving me from errors and infelicities of expression.

PART ONE

REALITY

1. The Ascent from Mass Poverty

In thinking about poverty, it is useful to make a distinction between three types: structural, conjunctural, and destitution.

The first—mass structural poverty—is what most concerns observers. It is the type that underlies the numbers calculated by various national and international agencies of the absolute poor—globally and in particular countries. Given the endowments of land, labor, and capital, and the existing technology, if per capita income is so low that any redistribution of income will merely lead to a redistribution of poverty, rather than its alleviation, mass structural poverty can only be eliminated by rapid economic growth.

By contrast, destitution and conjunctural poverty[1] require income transfers for amelioration if their sufferers are to survive. The major difference between these types of poverty is that while destitute individuals have no means of making a living and hence must receive permanent income transfers to survive, the conjunctural poor need temporary transfers, since their poverty is caused by climatic fluctuations (as is common in agrarian economies) or the trade cycle (in industrial economies) and can be expected to end with the upturn in the weather or the economy. These transfers can be from either private donors or the government, though much of the passion in continuing debates concerns the latter.

Ancient Mass Structural Poverty

Table 1.1, which summarizes Angus Maddison's estimates of the level of per capita income in different regions of the world (and separately for India, China, and Japan) from 1–2003 AD, shows that for most of human history until 1000 AD, the per capita income of the world and most of its regions was about $450 in 1990 purchasing power dollars per year. As the internationally accepted absolute poverty line is roughly $1 per day, this suggests that the level

Table 1.1
LEVELS OF PER CAPITA GDP, POPULATION, AND GDP: WORLD AND MAJOR REGIONS, 1-2003 AD

	1	1000	1500	1820	1870	1913	1950	1973	2003
Levels of per capita GDP (1990 international dollars)									
Western Europe	576	427	771	1,202	1,960	3,457	4,578	11,417	19,912
Western Offshoots	400	400	400	1,202	2,419	5,233	9,268	16,179	28,039
West	**569**	**426**	**753**	**1,202**	**2,050**	**3,988**	**6,297**	**13,379**	**23,710**
Asia	456	465	568	581	556	696	717	1,718	4,434
Latin America	400	400	416	691	676	1,494	2,503	4,513	5,786
E. Europe & f. USSR	406	400	498	686	941	1,558	2,602	5,731	5,705
Africa	472	428	416	421	500	637	890	1,410	1,549
Rest	**453**	**451**	**538**	**580**	**609**	**880**	**1,126**	**2,379**	**4,217**
World	**467**	**450**	**567**	**667**	**873**	**1,526**	**2,113**	**4,091**	**6,516**
Interregional Spread	1.4:1	1.2:1	1.9:1	2.9:1	4.8:1	8.2:1	13.0:1	11.5:1	18.1:1
West/Rest Spread	1.3:1	0.9:1	1.4:1	2.1:1	2.3:1	4.5:1	5.6:1	5.6:1	5.7:1
Population (millions)									
Western Europe	25	26	57	133	188	261	305	359	395
Western Offshoots	1	1	3	11	46	111	176	251	346
West	**26**	**27**	**60**	**144**	**234**	**372**	**481**	**610**	**741**

Asia	168	183	284	710	765	978	1,383	2,249	3,734
Latin America	6	11	18	22	40	81	166	308	541
E. Europe & f. USSR	9	14	30	91	142	236	267	360	409
Africa	17	32	47	74	90	125	228	390	853
Rest	**200**	**241**	**378**	**898**	**1,038**	**1,419**	**2,045**	**3,307**	**5,537**
World	**226**	**267**	**438**	**1,042**	**1,272**	**1,791**	**2,526**	**3,916**	**6,279**
% West/World	11.5	10.1	13.7	13.8	18.4	20.8	19.1	15.6	11.8

Levels of GDP (billions of 1990 international dollars)

Western Europe	14.4	10.9	44.2	159.9	367.5	902.2	1,396	4,097	7,857
Western Offshoots	0.4	0.7	1.1	13.5	111.5	582.9	1,635	4,058	9,708
West	**14.9**	**11.7**	**45.3**	**173.4**	**479.0**	**1,485.2**	**3,032**	**8,155**	**17,565**
Asia	76.7	84.9	161.3	412.5	425.6	680.7	991	3,864	16,555
Latin America	2.2	4.6	7.3	14.9	27.3	120.8	416	1,389	3,132
E. Europe & f. USSR	3.5	5.4	15.2	62.6	133.8	367.1	695	2,064	2,339
Africa	8.0	13.8	19.4	31.3	45.2	79.5	203	550	1,322
Rest	**90.5**	**108.7**	**203.2**	**521.3**	**632.0**	**1,248.1**	**2,303**	**7,868**	**23,348**
World	**105.4**	**120.4**	**248.4**	**694.6**	**1,111.2**	**2,733.3**	**5,337**	**16,022**	**40,913**
% West/World	14.1	9.7	18.2	25.0	43.1	54.3	56.8	50.9	42.9

SOURCE: Maddison (2007): p. 70.

of income of someone at the poverty line would be $365 per year. Given the pervasive social stratification in Eurasian agrarian economies, with a small upper crust of merchants, priests, and warriors having a higher income than the peasants whose labor provided the surplus to keep them in relative luxury, the mass of the population would have been at or below the poverty line. Thus for most of human history, mass structural poverty has been the norm.

Growth did occur in these premodern agrarian economies (see Table 1.2), but it was the extensive kind, with output expanding with population as new land was brought into cultivation, but leaving the per capita income virtually constant.

But even in these Eurasian agrarian economies there were periods of intensive growth, with output expanding faster than the population. This rise in per capita income was usually associated with the rise of empires. They enlarged the common economic space by integrating hitherto autarkic regions into a common market, leading to gains from trade and the division of labor emphasized by Adam Smith, as well as from technological exchanges. The increase in per capita income from this Smithian intensive growth, however, could not be sustained, as the economy reverted to a long period of extensive growth with a higher per capita income. With their climacteric, these imperial agrarian economies remained in equilibrium at a relatively high level. Only recently have the two major ones (India and China) begun generating unbounded Promethean intensive growth.

Table 1.3 shows the data for the three dominant Eurasian imperial systems in 0 AD—Rome, China, and India. Of these, only the two Asian imperial "states" survive to our day. Indian per capita income was probably the highest, since it had reached its climacteric with the imperial unification of the subcontinent by the Mauryas in the sixth century BC. Thereafter, per capita income stagnated because only extensive growth occurred until the British Raj introduced the first whiff of Promethean growth in the 19th century.

China did not experience its climacteric till the Sung unified the lands of the Yellow and Yangtze rivers in the 11th century, leading to a higher per capita income equilibrium than in India. China then entered a prolonged period of extensive growth, with output expanding in line with the steady increase in its population. Rome reached its climacteric during the reign of Augustus in the

Table 1.2
GROWTH RATES OF PER CAPITA GDP, POPULATION, AND GDP, 1–2003 AD
(ANNUAL AVERAGE COMPOUND GROWTH RATES)

	1–1000	1000–1500	1500–1820	1820–70	1870–1913	1913–50	1950–73	1973–2003
Per capita GDP								
Western Europe	−0.03	0.12	0.14	0.98	1.33	0.76	4.05	1.87
Western Offshoots	0.00	0.00	0.34	1.41	1.81	1.56	2.45	1.85
West	**−0.03**	**0.11**	**0.15**	**1.07**	**1.56**	**1.24**	**3.33**	**1.93**
Asia	0.00	0.04	0.01	−0.09	0.52	0.08	3.87	3.21
Latin America	0.00	0.01	0.16	−0.03	1.86	1.40	2.60	0.83
E. Europe & f. USSR	0.00	0.04	0.10	0.63	1.18	1.40	3.49	−0.02
Africa	−0.01	−0.01	0.00	0.35	0.57	0.91	2.02	0.32
Rest	**0.00**	**0.04**	**0.02**	**0.10**	**0.86**	**0.67**	**3.31**	**1.93**
World	**0.00**	**0.05**	**0.05**	**0.54**	**1.30**	**0.88**	**2.91**	**1.56**
Population								
Western Europe	0.00	0.16	0.26	0.69	0.77	0.42	0.71	0.32
Western Offshoots	0.05	0.08	0.44	2.86	2.07	1.25	1.54	1.08
West	**0.00**	**0.16**	**0.27**	**0.98**	**1.08**	**0.70**	**1.04**	**0.65**

(continued)

Table 1.2
(continued)

	1–1000	1000–1500	1500–1820	1820–70	1870–1913	1913–50	1950–73	1973–2003
Asia	0.01	0.09	0.29	0.15	0.57	0.94	2.14	1.70
Latin America	0.07	0.09	0.07	1.26	1.63	1.96	2.72	1.90
E. Europe & f. USSR	0.05	0.15	0.35	0.89	1.19	0.33	1.31	0.43
Africa	0.06	0.07	0.15	0.40	0.75	1.65	2.36	2.64
Rest	**0.02**	**0.09**	**0.27**	**0.29**	**0.73**	**0.99**	**2.11**	**1.73**
World	**0.02**	**0.10**	**0.27**	**0.40**	**0.80**	**0.93**	**1.93**	**1.59**
GDP								
Western Europe	−0.03	0.28	0.40	1.68	2.11	1.19	4.79	2.19
Western Offshoots	0.05	0.08	0.78	4.31	3.92	2.83	4.03	2.95
West	**−0.02**	**0.27**	**0.42**	**2.05**	**2.67**	**1.95**	**4.40**	**2.59**
Asia	0.01	0.13	0.29	0.06	1.10	1.02	6.09	4.97
Latin America	0.07	0.09	0.22	1.23	3.52	3.40	5.38	2.75
E. Europe & f. USSR	0.04	0.21	0.44	1.53	2.37	1.74	4.85	0.42
Africa	0.05	0.07	0.15	0.75	1.32	2.57	4.43	2.97
Rest	**0.02**	**0.13**	**0.29**	**0.39**	**1.60**	**1.67**	**5.49**	**3.69**
World	**0.01**	**0.15**	**0.32**	**0.94**	**2.12**	**1.82**	**4.90**	**3.17**

SOURCE: Maddison (2007), p. 71.

Table 1.3
GDP and Population for Ancient Powers, 0 AD

	GDP (in millions of 1990 U.S. dollars)	Population (in thousands)	GDP per capita
Roman Empire	20,961	55,000	381
China	26,820	59,600	450
India-1	33,750	75,000	450
India-2	55,146	100,000	551

Sources: Maddison (2001), pp. 241, 261, 264; Goldsmith (1984). Tons of gold converted into U.S. dollars at the average 1990 price; Lal (1989); 1965 dollars converted into 1990 dollars using GDP deflator.

first decades of the Christian century, when its imperial expansion ended. With the fall of the western empire to the barbarians in 476 AD, western Europe saw a steep fall in its living standards as economic disorder replaced the order provided by the Roman imperium. It did not reach the Augustan standard of living till the 16th century (Lal 2004).

The Rise of Capitalism

This slow western ascent began with the creation of an institution unique in the ancient Eurasian civilizations—capitalism. Though definitions of capitalism are still contested by social scientists, most of these conflate the existence of its agents—merchant capitalists—and instruments—markets, bill of exchange, banks, etc.—with the institution that arose only in the 11th century. Capitalists and their instruments have existed since at least 2000 BC in all the ancient Eurasian civilizations, as testified by Mesopotamian tablets of the *Karum*. But capitalists' property rights remained insecure. It was only when they were finally protected from the predations of the state that the institution of capitalism arose in one part of Eurasia in the 11th century (Lal 2006). I have argued in *Unintended Consequences* that this was due to two papal revolutions. A brief account of this emergence of capitalism follows.

Merchant capitalists were a necessary "evil" in all the ancient agrarian civilizations because of the social stratification that emerged for two major reasons. First, all the ancient Eurasian civilizations were centers of the sedentary agriculture practiced in the river valleys where they arose. But they were constantly under threat from two sets of nomadic roving bandits: from the Steppes in North Asia and the deserts of Arabia. Unlike the inhabitants of the settled agrarian communities, these nomads had not eschewed the predatory and warlike ways of our hunter-gatherer ancestors. They mounted periodic raids on the rich sedentary civilizations. To protect these riverine agrarian civilizations, wielders of the sword became a necessity (Lal 2004). These warriors sought to extend the boundaries of their states to naturally defensible borders, creating imperial polities—and these warriors needed to be fed.

This provides the second reason for Eurasian social stratification. In the ancient world (unlike much of Eurasia today), land was abundant, but people to work it were scarce. This meant that if attempts were made to tax peasants, implicitly or explicitly, they could flee these predations. It was necessary to tie them down to the land. Various institutions like serfdom, slavery, and the caste system were devised to achieve this aim, allowing an agricultural surplus to be extracted to feed the warriors who lived in towns (Lal 2005a). To justify these various forms of social control, "people of the book" (priests) arose to provide the cosmological beliefs that underwrote these civilizations. Thus social stratification of the wielders of the sword, the keepers of the book, and the yeomen of the plow emerged in all these Eurasian civilizations.

There was also the need to move the agricultural surplus from the villages to the towns, where the soldiers and priests lived. This service was provided by merchants and traders—the ancient capitalists. In the process, many of them became very rich. But their wealth was insecure, being subject to periodic raids by the predatory state. Nor was this predation unpopular. As risk takers and novelty seekers, these capitalists were seen as dangerous to the settled ways of stable agrarian societies. They were looked down upon and found socially unacceptable by the inhabitants of these civilizations.

It was the 11th-century legal papal revolution of Pope Gregory VII that provided a framework to protect the property of these merchant

16

traders. It created the church-state and all the modern institutions of capitalism. Through its canon law, enforced on recalcitrant princes by the threat of excommunication, the church-state protected property throughout Christendom from the predation of individual states. This made the property rights of capitalists secure and gave them freedom of action. This creation of all the legal and institutional requirements of a market economy eventually put the West on a different economic trajectory from its Eurasian peers. These institutions allowed capitalists to indulge in the "creative destruction" that Joseph Schumpeter saw as the hallmark of capitalism (Schumpeter 1950).

This 11th-century papal legal revolution was precipitated by an earlier papal family revolution in the sixth century, which also introduced what became a unique feature of the cosmological beliefs of the West compared with the other Eurasian civilizations—individualism.[2] The rise of individualism in turn led to the scientific revolution, the Renaissance, and with the institution of capitalism after the 11th-century papal legal revolution, the slow rise of the West. The Promethean growth engendered by the associated Industrial Revolution then began to end the West's age-old structural poverty.

This Promethean growth was based on the slow-rolling Industrial Revolution's harnessing a new source of energy to fuel the economy—fossil fuels (Wrigley 1988). Unlike land, the traditional source of all the energy utilized—mechanical, heat, protoindustrial—which, being limited, was subject to diminishing returns as the population expanded, the unlimited energy stored in fossil fuels allowed first the western end of Eurasia and then its new outposts in the Americas to escape from this age-old constraint on intensive growth. The rise in per capita incomes this permitted enabled these economies to banish the scourge of structural poverty.

Divergence and Convergence in Per Capita Incomes

Beginning in the 11th century, with its combination of capitalist institutions and individualistic values promoted by the twin papal revolutions, western Europe began the slow gradual economic ascent that is misleadingly called the Industrial Revolution. This led to the Great Divergence between the West and the Rest. Although

17

per capita income was roughly the same in 1000 AD, by 1973 it was 5.6 times greater in the West. This historically unprecedented acceleration of growth, first slowly and then from the mid-19th century spectacularly, allowed the West finally to eliminate mass structural poverty.

The emergence of European seafaring powers gradually brought much of the Rest into the ambit of the gunpowder empires of the West through various forms of imperial and colonial control. With the consolidation of British power after its victory over the French at Waterloo, and the adoption of classical liberalism in the mid-19th-century, the British, through their formal and informal global empire, created the first liberal international economic order (LIEO). This was the first period of globalization.

The 19th-century LIEO saw a distinctive pattern of international trade develop: with the "North" (mainly western Europe and later the United States) specializing in the new products and technologies of the Industrial Revolution and experiencing Promethean intensive growth, and the "South" (which included the current Third World and the areas of "new" settlement in the Americas and Australasia) specializing in primary products and experiencing Smithian intensive growth.

The three pillars of the 19th-century LIEO promoted by the British were free trade, the gold standard, and a legal framework for protecting international property rights. These allowed the worldwide expansion of trade and commerce. They also allowed the empire to fulfill a

> wider mission which can be summarized as the *world's first comprehensive development programme*. After 1815, Britain aimed to put in place a set of like-minded allies who would cooperate . . . [in creating] its vision of a liberal international order bound together by mutual interest in commercial progress and underpinned by a respect for property, credit and responsible government, preferably of the kind found at home [Cain and Hopkins 2002, 650; emphasis added].

And compared with the previous millennia, the results were stupendous. It was at the height of this 19th-century LIEO, from 1850–1914, that many parts of the Third World for the first time experienced intensive growth for a sustained period. Lloyd Reynolds in his survey of the economic histories of 41 developing countries dated the turning points when developing countries entered the era of intensive growth (with a sustained rise in per capita incomes), as compared with the ubiquitous extensive growth of the past (when output growth just kept up with population) as shown in Table 1.4.

Table 1.4
A TURNING POINT CHRONOLOGY

1840	Chile	1900	Cuba
1850	Brazil	1910	Korea
1850	Malaysia	1920	Morocco
1850	Thailand	1925	Venezuela
1860	Argentina	1925	Zambia
1870	Burma	1947	India
1876	Mexico	1947	Pakistan
1880	Algeria	1949	China
1880	Japan	1950	Iran
1880	Peru	1950	Iraq
1880	Sri Lanka	1950	Turkey
1885	Colombia	1952	Egypt
1895	Taiwan	1965	Indonesia
1895	Ghana	—	Afghanistan
1895	Ivory Coast	—	Bangladesh
1895	Nigeria	—	Ethiopia
1895	Kenya	—	Mozambique
1900	Uganda	—	Nepal
1900	Zimbabwe	—	Sudan
1900	Tanzania	—	Zaire
1900	Philippines		

SOURCE: Reynolds (1983), Table 1, p. 958.

Maddison sums up the achievements of this period as follows (Maddison 2001, 100):

> From 1870 to 1913 world per capita GDP rose 1.3% p.a. compared with 0.5% in 1820–70 and 0.07% in 1700–1820. The acceleration was due to more rapid technological progress, and the diffusionist forces unleashed by the liberal economic order of which the United Kingdom was the main architect. It was not a process of global equalization, but there were significant income gains in all parts of the world. Australia and the United States reached higher levels than the United Kingdom by 1913. Growth was faster than in the United Kingdom in most of Western and Eastern Europe, in Ireland, in all the Western Offshoots, in Latin America and Japan. In India, other Asia (except China) and Africa, the advances were much more modest, but per capita income rose more than a quarter, between 1870 and 1913.

The 19th-century LIEO died in the First World War on the killing fields of Flanders. There followed an interwar period marked by the gradual weakening of the British empire and its ability to maintain its global hegemony. With the new rising global hegemon—the United States—unwilling to take over the British responsibility for maintaining global order, a period of grave economic and political disorder followed—with a Great Depression and the Second World War. The turning inwards of most of the world in the 1930s dealt a fatal blow to the LIEO. Only after the second war, with the Americans willing to take on the global responsibility for world order, did a partial reconstruction of a new LIEO begin. But this second LIEO initially covered only the industrial countries, since much of the Third World, burnt by its close 19th-century integration into the global economy, turned inwards instead of embracing the openness advocated and gradually implemented by the new global hegemon.

The opening of China by Deng Xiaoping to the forces of globalization in 1979, and of India in 1991, with its steady move from the plan to the market, marks the beginning of the second era of globalization. The Third World debt crisis of the 1980s had already led many countries in Latin America and Africa to abandon their inward-looking dirigiste past—most often under World Bank and International Monetary Fund tutelage. With the implosion in 1991 of the countries of "really existing socialism" and their embrace of markets, by the early 1990s another global LIEO was in place. How did this changing global landscape over two centuries affect the growth of per capita income and the resultant fate of the world's absolute poor?

Mass Structural Poverty 1820–2000

The worldwide growth engendered by the first era of globalization marked the beginning of the global diminution of the mass structural poverty that had afflicted mankind for millennia. Bhalla (2002) has put together data on the changing extent of absolute poverty in the world, measured by the number of poor people with less than $1.50 per day in 1993 purchasing power parity (PPP) dollars. These estimates are given in Figure 1.1a for the resulting head count ratio (HCR)—the proportion of the world's population falling below this poverty line—from 1820 to 2000. The total numbers of those in absolute poverty for these years is charted in Figure 1.1b. Table 1.5 shows the changes in income and the reduction in the world HCR of poverty for various years.

Three periods can be broadly identified: the 19th-century period of globalization; the interwar period from 1929 to 1950, when globalization stalled and was reversed; and the period from 1950, when a new international liberal economic order was reconstructed. But since the Third World did not join this LIEO till 1980, the true second period of globalization begins in 1980. Bhalla then calculates what he calls the "poverty reduction yield of growth": the decline in the poverty HCR brought about by each 10 percent of growth in per capita incomes—the "bang for the buck" in poverty reduction. From Table 5, it is apparent that the head count poverty ratio was falling during both the 19th century and current periods of globalization, but rose during the period of anti-globalization in the interwar period. The highest yield in terms of poverty reduction has been since 1980, when the Third World started to integrate with the world economy. Africa is the only region where poverty has not declined, and it is also the region least integrated into the world economy. The largest decline in poverty has been in Asia, but Latin America and the Middle East have also seen declines in poverty (see Table 1.6). So poverty today is by and large an African problem (Fig. 1.2), and it

Figure 1.1
WORLD POVERTY 1820–2000

a.

Head count ratio for extreme poverty (percent)
($1.50 a day, 1993 PPP prices)[a]

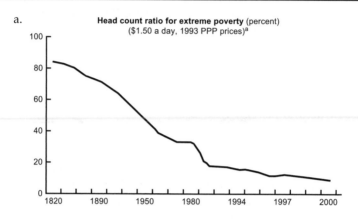

b.

Number of poor people (in millions)[b]

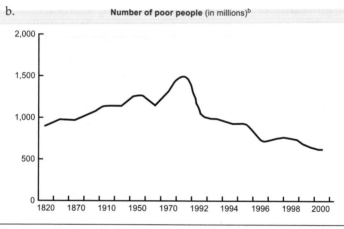

a. The poverty line used is $1.50 a day, national accounts means, 1993 prices. This is roughly equal to the popular $1-a-day, 1985-prices poverty line, when such a line is used in survey data. The $1.50-a-day poverty line incorporates within it the tendency for the rich to understate their expenditures to a greater degree than poor people, as well as the tendency for the rich to not be fully covered by surveys. b. Figures for the number of poor are computed by multiplying the estimated head count ratio by the world population.

SOURCES: Bhalla (2002), Figure 9.1, p. 144. Derived from Deininger and Squire (1996); World Income Inequality Database, available at http://www.wider.unu.edu/wiid; Asian Development Bank (2002); World Bank, World Development Indicators, CD-ROM. For years prior to 1950, data were taken from Bourguignon and Morrisson (2002).

Table 1.5
POVERTY REDUCTION YIELD OF GROWTH

Time Period	Income		Head Count Ratio		Yield
	Change	Equivalent 20-year Change	Change	Equivalent 20-year Change	
1820–50	11.1	7.4	−2.4	−1.6	2.2
1850–70	19.0	19.0	−6.1	−6.1	3.2
1870–90	22.4	22.4	−3.6	−3.6	1.6
1890–1910	27.1	27.1	−6.1	−6.1	2.3
1910–29	21.9	23.0	−9.3	−9.8	4.3
1929–50	16.6	15.8	17.3	16.5	−10.4
1950–70	51.3	51.3	−12.4	−12.4	2.4
1960–80	42.9	42.9	−4.6	−4.6	1.1
1970–90	28.2	28.2	−14.6	−14.6	5.2
1980–90	11.2	22.4	−13.6	−27.2	12.2
1990–2000	12.6	25.2	−9.7	−19.4	7.7
1980–2000	23.8	23.8	−23.3	−23.3	9.8
Mean		25.7		−9.4	3.5
Standard Deviation		11.6		11.5	5.6

NOTES: When a time period is either less or more than 20 years, the 20-year "equivalent" income or head count ratio change is presented, i.e., the actual change is multiplied by a fraction equal to (20 divided by the number of years): for example, figures for 1910–29 will be multiplied by (20 divided by 1 g). The yield of growth is defined as the decline in poverty (head count ratio) brought about by each 10 percent growth in per capita incomes (data up through 1950) or per capita consumption (data for 1950 to 2000). Both income and consumption figures are national accounts base. The poverty line used is $1.50 a day, national accounts means, 1993 prices, for data for 1950–2000.

SOURCES: Bhalla (2002), p. 145. Derived from Deininger and Squire (1996); World Income Inequality Database, available at http://www.wider.unu.edu/wiid; Asian Development Bank (2002); World Bank, World Development Indicators, CD-ROM. For years prior to 1950, data were taken from Bourguignon and Morrisson (2002).

Table 1.6
WHERE DID POVERTY DECLINE?

Region and Country	Population, 2000 (millions)	Change in Number of Poor People ($1.50-a-day poverty line)		
		1960–80	1980–2000	1960–2000
East Asia				
China	1,265	206.8	−727.0	−520.2
Indonesia	210	8.1	−67.4	−59.3
Thailand	61	−5.9	−7.4	−13.3
Vietnam	78	16.5	−24.9	−8.4
Total	**1,894**	**226.2**	**−841.0**	**−614.8**
South Asia				
Bangladesh	131	9.7	2.1	11.8
India	1,011	92.4	−207.2	−114.8
Pakistan	137	−7.9	−16.0	−23.8
Total	**1,355**	**101.2**	**−205.0**	**−103.8**
Sub-Saharan Africa				
Ethiopia	65	9.7	23.3	33.0
Kenya	30	4.9	5.6	10.5
Nigeria	129	11.3	50.9	62.2
Tanzania	35	6.6	12.4	18.9
Uganda	22	4.06	−1.76	2.31
Lesotho	2	−0.25	0.10	−0.15
Mauritania	3	−0.22	0.11	−0.11
Total	**661**	**70.6**	**173.8**	**244.4**
Middle East and North Africa				
Egypt	64	−11.8	−1.2	−13.0
Total	**374**	**−22.2**	**19.4**	**−2.8**

(continued)

Table 1.6
(continued)

Region and Country	Population, 2000 (millions)	Change in Number of Poor People ($1.50-a-day poverty line)		
		1960–80	1980–2000	1960–2000
Latin America				
Brazil	172	−14.1	8.9	−5.2
Mexico	97	−6.8	0.0	−6.8
Total	**518**	**−21.8**	**14.0**	**−7.8**
All less-developed countries	**4,928**	**348.2**	**−831.6**	**−483.4**

NOTE: The poverty line used is $1.50 a day, national accounts means, 1993 prices. This is roughly equal to the popular $1-a-day, 1985-prices poverty line, when such a line is used in survey data. The $1.50-a-day poverty line incorporates within it the tendency for the rich to understate their expenditures to a greater degree than poor people, as well as the tendency for the rich to not be fully covered by surveys.

SOURCES: Deininger and Squire (1996); World Income Inequality Database, available at http://www.wider.unu.edu/wiid; Asian Development Bank (2002); World Bank, World Development Indicators, CD-ROM.

is the behavior of its predatory elites, as well as their failure to join the globalization bandwagon, that explains most of today's poverty in the Third World. Thus, in 1980—when the number of the world's poor peaked—the majority of the world's poor were in Asia. Today they are in Africa.

It has also been claimed by the World Bank and others—particularly in the anti-globalization movement—that the growth which occurred in the latest period of globalization was not "pro-poor." Despite the rapid growth promoted by global integration, it is said, poverty was not reduced very much.[3] Bhalla shows that this is not true. He asks a simple question: Did the consumption of those considered poor in 1980 (the bottom 44 percent) grow faster than that of the rest of the population between 1980 and 2000—the second period

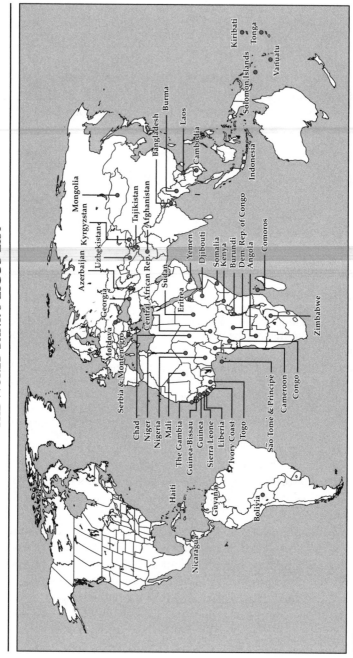

Figure 1.2
THE WORLD BANK'S LICUS LIST

The World Bank's LICUS list—Low Income Countries Under Stress—correlates closely to those countries that are regarded as failing, or in danger of failure. Poverty is not the only definiton of failure, but if prolonged, it is the largest predictor of it. These 48 countries are in the three lowest quintiles of the LICUS list.

of globalization? For the developing world as a whole, the poor increased their income twice as fast as those who were not poor. Thus the growth generated by globalization has not been anti-poor as the jeremiads claim. Instead, globalization and the rapid growth it promoted have reduced world poverty by historically unprecedented amounts. Growth has not merely "trickled down" to the poor: it has been a flood!

2. The Global Spread of Well-Being

Is this relatively benign picture of the changing lineaments of world poverty also supported by data on various social indicators relating to life expectancy, education, and health? Has the condition of the mass of humanity whose lives have been "nasty, brutish and short" changed markedly in the modern era?

Life Expectancy

Apart from the growth in per capita GDP, which measures the material dimension of human welfare, the quantity of life—longevity—also effects welfare. The United Nations Development Program (UNDP) has been calculating wider measures of well-being in its Human Development Index that include other nonmonetary factors. But these measures are deeply flawed because they are based on arbitrary assumptions made by official agencies (Philipson and Soares 2002). By contrast, Gary Becker, Philipson, and Soares (2005) have estimated measures of "full income" that include both the material measure (per capita GDP) plus longevity. The value of longevity is estimated through the revealed preferences of individuals in their market behavior. The resulting monetary value of longevity gains are added to the observed gains in per capita income to calculate "full income." The resulting changes in "full income" provide the monetary value of the full welfare gain as if it had all taken the form of income growth.

Becker and his associates find that for the 96 countries they have estimates for, between 1960 and 2000 there was an "average yearly growth in 'full income' of 2.8%, of which roughly three quarters are due to income per capita and one quarter to longevity." But the yearly growth of "full income" of the 50 percent of countries that were the poorest in 1960 was on average much higher at 4.1 percent, "of which 1.7 percentage points are due to health, as opposed to the richest 50 per cent of countries, for which the average yearly growth in 'full income' is 2.6 per cent, and only 0.4 percentage points are due to health" (p. 279). This means that, taking account of longevity (resulting from health improvements), welfare inequality across countries dropped substantially between 1960 and 2000 (Table 2.1).

Most of the improvements in health that contributed to increased longevity in poor countries were due to reduced mortality from infectious, respiratory, and digestive diseases and "congenital and perinatal conditions, mostly concentrated at early ages" (Becker, Philipson, and Soares 2005). By contrast, in rich countries there was a reduction in mortality from the diseases of the old: nervous-system, sense-organ, heart, and circulatory diseases. Thus, while the health improvements in poor countries were due to absorbing existing medical knowledge and techniques at low cost, those in rich countries were based on advances on the frontiers of medical technology. However, because of the AIDS epidemic in Africa, even though global health inequality declined from 1960 to 2000, most of this decrease occurred between 1960 and 1990, after which there was a slight increase in inequality in life expectancy between 1990 and 2000.

As with per capita GDP, there was initially a growing divergence and then convergence in life expectancy between the West and the Rest. The divergence began with rising longevity in the United Kingdom from the 15th to the 16th century. This divergence slowed at the start of the 20th century and then turned to convergence before 1950. Table 2.2 shows Maddison's historical estimates for life expectancy between the West and the Rest from 1000 to 2003 AD, and Table 2.3 shows these for India and the United Kingdom from the 14th century. A similar pattern is observed from the historical data (from 1870 to today) for Brazil and Russia (Kenny 2005, 5). What explains these changes?

Per Capita Food Supply

We need to look at the historical record on food supply and population. Until recently most of the world's working population was engaged in agriculture. Bairoch estimated that even in 1800, 75–80 percent of the working population in developed countries was in agriculture, with an even higher proportion in developing countries (Bairoch 1988, 287). In India in 1891, the rural population was 90 percent, and in China as late as 1949, it was 89 percent. The

Table 2.1

VALUE OF LIFE EXPECTANCY GAINS BY REGION OF THE WORLD AND GROUPS OF COUNTRIES, 1960–2000

	1960		2000		Value of Life Exp. Gains in Annual Income	Lifetime Present Value of Life Exp. Gains	Yearly Growth Rate of Full Income (percentage)
	Life Exp.	GDP p.c.	Life Exp.	GDP p.c.			
Europe & Central Asia	68	6,810	76	18,281	1,809	51,706	2.7
East Asia & the Pacific	42	1,317	71	5,866	2,600	60,957	4.8
Latin Am. & the Caribbean	56	3,459	70	7,161	1,365	36,935	2.3
Middle East & North Africa	48	1,935	69	5,525	1,817	46,076	3.4
North America	70	12,380	77	32,880	2,804	81,993	2.7
South Asia	44	892	63	2,346	635	15,504	3.1
Sub-Saharan Africa	41	1,470	46	1,573	72	1,612	0.3
Poorest 50% countries in 1960	41	896	64	3,092	1,456	33,673	4.1
Richest 50% countries in 1961	65	7,195	74	18,162	2,076	58,957	2.6
World	49	2,983	67	7,236	1,627	40,626	2.8

NOTES: Income per capita is GDP per capita in 1996 international prices, adjusted for terms of trade (Penn World Tables 6.1). Life expectancy is life expectancy at birth (World Development Indicators, World Bank). Regional averages weighted by country population. Sample includes 96 countries, comprising more than 82 percent of the world population. Value of life expectancy gains based on the authors' calculations.

SOURCE: Becker et al. (2005).

31

Table 2.2
LIFE EXPECTANCY, 1000–2003 AD
(YEARS AT BIRTH FOR BOTH SEXES COMBINED)

	World	West	Rest
1000	24	24	24
1820	26	36	24
1900	31	46	26
1950	49	66	44
2003	64	76	63

SOURCE: Maddison (2003: 31), updated from Population Division, U.S. Bureau of the Census.

per capita availability of food depended on agricultural productivity, which was low.

The limited availability of food led to lower life expectancy. In Roman times, life expectancy has been estimated to be about 25 years

Table 2.3
LIFE EXPECTANCY, HISTORICAL ESTIMATES FOR INDIA AND THE UNITED KINGDOM

Date	India	United Kingdom	India/United Kingdom (%)
1363	24	24.3	99
1543	24	33.7	71
1738	24	34.6	69
1813	24	40.8	59
1913	24.8	53.4	46
1931	26.8	60.8	44
1950	38.7	69.2	56
1999	63	77	82

SOURCES: Kenny (2005), derived from Maddison (2000), Preston (1975), and World Bank (2000). For 1364 (data for the period 1301–1425) 1543 (data for period 1541–46) United Kingdom, 1913 and 1950 India and United Kingdom are Maddison (2000). Data for 1931 are from Preston (1975). Data for 1999 are from World Bank (2001). India 1363 estimate is based on lowest historically recorded life expectancy in Maddison (2000).

(Bogue 1969, 566).This was close to the life expectancy estimated for France in 1750 (26 years). Fogel's estimate of per capita daily calorific supply at the beginning of the 18th century was 1,657 for France (2005, 1999). Britain's was higher, 2,095, as was its life expectancy of 32 years. Thus a daily per capita calorific supply between 1,650 and 2,000 calories, and a life expectancy of 25 to 30 years, was probably the fate of humanity throughout recorded history until about 1750 (Johnson 2000, 4).

It was a Western agricultural revolution beginning in the early 18th century in England that raised agricultural productivity and per capita food supplies. The agricultural revolution can be dated from the growth of urbanization, for without a rise in per capita agricultural output, the food surplus required to feed a growing urban population would not have been available. Beginning in the 18th century, first in England and then extending to Western Europe, urbanization grew. In 1300, Europe's urban population was about 10 percent and in 1800, 12 percent, but by the end of the 19th century, it had risen to 38 percent.

This urbanization was made possible by an agricultural revolution raising agricultural productivity in England and the Netherlands from 1750. There was also a significant rise in labor productivity. These productivity increases were the "necessary conditions for the Industrial Revolution, which was associated with, and may well have been advanced by, rapid population growth" (5). The increased supply of per capita calories from the mid-18th century led to the beginning of life expectancy increases in Europe, which were then accentuated with medical advances associated with the development of the germ theory of disease from the mid-20th century.

This increase in per capita calories in the West led to a growing divergence between it and the Rest. But, as can be seen from Table 2.4 on relative per capita calorific supply in India and Britain between 1700 and 1990, convergence in per capita food supplies between India (and many other parts of the Third World) and the West began in the 1950s. This was linked to both population growth and technical advances in the form of the Green Revolution.

Population and Technology

Thus for much of human history, mankind was caught in the Malthusian trap, with population held in check by the food supply.

Table 2.4
CALORIE INTAKE, HISTORICAL ESTIMATES FOR INDIA AND THE
UNITED KINGDOM

Date	India	United Kingdom	India/United Kingdom (%)
1700	1,650	2,095	79
1800	1,650	2,237	74
1934	1,800	3,042	59
1970	2,030	3,316	61
1990	2,243	3,282	68

SOURCES: Kenny (2005), derived from Johnson (2000), Geiger (1999), Bennett (1976), and Easterly (1999). Data for United Kingdom 1700 and 1800 are from Johnson (2000), for United Kingdom 1934 Geiger (1999), and for India 1934 from Bennett (1976). Johnson argues that calorie intake prior to the 18th century was probably in the range of 1,650 to 2,000 worldwide, and that Indian calorie intake was already increasing by the time of the first estimates made for 1934. This suggests that India was likely at the lower end of the world range in the 1700–1900 period, thus the estimate the 1,650 figure for India in 1700 and 1800. 1970 and 1990 data are from Easterly (1999).

But the check on food and hence population was not a shortage of land (subject to diminishing returns) but of labor. However, as Boserup has persuasively argued, population growth itself was the lever that led to induced innovations and the movement to more intensive agricultural techniques (1965). She argues that population pressure is a necessary but not a sufficient condition for technical change in agriculture (in the form of more intensive use of both labor and capital). She identifies the differing labor inputs per hectare of different agrarian systems by the frequency with which a particular piece of land is cropped. Thus, nomadic pastoralism is more labor and capital-intensive than hunting and gathering or the slash-and-burn-type agriculture practiced by many Stone Age tribes.

According to Boserup, different agrarian systems can be ranked in terms of their period of fallow on a spectrum from most primitive—slash and burn—to most advanced—multiple cropping with modern inputs. What distinguishes these systems is both the relative frequency with which a particular piece of land is cropped and the ensuing increase in direct and indirect labor inputs required to maintain a constant per capita food output. The crucial economic variable in different types of agrarian systems is the amount of labor required per unit of food (say, grain) produced. Thus, in those earlier agrarian systems where land is not scarce relative to labor, it is the yield per unit of labor rather than the absolute yield per hectare that is important for the farmer. In Europe, land was not scarce until the beginning of the 19th century, since until then, as Johnson (citing van Bath) reports, "Yields were calculated per unit of seed not per unit of land" (Johnson 2000, 6.)[1]

From about 10,000 BC, after our hunter-gatherer ancestors had occupied all the world's habitable areas for their land-intensive form of making a living, there was a momentous move with the invention of agriculture. During this earliest phase of agrarian evolution, the human population is estimated to have doubled to about four million. But it was the move to settled agriculture in about 8000 BC that was decisive for population expansion. These changes in systems of agriculture arguably occurred under the Boserupian pressure of a reduced per capita food supply once the "land frontier" for hunter-gathering had been reached. The domestication of plants and animals, and the invention of the plow about 2000 BC, led to the emergence of Eurasian agrarian civilizations. They were based on fairly intensive cultivation with annual cropping, which usually required irrigation and the annual deposit of silt from the flooding of the rivers around which these civilizations arose. A larger population could now be supported.

However, until 5000 BC, the area under crops was too small to have much effect on the size of the global population. Thereafter, a surge took place, with McEvedy and Jones estimating that "a gain of near 50% in the course of the 5th millennium B.C. and of roughly 100% in each of the next three millennia" (1978, 343). By 500 BC, global population had reached 100 million, but its growth began to slow. By the second century AD, the global population had reached 200 million. Thereafter, population stagnated until the medieval period, most likely because the optimum level had been reached for the available agrarian technology. The medieval population growth in western Europe (Figure 2.1) resulted from the political, technological, and cultural effects of the twin papal revolutions.[2]

But the medieval surge reached its Malthusian limits by 1300. This was followed by a population bust with the arrival of the bubonic plague carried on the hoofs of the horses of the Mongol hordes

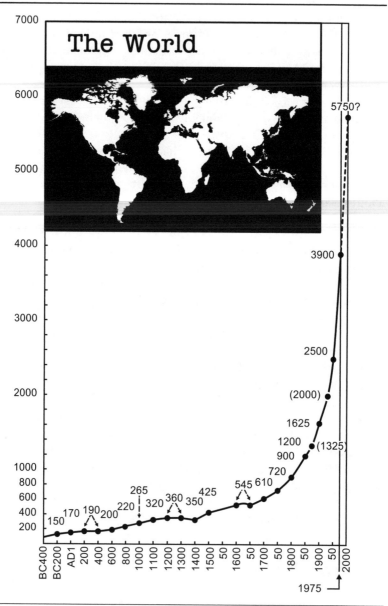

Figure 2.1
WORLD POPULATION (MILLIONS)

from Burma, in their sweep across Eurasia in the 14th century.[3] The medieval population cycle peaked at 360 million in 1200. This level "was not exceeded well into the fifteenth century" (346). But thereafter, with little growth in per capita output of agriculture, world population increased only slowly until the beginning of the 19th century. In the 18th century, population growth in Europe accelerated to 0.41 percent due to the agricultural revolution after 1750 involving various technological and institutional changes.

The increased per capita food supply in Europe, following the agricultural and industrial revolutions, led to better nutrition and a fall in mortality without any notable change in fertility. This in turn produced a 115 percent expansion of Europe's population in the 19th century, followed by the "demographic transition," which finally put an end to the Malthusian trap that had in the past halted population and economic growth.

The increase in per capita incomes in Europe and its offshoots, resulting from the Promethean growth promoted by the Industrial Revolution and the incorporation of the lands of the New World by the seafaring gunpowder European empires, also changed the fertility behavior of families. With the decline in mortality rates from better nutrition, strengthened by the medical advances flowing from the germ theory of disease, families came to realize that their desired family size could be achieved with lower live births. This led to a decline in fertility and eventually to fairly low natural increases in the population in industrialized countries.

Similarly in the Third World, the acceleration in population occurred after the fall in mortality, particularly for infants, with the transference of the new medical knowledge in the early parts of the 20th century. In 1960, the infant mortality rate for 30 low-income countries including China was 157 per thousand births. It declined to 62 in 1996 (United Nations Development Program 1998). By contrast, in 1900 the rate in the United States was 160 and in Europe ranged from 121 in Denmark to a high of 216 in Austria (Bairoch 1988, 231). Although the teeming slum-ridden cities of the Third World are seen as cesspools of poverty, in a sample of these cities with a population of over a million, the infant mortality rate was 60 per thousand births in the 1990s. In fact, while current developed countries historically had higher infant mortality rate in cities than in the rural countryside, because of the easy spread of infectious diseases and insecure water supplies and sanitation, the

Table 2.5
TOTAL FERTILITY RATE, MAJOR AREAS OF THE WORLD,
1950–55 AND 1990–95

	1950–55	1990–95	Decline
More developed areas	2.8	1.7	1.1
Less developed areas	6.2	3.3	2.9
China	6.2	1.9	4.3
India	6.0	3.6	2.4
Rest of Asia	6.1	3.4	2.7
Latin America	5.9	3.0	2.9
Northern Africa	6.8	4.0	2.8
Sub-Saharan Africa	6.5	5.9	0.6

SOURCE: Easterlin (2000), derived from United Nations Department of Economic and Social Affairs (1998, 12, 516, 518).

reverse is the case in the Third World (Brockerhoff and Brennan 1997, 24). As Johnson comments, "These data indicate both the large magnitude of the declines and the extent to which the improvements [in infant mortality] have been widely shared among many of the lowest-income families in the world" (2000, 11).

This decline in infant mortality was followed by the demographic transition, with a sharp decline in fertility, in the Rest (Table 2.5). "Compared with the historical experience of the West, fertility in today's less developed areas, like mortality, starts from higher initial levels and declines more rapidly," Easterlin writes (2000, 16). The lower fertility rate brings down not only the population growth rate but also the time women spend in childbearing, implying "a revolutionary enlargement of freedom for women" (16).[4]

A graphic picture of this demographic transition, which ended the age-old Malthusian Trap, is provided by the census data for India (which has one of the most reliable and long-run series of censuses going back to the British Raj) in Figures 2.2, 2.3, and 2.4. These data chart the crude birth and death rates, the infant mortality rate, the population growth rate, per capita GDP, and GDP over the 20th century. It can be seen that, as the theory of the demographic transition predicts, the decline in the death rate

Figure 2.2
BIRTH AND DEATH RATES FOR INDIA, 1901–2001

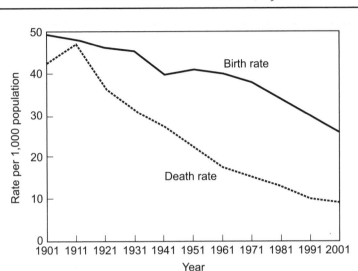

SOURCE: Lal (2005).

has been faster than the fall in the birth rate, so that population growth that began in the 1920s continued to accelerate until 1981. Since then, the birth rate has been declining faster than the death rate, induced by the even faster declining infant mortality rate. The population growth rate is now declining to replacement levels, with population expected to stabilize at 1.6 billion by 2045 (Lal 2008a). This fall has boosted the growth in per capita income, particularly after the rise in the GDP growth rate following the 1991 economic liberalization.

In *The Hindu Equilibrium*, I also provide an outline of agricultural growth in India on Boserupian lines, taking account of this changing demographic history. With a historically static population of about 140 million and the mild expansion of about 0.45 percent per year from the late 18th to the early 20th century, Indian agriculture faced a shortage of labor. Until 1921, the modest expansion of population was accommodated by extending the

Figure 2.3
GROWTH RATES OF POPULATION, GDP, PER CAPITA GDP, FOR INDIA, 1901–2001

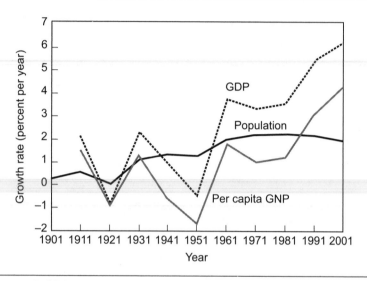

SOURCE: Lal (2005).

land frontier with relatively unchanged technology and cropping patterns. But with the increase in the population growth rate, followed by an increase in the rural labor force, the labor intensity of agricultural production increased. This largely consisted in double cropping and increased land-saving capital formation in the form of irrigation. But this intensification was reaching its limits in the 1970s. From the 1980s, this Boserupian process was replaced by the technical change that was introduced by the Green Revolution of the late 1960s.

The Scientific Revolution and the Growth of Knowledge

The Green Revolution was only one of the many forms in which the scientific revolution, unleashed with the rise of individualism in the West, has led to the systematized growth of knowledge, enabling

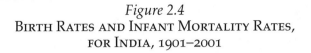

Figure 2.4
BIRTH RATES AND INFANT MORTALITY RATES,
FOR INDIA, 1901–2001

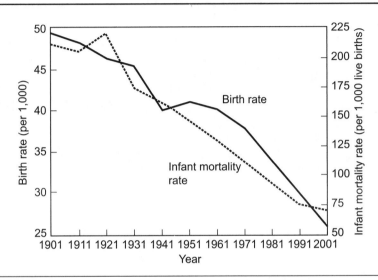

SOURCE: Lal (2005).

mankind to escape the Malthusian trap. This growth of knowledge accelerated, first, with the invention of the printing press, which allowed a much wider dispersion of the new learning, and then, in the 19th century, with the gradual expansion of institutions of learning to advance and transmit knowledge. The movement from village to town and the expansion of population meant that growing numbers of people could specialize in the production and dissemination of new knowledge.

The expansion of population also meant that, since intelligence is likely to be distributed along a bell curve, a growing number of people would likely be found in the right tail—that is, geniuses.[5] On the "genius theory," this implies that the growth rate of technology will be proportionawl to total population. Since there is historical evidence, as we have seen, for the Boserupian process, also implied is an endogenously induced technical change with the growth of

41

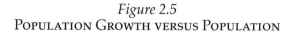

Figure 2.5
POPULATION GROWTH VERSUS POPULATION

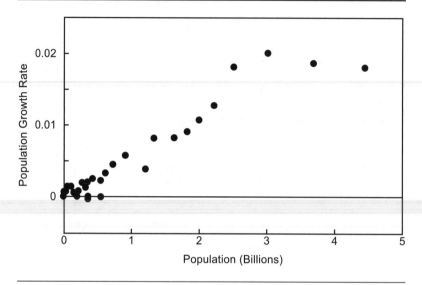

SOURCE: Kremer (1993).

population. However, with population limited by the available technology on Malthusian lines, the growth rate of population will be proportional to the growth rate of technology. Combining Boserup, Malthus, and the genius theory then implies that the growth rate of population will be proportional to the level of population (Lee 1988).

Kremer has charted this relationship in Figure 2.5 for the historical data on human population from 1,000,000 BC. He shows that this relationship held till recently, when the demographic transition led to a leveling off of the population growth rate. Since then, technological change depends on rising per capita incomes, which allow the financing of systematic research and development in modern-day universities and industries based on the scientific revolution.

Literacy and Education

An important measure of human well-being is the ability to read and write. Literacy aids in the transmission of knowledge, fueling its further advancement. England was *not* the pioneer in the spread of literacy and education in the West, as it was in income growth and improved life expectancy. Rather, Scandinavia and the United States led the way in the 19th century. These were also the areas to where industrialization spread from England, as their greater human capital allowed them to learn new methods of production more easily. Easterlin notes that the divergence in literacy within Europe goes back to the Protestant Reformation of the 16th century (2000, 19). Unlike Roman Catholicism, the Protestant sects emphasized the need for each individual to read the Bible for himself, and Anglican England followed the Roman Church. The invention of the printing press by Gutenberg aided this spread of literacy among these European Protestant countries. In England, the nonconformist sects took to reading. In the United States, the northern states settled by these sects saw the spread of literacy and education.

Globally, the Rest were soon to converge with these educational and literacy trends set in the West. This can be seen in the historical estimates of literacy rates in India and the United Kingdom in Table 2.6, the primary-school enrollment rates in India and the United States in Table 2.7, and the changes in the adult literacy rates

Table 2.6
LITERACY, HISTORICAL ESTIMATES FOR INDIA AND THE UNITED KINGDOM

Date	India	United Kingdom	India/United Kingdom (%)
1500		6	
1830		69	
1870		76	
1913	9	96	9
1950	19	99	19
1999	57	100	57

SOURCES: Kenny (2005), derived from Allen (2003), Webb (1963), Crafts (2000) and World Bank (2002). Estimate for 1500 based on extrapolation from Allen (2003), 1830 United Kingdom estimate based on Webb (1963), later data from Crafts (2000) and World Bank (2002).

Table 2.7
PRIMARY SCHOOL ENROLLMENT (% OF TOTAL POPULATION),
HISTORICAL ESTIMATES FOR INDIA AND THE UNITED STATES

Date	India	United States	India/United States (%)
1840		16.5	
1870	0.3	18.6	1.6
1913	1.9	17.9	10.6
1950	5.2	13.7	38.0
1990	11.8	12.4	95.2

SOURCES: Kenny (2005), derived from Mitchell (1998), Maddison (2001), and (for 1840 United States) Easterlin (1981).

in developed and developing countries between 1950 and 1995 in Table 2.8. As with other measures of living standards, Easterlin writes, "the rapidity of change in the less developed countries [in literacy and education] is often much greater than was true in the historical experience of the West" (20).

Table 2.8
ADULT LITERACY RATE, MAJOR AREAS OF THE WORLD,
1950 AND 1995 (%)

More Developed Areas	(1) 1950	(2) 1995	(3) Change, (2)–(1) (percentage points)
More developed areas	93	98	5
Less developed areas	40	70	30
China	48	82	34
India	19	52	33
Rest of Asia	24	72	48
Latin America	57	86	29
Northern Africa	12	53	41
Sub-Saharan Africa	17	56	39

SOURCES: Easterlin (2000), derived from UNESCO (1957) and World Bank (1999).

Summary

The convergence in per capita incomes and the historically unprecedented reductions in structural poverty imply that the Millennium Development goal of halving the percentage living on less than a dollar a day on a population-weighted measure has been achieved rapidly (Sala-i-Martin 2006; Bhalla 2002; World Bank 2004; Kenny 2005, 10). But as we have seen in this chapter, an even more rapid convergence has occurred in other measures of living standards encompassing life expectancy, nutrition, infant mortality, and literacy. Moreover, in the last half century, the rate of change in these indicators of well-being in the less developed countries has substantially exceeded those in the historical experience of western Europe. The ascent from the poverty that has plagued mankind, an ascent that began in the West in the 19th century, has now spread to the Rest at a speed unprecedented in human history. The end of world poverty is no longer a chimera. It is within reach.

3. Destitution, Conjunctural Poverty, and Income Transfers

Destitution

With mass structural poverty being ubiquitous, the problem of "poverty" historically has been confined to destitution. Most traditional agrarian, organic economies were labor-scarce and land-abundant. Destitution occurred when individuals lacked the labor power to work the land because they were physically disabled and had no families. This remains a major source of destitution in land-abundant parts of Africa.[1]

With population expansion and the emergence of land-scarce economies in Europe and in many parts of Asia, there arose "the poverty of the able-bodied who lacked land, work, or wages adequate to support the dependents who were partly responsible for their poverty" (Iliffe 1987, 5). Their poverty merges with mass structural poverty, and growth will, as it has, lead to its amelioration.

No estimates of worldwide destitution—as far as I know—are currently available. Michael Lipton's attempts to find some correlates of destitution in India based on village studies, however, show the extreme heterogeneity of this group. Dasgupta's seemingly reasonable assertion that widows are "routinely forced into destitution" in India (1993, 323) has been shown to be false by Dreze and Srinivasan, who find "in terms of standard poverty indices based on household per capita expenditure, there is no evidence of widows being disproportionately concentrated in poor households, or of female-headed households being poorer than male-headed households" (1995).

Conjunctural Poverty

This leaves the third type of poverty: conjunctural poverty. In organic agrarian economies, its main causes are climatic crises and political turmoil, and its most dramatic manifestation is a famine.

Since the Indian Famine Code was devised by the British Raj in the late 19th century, it has been known that to deal with what Sen labels the "entitlement failures" precipitating a famine (1982), the government should provide income directly (through public works or food-for work-schemes) to those suffering a temporary loss of employment. This administrative solution has eliminated famines in India.

The Industrial Revolution introduced its own source of conjunctural poverty in the form of the trade cycle and the unemployment that ensues during its downturns. But in primarily agrarian economies, like India, the seasonal unemployment of landless labor in rural areas is likely to be of greater importance than urban industrial unemployment. Rural public works programs like the Maharashtra Employment Guarantee scheme[2] have been effective both in preventing famines and in dealing with problems of short-run income variability (Ravallion 1991). Their success lies in the self-targeting made possible by their offering a wage that only the truly needy will accept.

Income Transfers and Poverty Alleviation

Income transfers are the only way to tackle destitution and conjunctural poverty. Traditionally, these have been provided by private agencies—the Church, private charity, and most important of all, transfers within extended families. However, these private transfers were replaced in most Western societies by public transfers through the welfare state. In assessing the case for Western-style welfare states in dealing with the continuing problems of destitution and conjunctural poverty, it is useful to first distinguish between social safety nets and welfare states.

The distinction essentially turns on the universality of coverage in a welfare state versus the restriction of benefits with a social safety net to the truly needy. The World Bank's *Poverty Reduction Handbook* noted two essential elements in any design of a social safety net: "identifying the groups in need of assistance and the means of targeting assistance to those groups cost-effectively." It went on to ask: "Are these questions for public policy, or are they adequately addressed by the traditional family network?" (World Bank 1992, 2–13).

The need for a social safety net—to be found in most economies—is not necessarily a reflection of morality or "market failures" but of the ubiquitousness of risk in people's lives and the possibility of reducing its individual burden through various forms of mutual aid. This could take various forms: from market processes like insurance to social institutions like the family. The term "social" needs to be clarified in this context. Though it has become coterminous with public (state) action, in its original sense it refers only to cooperative action—private or public. In this sense, to say there is a need for a "social safety net" does not prejudge whether this should be provided through private or public action.

Labor Market Risks

So what are the risks in labor markets against which mankind has sought some form of insurance through social cooperation, and how have these changed with different stages in economic development? Because most economies were agrarian organic economies, in which (until fairly recently) labor was scarce relative to land, there were two major types of endemic risk.

The first, a form of systemic risk, was related to the need to tie labor down to land, where various forms of intensive agriculture were feasible and profitable (largely in alluvial plains, for example, the Indo-Gangetic plain in India). Without this tied labor, less intensive and productive forms of agriculture would have had to be adopted. Various institutions—feudalism in Europe (Bloch 1965), the caste system in India (Lal 1988, 2005a)—evolved to deal with this systemic risk.

More ubiquitous were the cyclical risks associated with changing climate. Various institutional arrangements, like the jajmani system in India (Lal 1988, 2005a), sharecropping (Bardhan 1989), and interlinked contracts in other factor markets (Bardhan 1980), provided the ways to cope with these risks. Moreover, in these traditional societies unemployment and destitution as "normal" states were virtually unknown (Garraty 1978). Feudal societies were designed to provide a place for every member, and the local "society"—village, clan, or tribe—provided the requisite social safety net. The main risk, as in a famine, was of not being able to spread highly covariant risks across the local group. In traditional Indian village society, for instance, this risk was partly dealt with by acquiring relatives through marriage in geographically distant areas whose climatic risks would not be correlated with one's own. These geographically interlinked families could then expect the necessary transfers from their spatially distant relatives when they were suffering climatically induced falls in their income.[3] In other parts of the world, as Hugh Thomas notes (1979, 577):

> Among tribes, no doubt, a rough and ready concern for the sick and old marked most peoples. In settled communities, an essential part was the role played by the lord. A typical feudal provision was that of the Prussian code of 1795: the lord had to see to it that poor peasants were given education, [and] that a livelihood for such of his vassals as had no land must be provided and, if they were reduced to poverty, he had to come to their aid.

In Europe, the breakdown of medieval society and the subsequent agrarian and industrial revolutions brought major changes—not least because population expansion led, in addition to the destitution of those without any labor power (the handicapped and the old without any families), to (as noted earlier): "the poverty of the able-bodied who lacked land, work, or wages adequate to support the dependents who were partly responsible for their poverty" (Iliffe 1987, 5). They were the paupers, and altruism apart, it was the danger to civil order from vagrancy that lent urgency to the alleviation of their poverty once the link between poverty, crime, and vice was perceived. Their numbers were swelled by another form of conjunctural poverty that arose with the Industrial Revolution's trade cycle, and the unemployment that ensues in its downturns.

Finally, in most preindustrial economies, self-employment was and remains the dominant form of employment. A self-employed worker combines in his person and personal enterprise (or household) all those characteristics that, due to the division of labor, are separated in industrial firms: labor, entrepreneurship, and capital. A variation in the demand for the output produced by these factors of production will be reflected in an instantaneous change in the implicit marginal value products of the various factors. There cannot therefore be any "involuntary" unemployment of the self-employed, and hence no question of unemployment insurance for them. Only the income transfers to alleviate conjunctural poverty, and those that may be deemed necessary to provide merit goods—health, education, and possibly housing—as part of the social safety net will be relevant for them.

Imperfect Information, Insurance, and the Welfare State

Classical liberals have advocated the targeting of benefits to the indigent and the disabled. For various merit goods, these benefits involve in-kind transfers. This is the type of social policy package implemented in Pinochet's Chile, which not only succeeded in protecting the poor during that country's arduous transformation to a liberal market economy but also led to dramatic long-term improvements in its various social indicators.[4]

By contrast, welfare state advocates favor universality because it alone in their view provides a feasible means to create a social safety net. Some have argued that because of the ubiquity of imperfect information, markets for risk will be inherently imperfect (for example, Barr 1992). Hence, universal welfare states are required as part of an efficient solution to "market failure." It would take me too far afield to deal with this argument.[5] However, a few points are pertinent in the context of the economics of insurance.

The technocratic public economics school argues that because of imperfect information, the ideal insurance contracts that would exist in a "complete markets" Walrasian equilibrium cannot be offered in any real-world insurance market due to moral hazard and adverse selection. Hence, in Arrow's (1965) words, "Clearly further innovation is desirable in the provision of health insurance, and I see no convincing argument that, in the absence of alternatives, it is undesirable or unnecessary for it to take the form of an increased role for the government."[6] And Barr, in his survey of the welfare state (mainly pensions, income support, and public financing or provision of medical services), states that "a central theme is the importance of the literature on imperfect information in establishing an efficiency case for various types of state intervention" (Barr 1992, 742). But is this normative use of the ideal Paretian optima to judge how an actual market copes with moral hazard and adverse selection justified?

My UCLA colleague Harold Demsetz's negative answer is devastating (1989, 8):

> Moral hazard is identified by Arrow as a unique and irremediable cause of incomplete coverage of all risky activities by insurance. But in truth there is nothing at all unique about moral hazard and economizing on moral hazard

provides no special problems not encountered elsewhere. Moral hazard is a relevant cost of providing insurance. . . . A price can be and is attached to the sale of all insurance that includes the moral hazard cost imposed by the insured on the insurance companies. And this price is individualized to the extent that other costs, mainly costs of contracting, allow. The moral hazard cost is present, although in different amounts, no matter what percentage of the value of the good is insured. The moral hazard problem is no different than the problem posed by any other cost. Some iron ore is left unearthed because it is too costly to bring up to the surface. But we do not claim ore mining is inefficient merely because mining is not "complete." Some risks are left uninsured because the cost of moral hazard is too great and this may mean that self-insurance is economic. There is no special dilemma associated with moral hazard, but Arrow's concentration on the divergence between risk shifting through insurance and risk shifting in the ideal norm, in which moral hazard is presumably absent, makes it appear as a special dilemma.

In other words, much of this technocratic analysis smacks of "nirvana economics," which judges the real world by the standard of an unattainable perfection. The important question, as Demsetz (9) notes, is, "Do we shift risk or reduce moral hazard efficiently through the market place? This question cannot be answered solely by observing that insurance is incomplete in coverage. Is there an alternative institutional arrangement that seems to offer superior economizing?" This question is now being asked by theorists concerned with the positive economics of insurance. The answers they have come up with in designing their so-called "incentive compatible" contracts in the presence of moral hazard seem to mimic the market. Thus, Laffont (1989) finds that such a contract will have both coinsurance and deductibles as essential features!

What of adverse selection? As with moral hazard, there is no a priori case that can be made for any necessary inefficiency of the market solution when adverse selection is an essential feature of health or any other insurance market.[7]

Thus, this form of "nirvana economics" provides no credible justification for a welfare state.

Two Rival Philosophies

An implicit objective of those who argue against safety nets and in favor of universal welfare states is the distribution of income. Here it is useful to contrast two rival ethical and political traditions: classical liberalism and the distributionist egalitarianism, which continue to jostle for our attention and color the various policies offered for alleviating poverty.

Classical Liberalism

For the classical liberal, it is a contingent fact that there is no universal consensus on what a "just" or "fair" income distribution is, despite the gallons of ink spilt by moral philosophers on trying to justify their particular prejudices as the dictates of reason. Egalitarianism is therefore to be rejected as the norm for deriving principles of public policy.

This does not mean that classical liberals are immoral! After all, the greatest of them all, Adam Smith, wrote *The Theory of Moral Sentiments*. Both of the great moral philosophers of the Scottish Enlightenment—Smith and Hume—recognized benevolence as the primary virtue, but they also noted its scarcity. However, as Smith's other great work, *The Wealth of Nations*, showed, a market economy that promotes "opulence" fortunately does not depend on benevolence. It only requires a vast number of people to deal with one another even if they have no personal relationships. They need only observe the "laws of justice." The resulting commercial society promotes some virtues—hard work, prudence, thrift, self-reliance—that are inferior to altruism because they benefit the agent rather than others. But by promoting general prosperity, these lower-level virtues do unintentionally help others. Hence, the resulting society is neither immoral nor amoral.

A good government, for the classical liberal, is one that promotes opulence by promoting natural liberty through the establishment of laws of justice that guarantee free exchange and peaceful competition. The improvement of morality is best left to nongovernmental institutions.

But from Smith to Milton Friedman and F. A. Hayek, classical liberals have also recognized that society or the state should seek to alleviate absolute poverty. On the classical-liberal view, as my colleague Al Harberger has noted (1984), there could be an externality whereby the poor "recipient's consumption of particular goods or services (food, education, medical care, housing) or his attainment of certain states (being better nourished, better educated, healthier, better housed) that are closely correlated with an adequate consumption of such goods" enters the donor's utility function. Since it is the specific consumption of these commodities, not the recipient's "utility," that enters the donor's utility function, there is no "utility" handle that can be used, as there is on the alternative distributionist view, to allow distributional considerations to be smuggled into the analysis of poverty alleviation programs.

Thus, the indigent and the disabled are to be helped through targeted benefits.

Distributionist Egalitarianism

By contrast, the alternative technocratic approach to poverty alleviation is necessarily infected with egalitarianism because of its lineage. At its most elaborate, it is based on some Bergson-Samuelson-type social welfare function, laid down by Platonic Guardians.[8] Given the underlying assumption of diminishing marginal utility, any normative utility weighting of the incomes of different persons or households leads naturally to some form of egalitarianism. But this smuggling in of an ethical norm, which is by no means universally accepted, leads to a form of "mathematical politics." Poverty alleviation becomes just one component of the general problem of maximizing social welfare, where given the distributional weighting schema, all the relevant tradeoffs between efficiency and equity, including intertemporal ones, can be derived in terms of the appropriate distribution-cum-efficiency shadow prices (Little and Mirrlees 1974; Lal 1980). If the concern is solely with those falling below some normative "poverty line," this merely implies increases in the weighting of changes in consumption (income) of those who fall progressively below the poverty line.[9]

But this is a thin edge of a very big wedge as far as the defenders of the market economy are concerned. Besides leading to recommendations for all sorts of redistributionist schemes, it also leads to a vast increase in dirigisme. The alleviation of poverty, an end embraced by classical liberals, is put on a route leading to creation of a vast transfer state, which in the long run is incompatible with the market economy.

A usual riposte to the classical-liberal separation of alleviating absolute poverty from fostering income equality is that in theory a market-based growth process could lead to such a worsening of the income distribution that the poor could be immiserated. This view was strengthened by the so-called Kuznets hypothesis, which states that inequality is likely to worsen in the early stages of development before it declines, as per capita incomes rose towards current developed country levels. All empirical evidence contradicts the Kuznets hypothesis and its corollary that growth might not alleviate absolute mass poverty (Fields 1991; Squire 1993).

Public vs. Private Transfers

Are public (state) transfers needed, as the welfare state advocates claim, to deal with destitution and conjunctural poverty and, as some assert, even to deal with mass structural poverty? We need briefly to examine the relative efficacy of private versus public income transfers.

Private Transfers

Traditional societies have dealt with income risk primarily through kin-based transfers, reciprocity arrangements, and interlinked factor-market contracts. These methods have been fairly effective.[10] With the inevitable erosion of village communities, it is feared that these private insurance arrangements will break down and that no private alternative will be available to counter destitution and conjunctural poverty in increasingly atomistic industrial economies.

It is in this context that the role of private interhousehold transfers is of great importance. Cox and Jimenez (1990, 206) provide evidence to show that they are of considerable quantitative importance. For example:

> among a sample of urban poor in El Salvador, 33% reported having received private transfers, and income from private transfers accounted for 39% of total income among recipients. Ninety-three percent of a rural south Indian sample received transfers from other households. In Malaysia, private transfers accounted for almost half the income of the poorest households. Nearly three quarters of rural households in Java, Indonesia, gave private transfers to other households. About half of a sample of Filipino households received private cash transfers.[11]

Moreover, since the oil price rise of the early 1970s, the poor in South Asia and parts of Southeast Asia have found remunerative employment in the newly rich oil states and their remittances to their Third World relatives have helped alleviate their poverty (Swamy 1981). In the most recent period of globalization, the flow of such remittances from the 150 million migrants from the developing world has become a flood.[12] In 2010, it was estimated that these countries received $375 billion, which was about three times what they received in 2002. We discuss these international remittances and their effects on alleviating poverty in greater detail in the next section.

Private transfers have by now been largely crowded out by public transfers in the West. For the developing world, Cox and Jimenez have estimated the large potential for such crowding out by public transfer systems in Peru and the Philippines (1992, 1993). For example, the authors estimate that if a public transfer program were instituted in the Philippines to bring each poor household up to the poverty line, after private transfers adjusted, 46 percent of urban and 94 percent of rural poor households would remain poor!

In a recent study of private household transfers in rural India, Sharma and I estimated there is crowding out of 0.56 rupees in private transfers for every rupee of public transfer (Lal and Sharma 2009). Both for India and the Philippines, it has been estimated that the threshold (node) income at which the private "transfer function" switches from the altruistic motivation (which entails crowding out) to the exchange motivation (which does not) for transfers was close to the official poverty lines.[13] This implies that private transfers are only made to those below the official poverty line.

Moreover, the evidence suggests that private transfers are efficient. By relying on locally held information and on extra-economic motivations like trust and altruism, private transfers overcome many problems such as adverse selection and moral hazard, which have so exercised the "nirvana economics" market-failure school. As Cox and Jimenez, summarizing the empirical evidence conclude: "Private transfers equalize income; private transfers are directed toward the poor, the young, the old, women, the disabled and the unemployed" (1990, 216).

Public Transfers

Perhaps we should not worry about crowding out of private transfers if public transfers can do even better. Two merit goods—health and education—are the objects of major public transfers in nearly all developing countries. In addition, social security is important in many Latin American countries.

But the empirical evidence overwhelmingly suggests that the incidence of the benefits from subsidies for merit goods is generally regressive and that they are imperfect means of helping the poor (Selowsky 1979; Meerman 1979; Jimenez 1989). A 1992 World Bank study (Box 3.4) indicates that public transfers are not only less efficient at redressing poverty than private transfers; the former also crowd out the latter. The study

> traced public social sector expenditures for nine Latin American countries in the 1980s . . . [and] found that real per capita public social spending on health, education, and social security fell during some part of the 1980s in every country in the study. The share of health and education expenditures in total government expenditures also fell, even as that of social security rose. In spite of lower funding, and no apparent increases in equity and efficiency, social indicators generally improved in the 1980s.

Apart from obvious statistical and other biases that might explain this anomaly, the most plausible explanation provided is that it might be due to "the growing role of non-governmental organizations, and the response of the market oriented private sector to enhanced expectations and demand." In other words, there was probably a "crowding in" of more equitable and more efficient private transfers!

Political Economy of Transfer States

The "middle class capture" of the benefits of public expenditure is a feature of both the developing countries and the welfare states of the OECD (Goodin and Le Grand 1987). A systemic process is clearly at work. In fact, it is the political economy of redistribution in majoritarian democracies. In a two-party system, politicians will bid for votes by offering income transfers to some sections of the populace at the expense of others. Models of this political process (which need not assume democracy but merely the interplay of different pressure/interest groups [Stigler 1988; Meltzer and Richard 1981; Peltzman 1980]) show a tendency for income to be transferred from both the rich and the poor to the middle classes—the so-called "median voter." Even if public expenditures are initially intended to benefit only the needy, such programs in democracies have inevitably been universalized through the political process, leading to what are properly called transfer rather than welfare states, which primarily benefit the middle classes.

The poverty alleviation that may occur as a byproduct of the expansion of the transfer state is moreover bought at a rising dynamic cost. With the universalization of various welfare schemes, political entitlements are created whose fiscal burden is governed more by demography than by the conjunctural state of the economy. With the costs of entitlements rising faster than the revenues needed to finance them, the transfer state sooner or later finds itself in a fiscal crisis. This process is discernible both in developing and developed countries.

The Lal-Myint study showed how this process is clearly visible in the developing countries in our sample (Uruguay, Costa Rica, Sri Lanka, and Jamaica) that under the factional pressures of majoritarian democracies have created and expanded welfare states. All four welfare states were financed by taxing the rents from their major primary products. With the expansion of revenues during upturns in the primary product cycle, political pressures led to a commitment to entitlements that could not be repudiated when revenues fell during the downturn in the price cycle. The ensuing increase in the tax burden on the productive primary sector (to close the fiscal gap) led to a retardation of its growth and productivity, and in some cases to the killing of the goose that laid the golden eggs. Thus, while there was undoubtedly some poverty redress as a result of the expansion of these welfare states, over the long run, the entitlements damaged the economic growth on which they were predicated and hence eventually became unsustainable. Similar processes leading to the fiscal crises are found in many other developing countries.[14] Not surprisingly, many of these countries with overextended welfare states are now seeking to rein them in.

Similar problems are visible in the more mature welfare states of the OECD (Lal and Wolf 1986).[15] In some countries that had gone furthest down the public-welfare route, the late 1980s and 1990s saw growing questioning of the welfare state in the West—and in some cases its partial or virtual dismantling.

The United Kingdom, the European Club Med countries, and even the United States are now facing actual or potential debt crises due to their unsustainable entitlements, and these countries along with Ireland have begun to roll them back. But the United States still has to deal with its unsustainable health and Social Security entitlements, whose impact on the fisc will worsen with the aging of its population.

Policy Implications

What are the conclusions for policy that follow from this discussion?

The first is that nothing should be done to damage the existing private institutions and channels providing private transfers. "Forbear" should be the watchword for every proposed scheme that seeks to alleviate poverty through public transfers.

The second is that if public money is sought for transfer to the "needy," this is best done through private agencies. Particularly for the merit goods primary health care and primary education, even if there is a case for public financing, there is none for public production.

The third is that the very problems cited by "nirvana economics" as requiring public insurance—moral hazard, adverse selection, and monitoring—argue for fostering the alternative private route, which capitalizes on the comparative informational advantage of private agents with local knowledge. These private welfare channels can be promoted by various methods of public co-financing.

International Transfers

In addition to domestic transfers to deal with poverty, international transfers through remittances by migrants from Third World countries, various private philanthropic flows of capital from rich to poor countries and their citizens, and official flows from rich-country governments and international agencies (foreign aid) are also of importance when discussing poverty alleviation in Third World countries.

Figure 3.1
FLOWS FROM OECD DONOR COUNTRIES TO
DEVELOPING COUNTRIES, 1991–2010 (BILLIONS OF DOLLARS)

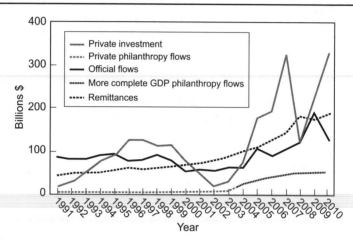

SOURCE: Hudson Institute (2012).

Recently, the Hudson Institute in Washington, D.C., put together a data set that tracks these various flows to the Third World from OECD donor countries. These trends are shown in Figure 3.1.

The figure indicates that apart from private investment flows (including direct investment, private export credits, portfolio investments, and bank credits) of $329 billion in 2010, remittances of $190 billion and private philanthropic flows of $56 billion together dwarf the official flows of $128 billion. As the figure shows, there has been a large and growing gap over the last 20 years between private and public financial flows to the Third World from the OECD-DAC (Development Assistance Committee) countries.

Over 80 percent of all DAC donor total economic engagement with the developing world is through private financial flows. (Hudson Institute 2012, 52). According to World Bank and OECD data, remittances, the most resilient flow to the developing world, have consistently been larger than ODA for much of the last decade (Hudson Institute 2009, 18).

We briefly discuss the evidence on the economic effects of private remittances and official foreign aid flows on poverty alleviation in the Third World.

Private Remittances

Remittances from all countries to developing countries were $375 billion in 2010. That amount is almost three times the total official development assistance sent by OECD countries to developing nations in 2010 (Hudson Institute 2012). Moreover, the official remittance numbers understate the full scale of global remittances since they do not include the money moving through informal, undocumented channels like the hawala system of informal currency transfer and hand delivery. These informal remittances are believed to "equal at least 50%, and perhaps more, of total official remittances" (Hudson Institute 2009, citing Ratha and Shaw 2006, Chapter 4).

These remittances have a substantial effect in reducing poverty. India, China, Mexico, and the Philippines were the largest recipients of remittances, accounting for 15 percent of the total official remittances received from all countries worldwide. But as figure 3.2 (based on data collected by International Fund for Agricultural Development for 2006) shows, nearly all parts of the Third World have benefited from private remittances.

About 80–90 percent of remittances are spent on food, clothing, shelter, household goods, debt payment, health care, and education. They have a marked effect in alleviating poverty. The World Bank has estimated that a 10 percent growth in per capita remittance income corresponds to a 3.5 percent decline in household poverty rates in developing countries (Adams and Page 2005). Household surveys in Uganda, Bangladesh, and Ghana found poverty was reduced by 11, 6, and 5 points, respectively (Ratha 2007). Studies have also found that remittance recipients experience significantly less severe poverty than those who do not receive remittances (OECD 2007).

Foreign Aid

The greatest passions continue to be aroused and the most ink spilled over the effects of foreign aid on growth and development, even though in terms of relative size, these public capital flows are now dwarfed by private ones. Nevertheless, over the years, as these flows have changed with shifting rationales, a huge worldwide poverty industry has grown up. This is where one finds the Lords of Poverty.

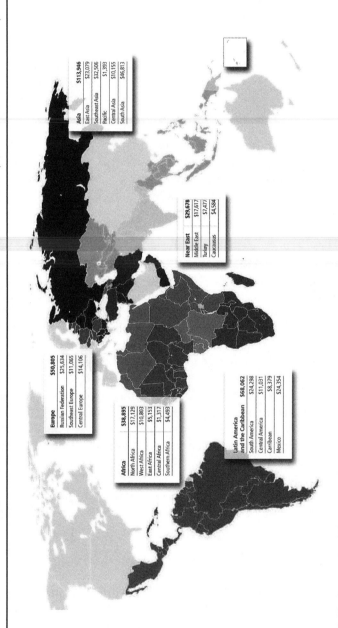

Figure 3.2
WORLDWIDE REMITTANCE FLOWS TO DEVELOPING COUNTRIES IN 2006 (MILLIONS OF DOLLARS)

Europe	$50,805
Russian Federation	$25,634
Southeast Europe	$11,065
Central Europe	$14,106

Africa	$38,895
North Africa	$17,129
West Africa	$10,803
East Africa	$5,153
Central Africa	$1,317
Southern Africa	$4,493

Latin America and the Caribbean	$68,062
South America	$24,298
Central America	$11,031
Caribbean	$8,379
Mexico	$24,354

Asia	$113,946
East Asia	$23,079
Southeast Asia	$32,506
Pacific	$1,393
Central Asia	$10,155
South Asia	$46,813

Near East	$29,678
Middle East	$17,617
Turkey	$7,477
Caucasus	$4,584

Total Remittances to Developing Countries: $301 billion.

Foreign aid as a form of capital flow is novel, both in its magnitude and its global coverage. Though there are numerous historical examples of countries paying "bribes" or "reparations" to others, the continuing large-scale transfer of capital from rich-country governments to those of poor countries is a post–World War II phenomenon. The origins of these transfers lie in the breakdown of the international capital market between the two world wars and in the rivalry for political allies during the Cold War.

The breakdown of the international capital market provided the impetus for the creation of the World Bank at Bretton Woods. Its purpose was to provide loans at market interest rates to poor countries that were shut out of Western capital markets—especially the largest, the United States. Their being shut out was the result of widespread defaults in the 1930s and the imposition of the U.S. government's "blue sky" laws, which forbade U.S. financial intermediaries to hold foreign government bonds. Meanwhile, European markets were closed through exchange controls; the United Kingdom, for example, maintained exchange controls until 1979. Official loans to poor countries at commercial interest rates, as laid down in the charter of the World Bank's parent, the International Bank for Reconstruction and Development, would have been justified purely on efficiency grounds to intermediate the transfer of capital from where it was less scarce to where it was scarcer.

This purely economic case was buttressed by political and, later, humanitarian justifications for concessional official flows, that is, loans with softer (concessional) terms on interest and repayment. As to the political reasons for giving aid, little can be added to Lord Bauer's devastating critique that instead of fostering Western political interests, foreign aid abetted the formation of anti-Western coalitions of Third World states seeking "bribes" not to go communist (1971, 1976). A statistical study concluded that "as an instrument of political leverage, economic aid has been unsuccessful" (Mosley 1987). The end of the Cold War has removed this political motive. Currently, advocates of foreign aid emphasize the humanitarian and economic case, though each rationale has seen many metamorphoses.

The humanitarian case for concessional flows was based on an analogy with the Western welfare state. The idea was that just as many people favor welfare to transfer wealth from the relatively rich to the relatively poor within a country, so they favor welfare to transfer wealth from relatively rich countries to relatively poor ones. But many commentators not necessarily hostile to foreign aid, for example, Little and Clifford (1965), emphasized that the humanitarian motives for giving aid may have justified transferring Western taxpayers' money to poor people, but not to poor governments: Money given to the latter may have no effect on the former. With the likes of Marcos of the Philippines, Bokassa of the Central African Republic, Abacha of Nigeria, and a host of other kleptocratic "tropical gangsters" in power, the money may simply be stolen (Klitgard 1990). According to William Easterly, despite over $2 billion given to Tanzania's government for roads, the roads did not improve. What increased was the bureaucracy, with the Tanzanian government producing 2,400 reports a year for the 1,000 donor missions that visited each year (Easterly 2004). Nor can the poor of the world claim a moral right to welfare transfers from the rich. While recipients of domestic welfare payments depend on the existence of a national society with some commonly accepted moral standard, there is no similar international society within which a right to aid can be established (Lal 1978, 1983).

The vast majority of foreign aid has failed to alleviate poverty. There are a few cases where it has improved the lot of poor people. The people of Martinique, for example, are probably better off because the French government provides a high percentage of their gross domestic product. Also, foreign aid helped wipe out river blindness in West Africa, protecting 18 million children (Easterly 2004). But a statistical study found that foreign aid "appears to redistribute from the reasonably well-off in the West to most income groups in the Third World *except* the very poorest" (Mosley 1987). This is consistent with the evidence (cited above) from both poor and rich countries that the middle classes tend to capture government transfers. The centralized bureaucracies of the Western aid agencies are particularly inept in targeting these transfers to the truly needy because they lack local knowledge. Not surprisingly, therefore, despite official aid agencies' continuing claim that their mission is to alleviate Third World poverty, they are increasingly subcontracting this role to nongovernmental organizations (NGOs). Whether this official embrace of NGOs is in the long-term interest is debatable (Lal 1996).

The political and humanitarian justifications for foreign aid are in tatters. What of the purely economic justifications? One was based on the "two-gap theory": the idea that foreign aid was required to fill one of two shortfalls—in foreign exchange or savings—that depressed the growth rates of developing countries below some acceptable limit (Lal 1972a). The alleged "foreign exchange" gap was based on dubious assumptions. One such assumption was "export pessimism," namely that poor countries could not generate many exports. Many development economists held this view despite a paucity of evidence for it (Lal 1983). Because both experience and theory have shown the irrelevance of this assumption, the "foreign exchange gap" justification for foreign aid has lost all force.

Nor has the "savings gap" justification proved to be any more cogent. Contrary to the theory that foreign capital is necessary to supplement fixed and inadequate domestic savings, the savings performance of developing countries shows that nearly all of them (including those in Africa until the early 1970s) steadily raised domestic savings rates since the 1950s (Lluch 1986). Since then, there has been a substantial increase in the savings rate in Asia, particularly in China and India. But after recovering from its decline in the 1980s, the savings rate in Africa (and in Latin America) has stagnated. In a World Bank study seeking to explain the poor savings performance of Africa, Elbadawi and Mwega (2000) concluded that foreign aid "is found to negatively Granger-cause[16] saving" (Loayza, Schmidt-Hebbel, and Serven 2000, 406). But this cannot be taken to be a causal explanation (for reasons set out in Chapter 6).

Moreover, the Lal-Myint study of 21 developing countries between 1950 and 1985 confirmed the common-sense expectation that differences in economic growth rates are related more to differences in the productivity of investment than to differences in investment levels.

Finally, statistical studies of the effects of foreign aid on growth and poverty alleviation have not been favorable (Easterly 2001). One found that after correcting for the link between aid and income levels and growth, the effect of aid on growth is often negative (Boone 1994). A survey of other such studies concludes that "there is now widespread skepticism that concessional assistance does have positive effects on growth, poverty reduction, or environmental quality" (Gilbert, Powell, and Vines 1999).

This is also hardly surprising. Except for sub-Saharan Africa, the World Bank finances less than 2 percent of the investment undertaken by developing countries (Krueger 1998). Most of its lending was to finance projects. The rates of return of more than 10 percent earned by these projects are not a measure of the true effects of the aid provided because money is fungible. A government can use aid to finance a high-yielding project that it would have undertaken in any case, and then use its own resources to finance a project with a low rate of return (say, more armaments). This problem led to the growth of "program" lending, which expanded in the 1980s along with the growth of "structural adjustment" loans. Program loans were based on a mutually agreed-on overall economic program undertaken by the recipient government. Structural adjustment loans were given in return for specific commitments to alter particular policies that damaged economic efficiency. Advocates of such loans hoped that by applying conditions to the program loans, they could give the governments an incentive to implement better policies by, for example, avoiding price controls, moving toward free trade, and reducing high marginal tax rates. That way, these advocates believed, foreign aid would improve economic conditions. But numerous studies have found that (Gilbert, Powell, and Vines 1999, F619):

> policy conditionality is ineffective. Not only is aid not necessarily used for what it is directly intended, but also, on average, it has no effect on growth, either directly, or indirectly through improved government policies. What matters is the policy environment, but lending appears to have little direct impact on this.

This is hardly surprising. As the adage has it, "You can lead a horse to water, but you can't make him drink." Governments make all sorts of promises to get the loan, but then renege on them once they have taken the money and run, as President Moi of Kenya demonstrated repeatedly in the 1980s. Moreover, the aid agencies do not call their bluff, for they are part of a large international "poverty alleviation" business from which many middle-class professionals derive a good living. These Lords of Poverty (Hancock 1989) depend on lending as much as possible and persuading the public in rich countries that these loans will help the poor. It is in the mutual interest of both the Lords of Poverty and the recalcitrant poor-country governments to turn a blind eye to the failure to make promised policy changes.

The latest justification for foreign aid is that, since the ex ante (before the fact) conditionality has failed, ex post (after the fact) conditionality should be used instead. In other words, rather than seeking promises for better future actions, governments should be judged by their past actions, and only those whose past policy environment has been better than that of their peers should receive aid. According to this rationale, not only will the laggards have a greater incentive to improve their policies, but aid will also be more effective. This is the rationale behind the latest U.S. foreign-aid agency, the Millennium Challenge Corporation.

There are two problems with this justification. The economic rationale for aid was to improve the economic performance of countries unable to help themselves. If the basket cases are to be left behind because of their predatory governments, what happens to the humanitarian arguments in support of aid? Second, and more important, with the opening of the world's capital markets to well-run developing countries, what incentive do these countries have to turn to the aid agencies—and their onerous procedures and conditions for loans—when they can borrow much more easily from a syndicate put together by the likes of Goldman Sachs? Any "neighborhood effects" whereby well-run countries are shunned by private capital markets because of their neighbors (as is claimed for Africa) can be readily countered by the aid agencies providing credit ratings for countries, just as Moody's does for the private sector. The large research capacity and information that governments provide the aid agencies would lend credibility to these ratings. No loans would be required.

There has also been an interminable attempt to provide econometric proof (or disproof) that aid fosters growth and alleviates poverty. As Deaton (in Banerjee 2007, 57) sums up in this highly dubious and inconclusive literature:

> isolating the role of aid . . . is clearly difficult, and a convincing demonstration may not be possible. Yet empirical work has improved considerably, and some of us who had previously discounted the econometric literature are beginning to think that indeed, there may be no effect to be found. Aid as we have known it has not helped countries to grow.

The foreign-aid programs of the last half century are an historical anomaly. They are part and parcel of the disastrous breakdown of the 19th-century liberal economic order during the interwar period. But just as a new liberal economic order is gradually being constructed—with a milestone being the collapse of the Soviet Union and its allies, and their growing integration in the world economic order—the various palliatives devised to deal with the dreadful woes bred by the past century's economic breakdown are becoming more and more redundant. Whether or not there was ever a time for foreign aid, it is an idea whose time has gone.

4. Political Economy

In the previous chapters, I have shown how the gradual embrace of what may be termed globalizing capitalism has—first in the West, and in the last half of the last century, in the Rest, led to a historically unprecedented reduction in world poverty and increase in well-being. But these overall trends hide the performance of many countries, mainly in Africa and Central Asia but also failed states like Burma, Haiti, and Laos, where what my old friend and colleague Paul Collier calls the "bottom billion" live. They are still mired in the age-old scourge of poverty and continually ravaged by the Four Horsemen of the Apocalypse.

How does one explain the failure of these countries to raise their populations' living standards when the mechanics of growth, the mainspring of the success of so many other Third World countries in alleviating poverty, are well known? The level and efficiency of investment, the rate of growth in the quality-adjusted labor force, the development by the advanced countries of new technology, and its absorption by the developing countries all require suitable public policies, like maintaining open economies, promoting investment in human capital, and providing a legal framework that promotes property rights and domestic order. The central question then becomes, as Lewis formulated it in his classic *The Theory of Economic Growth* (1955), why are these proximate causes of growth "found strongly operating in some societies but not in others, or at some stages of history but less so in others. What environments are most favorable to the emergence of these forces which promote growth" (11)? This was the central question we also asked in the Lal-Myint book, and in my *Unintended Consequences* and *Reviving the Invisible Hand*, I attempted to delve a bit deeper into this question. In this chapter, I summarize the results of this research.

Classificatory Schema

In Lal-Myint, we found it useful to categorize countries by a five-fold classification of polities and a three-fold classification of economies based on factor proportions. The latter were countries, which compared with the world endowment of capital, labor, and land, were classified as "labor-abundant," "land-abundant," and "intermediate." This allows an application of the three-factor trade-theoretic framework of Krueger (1977) and Leamer (1984, 1987) to yield a rich menu of alternative efficient development paths and the implied patterns of changes in the functional distribution of income (among the three factors of production: land, labor, and capital). As with capital accumulation and population growth, the factor endowments of the relevant countries change over time.

The Polity

The five-fold classification of the polity distinguished between the objectives of the government and the constraints on its activities. On the latter, two basic types were distinguished: the autonomous and the factional state. In the former, the state subserves its own ends. In the latter, it serves the interests of the "factions" that succeed in capturing the state.

Further subdivisions can be made among these two broad groups based on differing objectives. Amongst autonomous states, the first is the benevolent Platonic Guardian State of the "public economics" textbooks, seeking to maximize some social welfare function. The second is the predatory state, whose self-seeking can take the form either of the absolutist state attempting to maximize *net* revenue for the sovereign's use or the bureaucratic state maximizing public employment.[1]

A state is needed to provide the classical public goods of defense and justice. For their provision, a monopoly of coercive violence (including the power to tax) in its territory is needed. It is therefore best viewed as a natural monopoly providing these public goods. Being as self-regarding as its citizens (except for the Platonic Guardian version), the autonomous state's public goods-cum-tax equilibrium—which yields the net rents obtainable from the natural monopoly—will depend on the extent to which the natural monopoly is contestable from internal and external rivals. The greater the barriers to entry, the greater the net revenue the state can garner for its own purposes. But even if this contestability is very low, there will be a further constraint on the autonomous state's ability to levy confiscatory taxes. Particularly in developing countries, where a subsistence rural sector and an untaxable "informal" urban sector are common, as after-tax income decreases, the "prey" will at some stage exit the taxed sector and melt into the bush (as happened for example in Tanzania and Ghana in the 1960s and 1970s). While this puts an upper bound on the tax rate even when the state's natural monopoly is not contestable, in practice, depending on geography, military technology, and the internal legitimacy of its rulers, the maximum tax rate will be much lower and will depend on this degree of contestability.

Of the three types of autonomous states, the Platonic Guardian one provides the optimal level of public goods at least cost. The predatory state's tax-cum-public goods equilibrium will feature a net revenue maximizing tax rate (determined by the degree of contestability) and the provision of less-than-ideal amount of public goods in the absolutist version and an overprovision in the bureaucrat-maximizing version.

The factional state by contrast has no objectives of its own. It serves those of whoever is successful in its capture. Two major types can be distinguished: the oligarchic state and majoritarian democracy. The former limits the polity and hence the contestants for the state's capture, while the latter extends the polity to the adult population. As is well known from the median-voter theorem, the "predator" in a majoritarian democracy will be the median voters with their well-documented "middle class" capture of the unavoidable transfer apparatus that results in both developed and developing countries. Moreover, the tax rate will be the revenue-maximizing one based on the so-called Ramsey tax rule (Brennan and Buchanan 1980; Becker 1983, 1985; Lal 1990, 1994) as in the case of the autonomous predatory state, while the provision of public goods will be close to that of its bureaucrat-maximizing version (with pure public goods being supplemented with merit-good provision).

Where do four countries that have been or are failed states—Haiti, Burma, Zambia, and Nicaragua—fit into this classification? Clearly, Haiti is a classic predatory state, where one predatory "sovereign" (the two Duvaliers) were succeeded by someone (Aristide) who sought to become one. Zambia under Kaunda would also fit in this

71

category, but which since his fall is hovering between a factional state of the oligarchic kind and a continuation of the net revenue-maximizing predatory kind. Burma has clearly been a predatory state of the bureaucratic maximizing type, while Nicaragua after the ending of its civil war seems to be a majoritarian democratic factional state. Table 4.1 lists the classification of the states in the Lal-Myint study in these political categories.

Resource Endowments

In Lal-Myint, we also found that the initial resource endowment was more important in explaining divergent policy regimes and outcomes than the polity.[2] Thus, the labor-abundant countries (such as South Korea, Singapore, Taiwan, Malta), irrespective of their polities, had the easiest policymaking task. For them, the standard economist's policy prescription (based on the two-factor Hechsher-Ohlin model) of initially developing labor-intensive industries and then moving up the ladder of comparative advantage is easy to follow. There are three reasons for this.

First, this policy leads to politically desirable movements in the prices of factors of production (labor and capital). With wages rising as capital is accumulated, there is unlikely to be political resistance from the bulk of the population in factional states that realize the country's comparative advantage. All types of autonomous states will also find that even their predatory ends are better served by undertaking the development of their only resource—the human—on which their revenues and prosperity depend. The major task of government is to provide an adequate infrastructure to reduce the transaction costs of the relatively small-scale organizational units that will predominate in the earlier stages of their development.

Second, if the country is small, the limited size of the domestic market makes reliance on foreign trade inevitable. For the same reason, vertical import substitution is unlikely when the ubiquitous dirigiste impulse leads to some departures from free trade. This means that when a switch to free trade occurs, lobbies preventing competitive imports of intermediate inputs will not exist. The political costs of rectifying past mistakes are therefore likely to be lower than in the land-abundant or intermediate-group countries.

Third, their incremental comparative advantage is readily apparent to economic agents in both the private and public sectors. It is

Table 4.1
GROWTH AND TYPE OF POLITY

Region		Growth Rate	Autonomous State			Factional State	
				Predatory			
			Platonic	Rev Max	Bureau Max	Oligarchic	Democratic
As	Hong Kong	8.9	x				
As	Singapore	8.3	x				
As	Malaysia	6.9					x
As	Thailand	6.7		x			
LA	Brazil	6.6		x			
LA	Mexico	5.7			x		
ME	Malta	5.6					x
ME	Turkey	5.6	x				
ME	Egypt	5.4			x		
As	Indonesia	5.3		x			
LA	Costa Rica	5.0					x
LA	Colombia	4.7				x	
As	Sri Lanka	4.7					x
Af	Malawi	4.3	x				
LA	Peru	4.1				x	
Af	Nigeria	3.7					x
LA	Jamaica	3.3					x
As	Mauritius	2.9					x
Af	Madagascar	2.0				x	
Af	Ghana	1.3					
LA	Uruguay	1.1		x			x

Ranked in terms of growth performance. As = Asia, Af = Africa, LA = Latin America, ME = Middle East.

SOURCE: Lal and Myint (1996).

thus easier to pick "industrial winners," and the consequences of picking losers or policies that stimulate them are more immediately apparent—as with Singapore's ill-judged attempt to jump a few rungs on the ladder of comparative advantage through an artificial raising of wages in the 1980s.

Of the four "failed or failing states" noted above, only Haiti, with its population expansion relative to land, would seem to fall into the labor-abundant category. But with a failed state, there seems to be no obvious way in which even the basic public goods—law and order—required for any economic activity can be provided.

The comparative advantage of land-abundant and natural-resource-abundant countries is also likely to be clearer than for the intermediate group, but more difficult to realize than for the labor-abundant group of countries. This is for two reasons. First, with a higher supply price of labor than that of the labor-abundant countries (due to their more favorable land-labor ratios and abundant natural resources), their incremental comparative advantage is likely to lie in relatively capital-intensive projects. Public promotion may be required because of the large capital investments required and the need to develop scarce skills and absorb complex imported technology. The dangers of "bureaucratic failure" endemic to such promotion may then lead to a failure to realize their economic potential.

Second, if the rate of capital accumulation is not high enough, then with growing labor forces, their efficient development path could contain declining real wage segments. If the polity is subject to factional democratic pressures, this "equilibrium" time path of real wages could lead to political pressures to resist the requisite real-wage adjustments by turning inward. The polity could be at odds with the economy, with political cycles of economic repression (during factional "populist" political phases) followed by liberalization (during autonomous political periods).

Third, given the political imperative of avoiding the "falling wage" segments of their development paths, such countries have attempted Big Push development programs, often financed by foreign borrowing. These have often pushed them into a fiscal and debt crisis and then a growth crisis.

Finally, given the rents available from natural resources, the inevitable politicization of their disbursement leads to "transfer states" that inevitably bear harder on the revenue-generating sector when terms of trade decline, while raising entitlements when they improve. Thus, natural resources may prove a "precious bane" leading to polities that tend to kill the goose that laid the golden eggs.

The story of Zambia, Congo, and other natural-resource-rich African and Central Asian countries, as well as the travails of South Africa and Russia, would fit these patterns in the political economy of natural-resource-abundant and land-abundant countries. The story of Burma would also fit to some degree, but it is also strongly conditioned by the predatory nature of the state. However, as the shining example of Botswana, with its rich diamond deposits shows, natural resources are not always a "precious bane."

Finally, the intermediate resource endowment group has the most difficult task in terms of development policy. Its incremental comparative advantage is more opaque, so "mistakes" are not so easily recognized or rectified, particularly by the public sector, which in the absence of any bankruptcy constraint resists the exit of inefficient firms. Additionally, this group is also more likely to face situations in which the polity is at odds with the pursuit of its comparative advantage. Two of the largest developing countries—India and China—fall into this category (Lal 1995).

Crisis and Reform

There is also overwhelming evidence that, as I first hypothesized (Lal 1987), a "crisis" provides an important impetus for initiating economic reform (Lal-Myint 1996; Little et al. 1993; Bruno and Easterly 1996). China and India are the two major examples of countries whose past dirigisme led to growth crises, which led to reforms with their embrace of globalizing capitalism: in China in the late 1970s and in India in 1991. This move from the plan to the market led to a rapid acceleration of economic growth and the largest reduction in absolute poverty in human history.

In these cases of "crisis"-induced reforms, there are important parallels with the liberalization of the mercantilist anciens régimes in the late 18th and 19th centuries (Hecksher 1955; Lal-Myint 1996). One unintended consequence of past mercantilism and contemporary neomercantilism is that while both were motivated by the desire to establish "order" and then "nations" by expanding the span and scope of government control, after a certain stage, increased dirigisme bred disorder. As economic controls become onerous, people attempt to escape them through various forms of avoidance and evasion. This has a devastating effect on the state's fiscal base.

The first sign of an impending crisis is fiscal, with the accompanying un-Marxian "withering away of the state." Economic liberalization is undertaken to regain control over what seems to have become an ungovernable economy and to restore the fiscal base. But there may be a lot of ruin in countries—as the decades-long crisis in Ghana demonstrated. Moreover, if even half-completed reforms allow this crisis of the state to seem manageable, there is no further incentive for predatory states to continue with liberalization.[3]

This suggests that a crisis usually provides a small window of opportunity for liberalizers. A "big bang" may therefore be desirable to smash the equilibrium of rent-seeking interest groups that have a stake in maintaining the past system of dirigisme. It had been thought that to stiffen the government's spine in this unenviable task, sweeteners that ease its fiscal problem, in the form of "conditional" soft loans and grants from multilateral and bilateral donors, might be useful. But the emerging consensus from the sorry experience of "conditional" lending is that, invariably, unless the government has decided to bite the bullet, which inevitably involves rescinding the politically determined income streams its past dirigisme has created, predatory governments just take the money and run. The recent sad history of aid to Russia and Kenya for instance would support this judgment. So, as noted, it is now recommended that aid be given only to those who ex post are known to have reformed (Collier and Gunning 1999)!

Political Habits

An obvious question following from this discussion is: Why do countries have the political forms we observe? A second and related question is whether, apart from the market, other Western "habits of the heart," in particular democracy, need to be engendered to aid development and redress poverty.

My Ohlin lectures tried to provide a cultural explanation (Lal 1998). I distinguish between two aspects of a culture: its material beliefs, which are concerned with ways of making a living, and its cosmological beliefs, which, in Plato's words, relate to "how one should live." There is considerable cross-cultural evidence that material beliefs are fairly malleable—when the environment changes they can rapidly alter. By contrast, there is greater hysterisis in cosmological beliefs, and it seems they are related to the beliefs of the parent language group from which the culture emanated.

Cosmological beliefs are also important for the polity. No matter how tyrannical and predatory the state, it must command some general acceptance of its legitimacy by the general populace. For an ancient state, this general acceptance of its right to rule, and the political form that is considered legitimate, depend on ancient political habits. To understand these political habits and hence the feasibility of different political forms, we need to look at the history and cosmological beliefs of the people.[4]

China and India

I also argued in *Unintended Consequences* that the political habits of different cultures were formed as much by the geography of where the relevant culture was formed as by any ideology. Thus China, in its origins in the relatively compact Yellow River valley and constantly threatened by the nomadic barbarians from the Steppes to its north, developed a tightly controlled bureaucratic authoritarianism as its distinctive polity, which has continued for millennia to our day.

By contrast, Hindu civilization developed in the vast Indo-Gangetic plain, protected to a greater extent by the Himalayas from the predation of barbarians to the north. As I argued in *The Hindu Equilibrium*, this geographical feature (together with the need to tie down the then-scarce labor to land) accounts for the traditional Indian polity, which was notable for its endemic political instability among numerous feuding monarchies and its distinctive social system embodied in the institution of caste. The latter, by making war the trade of professionals, saved the mass of the population from being inducted into the deadly disputes of its changing rulers. And the tradition of paying a certain customary share of the village output to the current overlord meant that any victor had little incentive to disturb the daily business of his newly acquired subjects. The democratic practices gradually introduced by the British have fitted these ancient habits like a glove. The ballot box has replaced the battlefield for the hurly-burly of continuing "aristocratic" conflict, while the populace accepts with weary resignation that its rulers will take—through various forms of rent-seeking—a certain share of output to feather their own nests.

The Americas

Next, consider the Americas. Both North and Latin America shared similar resource endowments, with an abundance of land and a scarcity of labor. Whereas much of development economics is concerned with labor-surplus economies of relevance to Asia, it is the economics of land-abundant, labor-scarce economies that is relevant for the New World. A seminal essay by Domar (1970) provides the necessary theoretical framework. He cogently argues that in a land-abundant economy, free labor, free land, and a nonworking upper class cannot coexist. Any two can exist, but not all three.

Thus, consider the case where land and labor are the only two factors of production. Land is so abundant that there are no diminishing returns to labor, whose marginal and average product are the same. If employers seek to hire labor, they will have to pay a wage equal to this common marginal and average product of labor, leaving no surplus rents from land for the employer. Hence, the agrarian form that will emerge is family labor-based farms, as any form of hired labor or tenancy will be unprofitable, and landlords—who have to depend on one or the other—cannot exist. A government, by imposing direct or indirect taxes on this independent peasantry, could support a nonworking class of retainers, but the latter or an independent nobility of landlords could not support themselves from land rents—since none would be available. Economic expansion based on an independent yeomanry was the form that North American development and its agrarian structure took in the colonial period.

Next, suppose the government wants to create an independent class of landowners and grants the chosen few sole rights of ownership to land. If the peasants are free to move, competition among landlords will drive the rural wage up to the marginal product of labor, which is close or equal to its average product because of the abundance of land. There will be little or no surplus left for the landlords. To provide this surplus, some means will have to be found to restrict or abolish the peasants' freedom to move. Various forms of tying labor down to land—serfdom, slavery, and the caste system—emerged in the great agrarian civilizations. They created a landowning class that derived a rent not from land but from the peasants by expropriating a large part of their income above a subsistence level.[5]

Finally, as the labor force expands from natural increase and/or migration and land becomes scarce relative to labor, diminishing returns to labor appear with the marginal product of labor being less than the average. This allows landlords to obtain the rents from land and an assured labor supply to work it at a wage equal to its marginal product or else through various forms of tenancy.

The land-abundant U.S. subcontinent was gradually tamed by the gradual westward spread of the family farm. In Latin America, "a society of small farmers failed to take shape. Spain could not export many, and in America the lure of mines, the possibilities of large-scale, preemptive acquisition of land, and the opportunities for exploiting Indian and African labor militated against such a design" (Morse 1964, 128).

Equally important were the differing ecological conditions for agriculture in North and South America. In the north, unlike the tropical parts of the Americas, grains were the most suitable crops for cultivation. These have constant returns to scale in their production, unlike plantation crops such as sugar, which have increasing returns to scale. The same is true, to a lesser extent, of tobacco and coffee (Engerman and Sokoloff 1994; Solow 1991).[6] Where climatic conditions in the Americas were suitable for cultivating tropical crops, the use of coerced labor had enormous cost advantages over free labor, which led to great social and economic differentiation in society with large inequalities of income and wealth.

By contrast, given its factor endowments (including the climate), in most of the United States (except for the South), the family farm became the backbone of the colonial economy, and a society with fairly egalitarian mores could develop. That these factor endowments, rather than the cultural differences between the Protestant North and Catholic South, were responsible for the development of these different types of societies in the Americas is illustrated by the case of the Puritan colony of Providence Island, which developed the Caribbean and Latin American pattern of land ownership and settlement rather than the North American one of its coreligionists (Kupperman 1993).

These cultural differences, however, were vital in the different polities that were established in the areas of Iberian and Anglo-Saxon colonization. Morse (1964) argues that Spain after the reconquest (from the Moors) was a patrimonial state in which feudalism never developed fully. It was a centralizing state without the decentralization of rights of the manorial system.

The patrimonial rather than feudal states that Latin America inherited were further distinguished by their Catholic lineage. Whereas in the Protestant colonies—as Luther succinctly expressed in his "Open Letter to the Christian Nobility"—the duty of Christians who found themselves in a land populated by pagans "was not to convert the pagans but to elect their own religious leaders, [the] American Indians were to be tamed or exterminated. Moreover, the idea of salvation of one's neighbor never enters the Calvinist ethic because only divine grace, not human action, can save man. As the intermediaries between the individual conscience and God are suppressed, the evangelizing mission of Christianity disappears" (Paz 1988, 27).

By contrast, evangelism was the public justification for the conquest and for the Spanish and Portuguese domination of Latin America. New Spain, even more than its parent state, adopted the neo-Thomism developed by Suarez and his disciples as part of the Catholic Church's revitalization during the Counter Reformation. This provided an ideological justification for the patrimonial state. Society is considered to be a hierarchical system in which every person and group "serves the purpose of a general and universal order that transcends them" (Morse 1964). This hierarchy is part of a universal and natural order and not the product of any social contract. The sovereign is responsible to God, not to society, even though his authority originates in the people. "Neo-Thomism was a philosophy destined to offer a logical and rational justification of the Christian revelation. In turn, the teaching and defense of the Christian revelation formed the basis of the Spanish empire. Religious orthodoxy was the foundation of the political system" (Paz 1988, 30). Its economic correlate was corporatism.

This political and economic system was par excellence an "enterprise" association, as delineated by Oakeshott (1993). By contrast, the Protestant colonies were relatively indifferent to religious orthodoxy. Thus, Luther maintained that if in the colonies a group of Christians had no priest or bishop among them, they should elect one of themselves as a priest, and this election would not only legitimize their authority but also consecrate it (Paz 1988; Morse 1964). As Paz notes (27), "Nothing similar exists in all of Catholic tradition."

Thus, in the Protestant North a pluralist society developed, with the view that

> the world is composed not of one *highly differentiated society* for which certain common forms, acts, and ceremonies are a needed binding force, but of a *multitude of unrelated societies,* each of them a congregation of similar persons which in finite time and place are ordered by the declarative terms of a compact rather than by common symbolic observances [Morse 1964, 152].

This allowed the notion of the state as a civil association in Oakeshott's terms to develop, with the state as the umpire between many competing interests. This difference in cosmological beliefs explains the observation by political scientists that "politically, North Americans confine their feuds primarily to selecting officials and debating public policies, but in Latin America feuds are more fundamental . . . democrats, authoritarians, and communists . . . all insist they know what is best for themselves and their neighbors" (Wynia 1990, 3). This "universalism" of the neo-Thomist tradition was further strengthened by the attempt of the Jesuits in Latin America (and in other parts of the world) to promote a religious syncretism that would lead to a "unification of diverse civilizations and cultures . . . under the sign of Rome" (Paz 1988, 39).[7]

This fundamentalist universalism also provides, in my view, an explanation for the continent-wide swings in political and economic fashions over the last 200 years.[8] In the postwar era, the pronouncements of the Economic Commission of Latin America (ECLA) have been accorded the status of gospel truth. When it advocated dirigisme, this became the policy for most of Latin America. When in the early 1990s ECLA endorsed economic liberalism, that became the new gospel. More than other parts of the world, therefore, a universalist ideology matters in Latin America. This seems to be very much part of the story of the wild swings in ideology and policy to be found in many Latin American countries to this day. Therefore, instead of searching, as political economists do in other western societies, for the changing equilibrium of interest groups, in Latin America one needs to explain how these intellectual swings of "fashion" take place, since they are rather like religious conversions—Menem in Argentina and Cardoso (and Lula) in Brazil being outstanding examples.

This penchant for universalist ideological beliefs has also meant that there is a continuing dissonance between the Latin American social reality of extreme inequalities, which are the result of its ecological and political heritage, and its Christian cosmological beliefs emphasizing equality—which it of course shares with the North. There is no such northern dissonance, since both for ecological and political reasons, a uniquely egalitarian social and political society developed there.

In this context, it is worth noting the important difference between the cosmological beliefs of what became the Christian West and the other ancient agrarian civilizations of Eurasia. Nearly all of these believed in some form of hierarchical social order, which for instance in Hindu India—with its belief in reincarnation—was rationalized as resulting from the system of "just deserts" for one's deeds in the past life. By contrast, alone among the Eurasian civilizations, the Semitic ones (though least so the Jewish) emphasized the equality of men's souls in the eyes of their monotheistic deities. Dumont has rightly characterized the resulting profound divide between the societies of homo aequalis, which believe all men are born equal (as the philosophes and the American constitution proclaim) and those of homo hierarchicus, which believe no such thing (Dumont 1970).

This matters for the polity. With the rise of demos, those societies infected by egalitarianism have a greater propensity for the populism that damages economic performance than do the hierarchical societies. If, as in Europe, the granting of democratic rights can be phased in with the growing economic and social equality that modern growth helps to promote, then the political effects of the dissonance between an unequal social reality and egalitarian cosmological beliefs can be avoided.

In the colonial and 19th-century patrimonial states of Latin America, this dissonance was avoided by, in effect, restricting the polity to the property-owning classes. But if, as in the 20th century, the polity, while still in the early stages of modern growth, is expanded by incorporating the "dangerous classes" through an extension of democratic rights to the whole populace, this dissonance can, as it has, lead to political cycles of democratic populism, followed by authoritarian repression as the distributional consequences of the populist phase are found unacceptable by the "haves." By contrast, hierarchical societies can more easily maintain majoritarian democracies, however corrupt and economically inefficient—as the notable example of India shows—despite continuing social and economic inequalities. Thus, as many Latin American commentators[9] have noted, the historic and continuing inequalities of Latin America make democracy insecure, largely—I would argue—because of the dissonance between "society" and "cosmology" noted above.

Sub-Saharan Africa

Finally, consider sub-Saharan Africa, where most of the world's failed states and today's world poor are to be found. Although the Four Horsemen of the Apocalypse have ravaged Africa, they are (as Easterly has noted) still rare occurrences (see his Table 2). The major point to be noted about African states is their artificiality. They are the result of the 19th-century colonial Scramble for Africa and lack the ancient homogenous tribal identity of a state with a loose association, the necessary governance being provided by tribal chiefs; nor have they succeeded in behaving like imperial states, which historically have provided a means of welding a multitude of ethnic and religious groups into a functioning state.

I have elsewhere distinguished two major types of imperial state (Lal 1999, 2004): 1) the genuinely multiethnic states such as the Austro-Hungarian and Ottoman empires, which were mainly concerned with maintaining their Pax over a certain geographic space with no attempt to change or homogenize the "habits of the heart" of their constituent communities, and 2) the homogenizing empire, best illustrated by the Chinese, who created a fictitious homogenized Han identity out of the ethnically diverse people they incorporated. In our day the best example is the United States, which has created a homogenized American identity through its "melting pot" of diverse races and cultures. Then there are the "nation states" of the Renaissance princes, the United Kingdom, France, and Spain, which used mercantilist devices to incorporate different groups into a "nation."

It is this last model that the African elites seemed to follow after independence, and with their charismatic leaders, there seemed some hope that they might succeed. But given their resource endowments, the inevitable politicization of rents in states with continuing tribal and other ethnic rivalries has led to civil wars. In fact there seems to be an emerging statistical law about civil wars: an inverted U-shaped relationship between ethnolinguistic fragmentation in a state and the risk of civil war, the most homogenous (every group with its own state) and the most fragmented (as in a multiethnic empire) being at least risk of civil war (Collier and Hoeffler 1998; Collier and Sambanis 2003).[10] In this context, the idea that constitutions and democratic forms could contain the bloody conflicts in order to capture the state and the booty it affords is laughable. Much better to either reconvene a new Congress of Berlin—run by Africans—to recreate tribally homogenous states, which, as the shining example of Botswana shows, could prosper, or else hope that some African state will establish a multiethnic empire and its Pax over much of the continent!

Nevertheless, a number of cross-sectional statistical studies claim to have found a relationship between democracy and development.[11] But the statistical proxies used for the political variables in these studies do not inspire much confidence and are further plagued by the econometric problem of identification. In fact, in the Lal-Myint study, we found no relationship between the form of government and economic performance during the 30-year economic histories of the 25 developing countries that we studied. Rather than the polity, the initial resource endowment, in particular the availability or lack of natural resources, was a major determinant of policies that impinged on the efficiency of investment and thereby the rate of growth (as noted above). The difference in performance was further explained by the other major determinant of growth: the volume of investment. Thus, while the efficiency of investment in India and China during both their dirigiste and more economically liberal periods (till recently) was about the same, China's investment rate has been about twice India's, resulting in its growth rate also being twice as high. But in the 1990s, both the savings and investment rates and the efficiency of investment have increased, with Indian growth rates converging on the Chinese. The difference in Chinese and Indian savings rates might be taken as providing some support for the view that democracies will have very high rates of time preference as compared with dictatorships. But considering dictators like Mobutu of Zaire or Marcos of the Philippines, it would be difficult to sustain this view.

Effects of Globalization

Finally, we can examine the effects of the current episode of globalization on economic policymaking in developing countries, on which their economic growth rates and then poverty reduction depend. There is a view that globalization will lead to the withering away of the state. This view is as unjustified as the hope of the

Marxists that their communist paradise would lead to a similar—for them desirable—outcome. Two points need to be emphasized.

First, integrating with the world economy is still a matter of choice for every state. The reason so many are increasingly treading this path is the unparalleled popular opulence it offers. Some, like Cuba and North Korea, have chosen to turn their backs on the global economy, with predictable dire outcomes for their populace. Nor is there something new about globalization. In the past, it has been associated with the creation of empires that have brought hitherto disjointed economic spaces into a common economic area under their Pax, allowing the gains from trade and specialization emphasized by Adam Smith to generate what I call Smithian intensive growth. But these periods of globalization are not irreversible, as witness the 19th-century LIEO created under British aegis, which was destroyed in World War I. Whether the current global financial crisis will lead to a similar unraveling of globalization remains an open question.

Second, the processes of globalization, in particular the integration of capital markets, do increase the contestability of both states and corporations. For the degree of contestability depends, in both cases, on the barriers to entry against potential new entrants and barriers to exit for existing customers. Current fears that a globalized economy will be monopolized by large multinationals are thus unfounded, as globalization, by increasing contestability, will make even the largest of this species behave in a competitive manner.

Similarly, the predatory state (in all its forms) will find that globalization will force it to reduce the net revenues it can extract from its populace for its own purpose. Ideally, it will force them to act like the Platonic Guardian State, which only taxes its citizens enough to provide the essential public goods with a balanced budget.

Finally, in a globalized world, size does not matter as long as the global public good of defense against external predators is ensured by a global hegemon. In parts of the world, including much of Europe, where this external threat has almost disappeared, we are witnessing the unraveling of the ancient nation-states, for example, the United Kingdom, Spain, and Belgium. For many developing countries, such a happy outcome is unlikely, partly because of the reluctance of the current hegemon—the United States—to enforce its Pax if doing so requires it to expend its own men and materiel. Although the U.S. reaction to the savage events of September 11, 2001, seemed to change this attitude, with the Iraqi debacle, the stalemate in Afghanistan, and the burgeoning fiscal deficit, it is uncertain how long the United States will be willing and able to maintain global order.

So in much of the Third World, where the old impulses for territorial aggrandizement are not extinct, maintaining a national identity coterminous with the territorial nation-state will remain important, and hence the nation-building impulse that fueled much dirigiste neomercantilism will remain in place. But to the extent that globalization forces the depoliticization of economic and social life, it also makes it less important to capture the levers of economic power in order to make a living for oneself or one's constituents. This means that domestic politics will need to cater less to the economic interests of particular groups and could become less fissiparous. The state can then more easily become a "civil" rather than an "enterprise" association in Oakeshott's terms. This should reduce the tensions between a national identity fostered by a perceived external threat and that of belonging to a particular caste, tribe, or other narrow group seeking to garner more of the gains in the political redistributive game for itself. All this of course assumes that there is a functioning state in the first place. For the failed states in which a large number of the "bottom billion" live, until a viable state is created by the two routes outlined above, globalization in itself offers no panaceas.

It might be thought that the global financial crisis of 2008 will end the current period of globalization and that the crisis exposed the failings of the classical-liberal policy package. Both arguments in my view are mistaken. After a short dip, the growth rates of many developing countries (in particular India and China) have picked up to where they were before the crisis—and not because they retreated from globalization or the classical-liberal package. It is in the West, particularly in the United States—the epicenter—that there could be calls for protection and increased dirigisme. But to date, there are no signs that the West is going to revert to the closed economies instigated by the U.S. interwar Smoot-Hawley tariff.

Nor was the crisis due to purported "market failures." It was due to misguided monetary policies in the United States, the attempt by public authorities to put low-income people and poor credit risks on the property ladder and the creation of considerable moral hazard by bailing out bankrupt financial firms.[12] So adopting the classical-liberal package and joining the globalization bandwagon still remains the best means for developing countries to continue their ongoing ascent from poverty.

PART TWO

MYTHS

5. The Numbers Game

In April 2007, in its World Development Indicators, the World Bank announced that there were 986 million in extreme poverty (living on less than $1 a day). For the first time, the world's poor were less than the billion that was the basis of Paul Collier's popular book, *The Bottom Billion*. Then in August 2008, the World Bank announced that the number of poor were 1.4 billion, with Chen and Ravallion declaring that the "developing world is poorer than we thought" (2008, 1). How had the number of the world's poor increased by over 400 million in a year?

To understand this numbers game, we need briefly to look at the source of the poverty data of which the World Bank remains the custodian. The poverty numbers are derived from periodic surveys done by the International Comparison Program (ICP) and summarized in a series of Penn World Tables (PWT) by the researchers based at the University of Pennsylvania, with funding from the World Bank. The ICP produces estimates of countries' real GDP at purchasing power parity (PPP) index relative to a reference country, usually the United States. It provides internationally comparable estimates of the quantity (volume) of output of different countries.

Thus, the ICP estimates relative national price levels by using an absolute-price-comparison approach. Using a detailed sample of commodities, matched sets of prices of individual commodity groups are constructed in a particular country relative to a reference country. These are then weighted by the expenditure shares usually of the reference country to obtain the real value of the consumption basket of the particular country in domestic currency, which when divided by the value of same consumption basket at the prices of the reference country gives the PPP index for that country.[1]

There are numerous practical and theoretical problems in making these price comparisons to derive the PPP dollar values, particularly for goods and services such as housing that do not enter international trade. But this need not concern us.[2] What is important to note is that the PPP numbers are meant to provide a measure of the real size of an economy relative to the United States and relative differences in their per capita income and consumption. The resulting PPP estimates of per capita consumption allow the World Bank and others to derive the dollar-a-day poverty numbers reported in Chapter 1. They have formed the basis for all the discourse on the changing profile of poverty in the world.

The ICP has provided these PPP adjustments for several years: 1970, 1985, 1993, and the last one carried out in 2005. On the basis of this latest survey, the World Bank's estimates of the PPP value of most Asian countries' GDP in 2005 was reduced by 40 percent compared with that from the earlier 1993 survey. The major downgrades were for China (−40 percent), India (−36 percent), Bangladesh (−44 percent), and the Philippines (−43 percent). Other non-Asian countries with large downgrades included Ghana (−32 percent) and Uganda (−42 percent). It is worth noting that these were among the fastest growing economies at market exchange rates, and we would have expected to see large reductions in their poverty levels. But although, with the revisions, their absolute poverty numbers were higher in 2005 than those based on the earlier 1993 ICP survey, their fast growth has still reduced their poverty rates. Hence, Chen and Ravallion's subtitle, "No less successful in the fight against poverty."

So how does the World Bank explain this rise in the estimate of world poverty in 2005, particularly in Asia? In its *Background Document—Frequently Asked Questions*, it explains that "this is the first time China has participated in the ICP." But, as Surjit Bhalla (2008) reasonably asks, how can this explain the downgrades of PPP incomes in other countries? India has participated in the ICP surveys since its inception in 1970. There also seems to be a systematic bias in the downgrades, as can be seen from Table 5.1 derived by Bhalla. This shows the estimates of PPP annual per capita income in 2005, based on the previous 1993 ICP survey and the latest 2005 survey. It shows that of all regions, the new income estimates for Asia deviate the most from the older estimates. The new estimates for developed and Latin American countries are nearly the same as the older ones,

Table 5.1
How Sensible Are the New Estimates of World and
Country Incomes?

Region	Number of Countries	Annual Income Level in		% Deviation (Old/New)
		Old (1993)	New (2005)	
Developed economies	23	28239	28753	2
Russia & Eastern Europe	28	9060	7155	−17
Asia, excluding Japan	31	4916	3061	−41
Latin America	34	7453	6711	−7
Africa & Middle East	63	3452	3020	−11
Total	179	8363	7170	−25

Notes: Percent deviation is the percent by which new (2005) PPP estimate of income varies from the old (1995) PPP estimate.
Source: Bhalla (2008), Table 1. From PPP data, World Bank.

while those for eastern Europe, including the former Soviet Union and sub-Saharan Africa, are about 13 percent lower. As Bhalla notes:

> For 148 countries [out of the 179 country estimates], developed and developing, the new is much like the old; on an aggregate basis, only 7% lower. But for Asia, we have a different metric—incomes are reported to be 41% lower, and it does not matter whether India and China are included or excluded.

This general downgrading of Asian PPP incomes as a whole follows from the Chinese downgrade. Maddison notes that in this first ICP exercise involving China, it submitted estimates of the price level in 11 cities rather than a national average. He states that "in aiming at comparability with advanced countries, the Chinese statisticians probably made a disproportionate selection of items at the higher end of the product range. Thus, they failed to get a representative consumption profile of the average Chinese household" (2008a, 9).

This is further complicated by the large disparity in income levels in different Chinese provinces, as well as the large differential between urban and rural prices—problems that also plague the estimates for other large, regionally diverse economies with substantial rural populations, like India.[3]

One way of testing the plausibility of the latest World Bank PPP estimates of incomes in Asia is a route taken by both Maddison and Bhalla. Maddison reports that taking the World Bank-level estimates for 2005 with his growth estimate of a 12.5-fold increase in China's per capita income between 1950 and 2005, he gets "per capita GDP of EKS (Elteto-Koves-Szulc method) $4,091 in 2005 and EKS $326 in 1950. However, if we measure the intertemporal change in 1990 Geary-Khamis (GK) units using the World Bank's 2005 China/U.S. ratio of 10 percent, Chinese per capita GDP in 2005 would be GK $3052 and $243 in 1950. Both 1950 estimates are well below subsistence level. The implausibility is bigger if one believes the official estimate of per capita GDP growth (21-fold over 55 years)" (Maddison 2008a).

Bhalla performs a similar exercise for Asia, using the per capita daily consumption in 1950 implied by the new ICP-based PPP-income-level estimates for 2005 (see Table 5.2). The World Bank defines per capita consumption of less than $1.08 in 1993 prices as

Table 5.2
"NEW" ESTIMATES OF PER CAPITA PER DAY
CONSUMPTION IN 1950

Region	Bottom 20%	20–40%	40–60%	60–80%	All
Asia, excluding Japan	0.25	0.32	0.4	0.49	0.71
Latin America	0.34	0.5	0.7	0.97	2.32
Africa & Middle East	0.42	0.59	0.77	1.02	2.07
Total	0.28	0.37	0.47	0.6	1.08

NOTES: Consumption levels are person per day in 1993 PPP dollars, according to the new World Bank estimates of individual country and global income. The poverty line is $1.08 per person per day.

SOURCE: Bhalla (2008), Table 2.

barely enough to survive[4] The implied average level of consumption in all of Asia is only 0.71 1993 PPP dollars per capita per day. Thus, if the bottom 80 percent of the Asian population, with an average daily per capita consumption of less than half the minimum poverty line, is at 1993 PPP $0.49, most Asians would have been dead in 1950![5]

Srinivasan (1994) also noted a similar anomaly concerning Chinese GDP. The World Bank's *World Development Indicators* 1992, Table 1.1, reports that "in 1990 India and China had GNP per capita of U.S.$350 and U.S.$370 respectively and the average annual rate of growth of GNP per capita was 1.9% in India and 5.5% in China. Taken together, these levels and rates of growth would imply that China's per capita GNP was about 40% of India's [in 1965]! No knowledgeable observer of the two countries would subscribe to this ranking" (10).

This would seem to have been a precursor to what Deaton and Heston describe as "suspicions that the government of China wished simultaneously to exaggerate its growth rate and understate its level of per capita GDP" for political reasons.[6] Bhalla's conjecture is that, given China's policy of maintaining an undervalued exchange rate to promote export-led growth, the reduction in China's GDP in dollars adjusted for PPP and increase in the number of its poor in extreme poverty was "an attempt by the international organizations, and China, to portray China as *not* so rich in order that its exchange rate did not appear so undervalued."[7] For it is well known that an increase in per capita income leads to an appreciation of the exchange rate. So a lower PPP income would require less of an appreciation of the Chinese yuan, a useful tactic to resist the pressure from the United States and other trading partners for currency appreciation.

If this suspicion were justified, it would also explain the downgrading of all other Asian PPP per capita incomes. Having reduced China's by 40 percent, it would have stretched credulity even further if Indian per capita income had been kept the same, so that its ratio to the Chinese would have risen by 40 percent.

The most important lesson from this numbers game is that with the growing politicization of the international agencies, their professional rectitude can no longer be taken for granted.[8] The so-called "scientific data" they produce are now a highly political product. Hence, the carefully sifted and transparently analyzed intertemporal data produced by independent researchers like Maddison and Bhalla (which I have used in Chapter 1) provide a more credible anatomy of the dimensions of changing global poverty levels than the "official" numbers peddled by the international organization.

However, it should be noted that in its latest update to its estimates of consumption poverty in the world, the World Bank (2012) found that the $1.25 a day poverty rate in developing countries "had fallen to half of its 1990 value by 2010." That reaches the Millennium Development Goal of cutting the 1990 incidence of expected poverty in half by 2015. The $1 a day poverty rate was halved by 2008, this despite the financial crisis.

In addition, there are the inherent fragility and shortcomings of the ICP numbers lucidly detailed recently by Deaton and Heston. Despite this and the periodic warnings of the need to go behind the aggregate macroeconomic statistics for developing countries, the Penn World Tables based on the ICP have become the workhorse for myriad cross-country regression exercises by development economists. Hence, an ongoing exercise by two IMF economists—reported by Deaton and Heston—is of interest. The economists' preliminary results show that it is probably safe to use the PWT for analysis of long-term growth trends over 40-year intervals, but unsafe to do so for shorter periods and for dynamic processes for countries that are not classified as A and B in terms of quality grades by the PWT and that are mainly developing countries. This makes much of the last two decades' empirical econometric research that relies on these dubious global databases (including the PWT) highly unreliable. In the next chapter, I turn to this statistical snake oil being peddled by so many development economists in their search for panaceas for global poverty.

6. Statistical Snake Oil

A mania for finding quantitative certainty from various statistical models has been around since the mid-1960s, and it now infects many aspects of macroeconomic development and health policy. The recent credit crunch has exposed the failings of the quantitative risk-management models, which had previously led to the Long-Term Capital Management crisis. Curbs on carbon emissions are being promoted on the basis of highly insecure climate-change models (see Chapter 11 in my *Against Dirigisme* and Chapter 10 below). Mindless correlations of medical epidemiology are leading to numerous ridiculous health scares. The U.S. push for democracy in the world is based on political scientists' purported statistical correlations showing that democracies do not fight each other (a claim shown to be spurious in my *In Praise of Empires*).

This statistical snake oil is now being peddled by young development economists, in large part by their attempts to provide an answer to the question: Does foreign aid promote economic development and alleviate poverty? They use atheoretical econometric techniques to devise various unpersuasive answers to this question, citing the authority of peer-reviewed journals in which they publish their results and validate their findings. But what can we learn about the means to alleviate poverty from these atheoretical econometric studies based on using instrumental variables (IV) in the macroeconomic cross-country regressions that have proliferated in the journals, or the latest "empirical" fad in development microeconometrics: randomized controlled trials (RCT)?

When I was learning my econometrics at the feet of Terence Gorman and Alan Walters at Oxford in the early 1960s, it was drummed into me and my classmates that one had to begin with a theoretical model whose predictions depended on statistical estimation of its parameters, taking account of standard estimation problems like identification, serial correlation, and multicollinearity. Since most of the regressions in those days had to be done on hand-held calculators, or by punching hundreds of cards to be used on gigantic computers whose power was less than any standard PC today, one had to take immense care to ensure the robustness of the data one was using and the functional form one was estimating in order not to waste one's time. The PC revolution has meant that any researcher can now run millions of regressions on large, readily available data sets of highly variable quality, covering countries of different sizes, institutions, and histories, and obtain some statistically significant result or other, which one of the myriad of social science journals will be happy to publish. Common sense, the qualitative judgments that allow us to recognize meaningless or unpersuasive results, and specific knowledge (including historical) of the numerous countries thrown into the statistical regression sausage machine seem to have gone out of the window.

Causality

The problem of course is the difficulty of assigning causality in the social sciences, where J. S. Mill's "method of difference," which underlies the controlled experiments of the physical sciences to determine cause and effect, cannot be applied. It would take me too far afield to outline the different stances on causality in economics and econometrics.[1] The two major approaches to causality in economics go back to Hume and Mill. Hume believed that all ideas are based either on logic or sense experience and that observation of a constant conjunction of particular temporal sequences does not give us secure grounds to infer a general rule.

By contrast, Mill distinguished between what he called the "method of agreement" and the "method of difference" (two of his five methods of experimental inquiry). The method of difference is the normal method used in the experimental sciences. By this, "one can try to establish that several cases have in common a set of causal factors, although they vary in other ways that might have seemed causally relevant." The method of agreement by contrast deals with "cases in which the phenomenon to be explained and the hypothesized cause are both present to other cases in which the phenomenon and the causes are both absent, but which are otherwise as similar as possible to the positive cases" (1843, 219). Mill emphasized that the method of difference is by itself a more powerful method for establishing valid causal connections, but that "on those subjects where artificial experimentation is impossible . . . our only recourse of a directly productive nature [is the method of agreement], while in the phenomena which we can produce at pleasure, the method of difference generally affords a more efficacious process which will ascertain causes as well as mere laws" (219).

Mill also claimed that the basic principles of economics are known a priori, as it is a science of an aspect of human conduct of which we have firsthand experience through introspection. Thus, utility and profit maximization would be such basic a priori principles. When these basic principles are combined with assumptions about the structure of an economic system, deductive conclusions can be derived. The theory-based structural econometric models pioneered by the Cowles Commission are the direct descendants of Mill's epistemology. The structural parameters of the resulting economic model can be estimated and used to answer well-posed economic questions. As part of the problem of "identification" in these models, instrumental variable techniques (IV) were developed.[2]

But as Heckman and Urzua note, "After 60 years of experience with fitting structural models on a variety of data sources, empirical economists have come to appreciate the practical difficulty in identifying, and precisely estimating, the full array of structural parameters that answer the large variety of policy questions contemplated by the Cowles Commission economists" (2009, 2).

This led to a revival of an alternative approach based on Humean skepticism, but with a twist. This is the atheoretical inferential approach to causality, like the Granger causality pioneered by Clive Granger, which is purely data based and does not rely on any background economic theory. This is part of the modern probabilistic approach to causality, "which is a natural successor to Hume. Where Hume required constant conjunction of cause and effect, probabilistic approaches are content to identify cause with a factor that raises the probability of the effect" (Hoover 2008, 4). The IV regressions, which have run riot in the recent empirical literature on development, are an application of this atheoretical approach.

Instrumental Variables

The most penetrating critique of this IV approach in the development literature is by Deaton (2009). Deaton, based on Heckman, argues that the atheoretical IV is rooted in failing to distinguish between "exogenous" and "external" variables. He and Heckman argue that "exogenous" variables satisfy

> the orthogonality [uncorrelated] condition[3] that is required for consistent estimation in [the] instrumental variable [IV] context. . . . An instrument that is *external* but not *exogenous*, will not yield consistent estimates for parameters of interest, even when that parameter is constant. . . . Natural or geographic variables . . . are not affected by the variables being explained, and are clearly external.[4] So are historical variables—the mortality of colonial settlers is not influenced by current institutional arrangements in ex-colonial countries (Acemoglou, Johnson, Robinson (2001), nor does the country's growth rate today influence which country they were colonized by (Barro (1998). *Whether any of these instruments is exogenous depends on the nature of the equation of interest, and is not guaranteed by its externality. And because exogeneity is an identifying assumption that must be made prior to analysis of the data, no empirical tests are possible* [emphasis added].

This puts a coach and horses through the host of cross-section regressions trying to use atheoretical methods based on external but not truly exogenous IVs, which have proliferated in studies of institutional and historical factors in the process of growth and development.

Natural Experiments

Similar objections apply to many of the studies of natural experiments using IV estimation, which have also proliferated in recent years. Here there is an additional problem concerning heterogeneity. As Heckman puts it: "Any valid application of the method of instrumental variables for estimating . . . treatment effects in the case where the response to treatment varies among persons requires a behavioral assumption about how persons make their decisions about program participation. The issue cannot be settled by statistical analysis" (Heckman 1997, 449). He quotes an oft-cited study of a "natural experiment" by Angrist (1990) of the effects of military service on earnings, using Vietnam draft lottery numbers as instrumental variables. In 1969, the lottery randomly assigned different draft numbers to persons with different birth dates. The higher the number, the more likely they were to escape the draft. But if the rate of return to schooling differs among potential draftees, "the instrument (the draft lottery number) fails to be exogenous because the error term in the earnings equation depends on each individual's rate of return to schooling, and whether or not each potential draftee accepted their assignment—their veteran's status—depends on that rate of return" (Deaton 2009, 8).[5] So the instrument is not a random number and not necessarily uncorrelated to the error term in the earnings equation.

A more relevant example from the development literature is in a "natural experiment" by Urquiola and Verhoogen (2009) for Chile, on whether schoolchildren do better in smaller classes. This replicates another oft-cited study by Angrist and Lavy (1999) for Israel. In both Israel and Chile, there is a set maximum class size. If the number of children enrolled is greater than this number, say 40, then extra teachers must be found for another class. So with increasing enrollment, actual class sizes will follow a saw-tooth pattern. The graph will start off along a 45 degree line, then, when enrollment rises to 40, it will fall discontinuously to 20, thereafter rising along a 45 degree line until enrollment reaches 80, and so on. When test scores are plotted against enrollment, the opposite pattern is found, with scores rising at each of the discontinuities, when class size falls. But if children are not all the same, it is unlikely that the effect of lower class size is the same for all children. "This raises the possibility that the variation across discontinuities may not be orthogonal [uncorrelated] to other factors that affect test scores" (Deaton 2009, 22). More information is needed on how children end up in different classes. This is what a study for Chile in a similar quasi-experiment does. It finds that, as parents care about whether their children are in smaller classes, there is sorting across the boundary of classes with 40 and 20 children, so that

> the children in smaller classes have richer, more educated parents than the children in the larger classes . . . so that some of the differences in test scores across class size also come from differences in the children that would be present whatever the class size. . . . This [shows] why it is so dangerous to make inferences from natural experiments without understanding the mechanisms at work [Deaton 2009, 22–23].

Randomized Controlled Trials (RCTs)

The method closest to Mill's Principle of Difference is the method of randomized controlled trials (RCT), which has been claimed as the "gold standard" for generating evidence in medicine and now is claimed to be so by a new school of development economists based around the Poverty Lab at MIT. With this method, a randomized "treatment" group is administered the recommended policy (treatment), while another randomized control group is not. The difference between the means of the resulting effects in these two groups is then taken as a measure of the effectiveness of the treatment. Randomization is meant to ensure that causal factors other than the treatment administered are distributed equally in the two groups, while various forms of blinding are used to eliminate other forms of bias, like selection bias. This method is claimed to be superior to econometric evidence and free of the associated methodological criticisms. Also, it is not dependent on any theory.

But in medicine, the claim that clinical trials based on RCT provide the only valid scientific evidence is increasingly being questioned (Worrall 2002; Cartwright 2007a). The same is true of this latest turn in empirical development economics. The problem, as with the natural and quasi-experimental method, is the one of heterogeneity within the subgroups in the treatment and control groups. In purely physical processes, evidence based on controlled experiments can rightly assume that the "treatment" effects in the two groups are identical. But in medicine (and in economics), this cannot be assumed. Thus, a drug that passes a well-conducted RCT may well be curing people in the "treatment" group, on average, even while it is killing some in a subgroup. Moreover, there is no guarantee that treating the general population with the RCT-validated "treatment" will have the same effect. Thus, the drug Opren to treat arthritis passed the RCT (explicitly restricted to 18- to 65-year-olds) with flying colors, but when administered to the older population that normally suffers from arthritis, there were a number of deaths from renal failure, and the drug was withdrawn!

There are further practical problems with the method. The double-blinding method, whereby neither the experimenter nor the subjects know who is receiving the treatment and who a placebo, is often not feasible. Subjects may be able to decipher the randomization and take the treatment on the sly even if they are in the placebo control group. As Heckman has noted, in agronomy, "plots of grounds do not respond to anticipated treatments of fertilizer, nor can they excuse themselves from being treated." For human subjects, the higher the stakes, the greater will be the attempt to escape the trial assignments, "so that deviations from assignment cannot be treated as random measurement error, but will compromise the results in fundamental ways (Deaton 2009, 37). The technical fixes to overcome this involve instrumental variables. But this brings all the associated econometric problems, and the claimed scientific superiority of the RCT method disappears.

Moreover, randomization itself can be a problem in practice. Deaton cites a flagship study of this "new" development economics: Miguel and Kremer's (2004) study of intestinal worms in Kenya. They found that deworming was a highly effective way to reduce school absenteeism. Since children infect one another, a school-based program was more effective than individual treatment. But as Deaton discovered (39), on asking Michael Kremer (in private correspondence),

> local parents would not permit the use of random numbers for assignment, so that assignment to these groups was done in alphabetical order. . . . Alphabetization maybe a reasonable solution when randomization is impossible, but we are then in the world of quasi-or natural experiments . . . [and] as is true with all forms of quasi-randomization, alphabetization does not guarantee orthogonality [no correlation] with potential confounders. [That is, this is no longer an RCT but the type of natural experiment with instrumental variables discussed above (the instrumental variable being alphabetization).]

But having eschewed any theoretical foundations, the best RCTs, while perhaps useful in showing what works in specified circumstances, cannot tell us why it works. This makes them useless for learning about the processes or mechanisms of economic development or poverty alleviation. As Deaton rightly concludes (44):

> In the end there is no substitute for careful evaluation of the chain of evidence and reasoning by people who have the experience and expertise in the field. The demand that experiments be theory-driven is, of course, no guarantee of success, though the lack of it is close to a guarantee of failure.

This echoes the conclusion of Heckman's masterly survey of the evolution of econometrics in the 20th century and the various strategies empirical economists have employed to derive causal parameters for policy analysis:

> No successful mechanical algorithm for discovering causal or structural models has yet been produced, and it is unlikely that one will ever be found. At the same time, it is unlikely that the quest for a mechanical algorithm for determining causality from data will ever be abandoned. . . . The best empirical work in economics uses economic theory as a framework for integrating all of the available evidence, tacit and algorithmic, to tell a convincing story [Deaton 2009, 89].

Economics Is Not Like Physics

This is also the message of my distinguished UCLA econometrician colleague, Ed Leamer, in his recent guide for MBAs to empirical macroeconomics (2009).[6] Echoing Hayek's claim that unlike the "hard" sciences like physics, where specific predictions are possible, in the social sciences all one can make are pattern predictions. Leamer recommends a three-stage method. First, look at the patterns, then at plausible stories, and only then do the logical and mathematical analysis. Unlike the official empirical rhetorical advice to follow the scientific practice of "theory and evidence," Leamer instead suggests "patterns and stories." The former

> suggests an incessant march towards a level of scientific certitude that cannot be attained in the study of the complex self-organizing human system that we call the economy. The words "patterns and stories" much more accurately conveys our level of knowledge, now, and in the future as well. It is literature not science [3].

This echoes the views of Hayek, who has argued that the "physics envy" of economists is misplaced. Physics has developed by substituting a new classification for our sensory perception,

> which groups together not what appears alike but what proves to behave in the same manner in similar circumstances. . . . [This] new classification based on consciously established relations between classes of events is perhaps

the most characteristic aspect of the procedure of the natural sciences. . . . [It] renders it impossible to express observable occurrences in language appropriate to what is perceived by our senses. The only appropriate language is that of mathematics, that is the discipline developed to describe complexes of relationships between elements which have no attributes except these relations" [Hayek 1979, 31–3].

By contrast, the social sciences "deal not with the relations between things, but with the relations between man and man" (39). Of course, there are aspects of the "life of men in groups" that are not different from those of the natural sciences, like genetics, disease, or demography. "Wherever we are concerned with unconscious reflexes or processes in the human body there is no obstacle to treating and investigating them 'mechanically' as caused by objectively observable external events" (42). But in the social sciences (or moral sciences as they used to be called), this situation is different. They "are concerned with man's conscious or reflected action, actions where a person can be said to choose between various courses open to him" (43). Unlike the "objective" facts studied by the natural sciences, "social" facts are (47):

> beliefs or opinions held by particular people, beliefs which as such are our data, irrespective of whether they are true or false, and which moreover, we cannot directly observe in the minds of the people but which we can recognize from what they do and say merely because we have ourselves a mind similar to theirs.

The natural sciences are thus concerned with phenomena of "unorganized complexity," whereas the "social sciences" are concerned with "organized complexity. In the former, an explanation about the workings of the structure can be provided by "the relative frequency, or the probability, of the occurrence of the various distinctive properties of the individual elements." In the latter,

> we cannot replace the information about the individual elements by statistical information, but require full information about each element if from our theory we are to derive specific predictions about individual events. Without such specific information about the individual elements we

shall be confined to mere pattern predictions—predictions of some general attributes of the structures that will form themselves, but not containing specific statements about the individual elements of which the structures will be made up [Hayek 1974, 17–18].

This is not to reject the mathematical method in economics, which has the great advantage

that it allows us to describe, by means of algebraic equations, the general character of a pattern even when we are ignorant of the numerical values which will determine its particular manifestation. We could scarcely have achieved that comprehensive picture of the mutual interdependence of the different events in a market without this algebraic technique. It has led to the illusion, however, that we can use this technique for the determination and prediction of the numerical values of those magnitudes; and this has led to a vain search for quantitative or numerical constants. This happened in spite of the fact that the modern founders of mathematical economics [like Vilfredo Pareto] had no such illusion [18–19].

Relying on pattern prediction does not mean that the resulting method is unscientific. In the social sciences,

as we advance we find more and more frequently that we can in fact ascertain only some but not all the particular circumstances which determine the outcome of a given process; and in consequence we are able to predict only some but not all the properties of the result we have to expect. Yet, we will still achieve predictions which can be falsified and which therefore are of empirical significance [25].

But this limitation to pattern prediction means the hope that nature can be increasingly controlled by human design, as in the natural sciences, cannot apply to the social sciences. We cannot hope that its advances, in Hayek's words, "would soon enable us to mould society entirely to our liking." Moreover,

the confidence in the unlimited power of science is only too often based on a false belief that the scientific method consists in the application of a ready-made technique, or in initiating the form rather than the substance of scientific procedure, as if one needed only to follow some cooking recipe to solve all social problems [22].

This is a charge which applies, as we have seen, to the young "empirical" development economists of our day.

Nobel laureate Robert Solow (1985, 328) too has questioned the belief among "the best and brightest in the profession . . . [that] economics is the physics of society." He argues (328) that

> the attempt to construct economics as an axiomatically based hard science is doomed to fail . . . [as] the classical hard science devices for discriminating between competing hypotheses are closed to us. The main alternative device is the statistical analysis of historical time series. But then another difficulty arises. In order to distinguish between complex and subtle competing hypotheses, many of which "are capable of fitting the data in a gross sort of way[,] . . . we need long time-series observed under stationary conditions. . . . [But] much of what we observe cannot be treated as the realization of a stationary stochastic process without straining credulity."

He then "recommends" marrying the tools of the economist with "the ability [of the economic historian] to imagine how things might have been before they became as they now are" (331). This is pretty close to the classical method of economic analytical economic history used in the Lal-Myint volume and whose results were summarized in various chapters of Part 1. It may be useful briefly to recapitulate the logical basis of the resulting "comparative studies" method that has been the most fruitful one, in my judgment, in the study of the development process.

The Logic of Comparative Studies

Comparative studies are a form of comparative historical analysis that has a distinguished pedigree in social science.[7] J. S. Mill sets out the logic of these studies explicitly in his *A System of Logic* (especially Book 3, Chapter 8), and this comparative method was applied with great skill by Alexis de Tocqueville in *Democracy in America* and by Marc Bloch in *Feudal Society*.

The method is particularly suited to the empirical study of problems of growth and development, as John Neville Keynes (Maynard's father) noted at the turn of the last century (1890, 283–84). He wrote:

> There are in fact few departments of political or social science in which the a priori method avails less than in economic development. . . . In more general problems relating to economic growth and progress the part played by abstract reasoning is reduced to a minimum, and the economist's dependence upon historical generalizations is at a maximum. . . . For only by the direct comparison of successive stages of society can we reasonably hope to discover the laws, in accordance with which economic states tend to succeed one another or to become changed in character.

The evolution of institutions is likely to be central in explanations of differing growth performances, and in my *Unintended Consequences* and *Reviving the Invisible Hand*, I have provided my own comparative historical story of this evolution, which is summarized in the previous part of this book. This is in contrast with the black boxes that "institutions" have become when serving as explanatory variables in much of current empirical development economics based on IVs in cross-country regressions, which are discussed in the next section.

Cross-Country Regressions

By contrast, the development literature is now filled with cross-country regressions using IV to explain various aspects of the economy, in particular the role of institutions. But what are institutions? In Chapter 4, discussing political habits, I had made the distinction between the cosmological and material beliefs of different cultures based on my *Unintended Consequences*. This distinction also helps us to understand institutions, which is as murky a concept as "culture."

For institutions broadly defined consist of informal constraints on human behavior, like cultural norms or the more purposive formal ones embodied in particular organizational structures—including formal rules embodied in, for instance, the common law, which forms a spontaneous order in Hayek's sense, having evolved without any conscious design.

But as soon as we start talking about constraining human behavior, we are acknowledging that there is some basic human nature to be constrained. It would take me too far afield to discuss what we now know about human nature as a result of the findings of evolutionary psychologists, neuroscientists, and geneticists (Pinker 2002; Boyd and Silk 2003). But if as a first cut we accept the economists' model of *homo economicus*, which assumes that human beings are motivated purely by self-interest, then the function of institutions is to constrain such self-seeking behavior. There is a close relationship between institutions and "transactions costs," a concept even more slippery than institutions. For as Robin Matthews (1986) has argued, "To a large extent transactions costs are costs of relations between people," and institutions are par excellence ways of controlling the interactions between people.

The distinction between material and cosmological beliefs translates into two distinct types of transactions costs. The first are those associated with the efficiency of exchange, which relate to the cost of finding potential trading partners. The second are concerned with policing opportunistic behavior by economic agents and enforcing the execution of promises and agreements.

We need to see how material and cosmological beliefs have evolved in different cultures if we are to understand institutional change. But in much of the recent statistical development literature relying on cross-country regressions, institutions are black boxes.

To see how vacuous the results are, consider just one recent example. An article by Angeles purports to have established empirically that colonialism is the major explanation behind the differing inequality among nations (Angeles 2007). Income inequality was higher in colonies where European settlers were a larger share of the population (as in Africa and Latin America) without being a majority (as in what he calls "New Europe": Australia, Canada, New Zealand, and the United States). Two questions arise.

The first is, assuming that Angeles is right, so what? Does this mean that colonialism was bad for the Third World? As he himself recognizes, even if colonialism resulted in highly unequal societies where European settlers were a large minority of the population, this does not imply that they had poorer growth records, or that the poor majority of the population was less well-off in absolute terms than in what he terms "peasant economies," where the European settlers were either absent or a small minority.

Surely, apart from those dogmatic egalitarians who would cheerfully trade off growth and/or the reduction of absolute poverty for their supreme value, equality, most people would see colonialism as being beneficial if it had raised growth rates and reduced absolute poverty irrespective of what it did to the Gini coefficient. So Angeles provides no reasons for taking a jaundiced view of the economic record of empires and colonialism in general, judging by their effects on the well-being of the majority of the population in their dominions.

The second question is whether Angles's thesis is persuasive. I don't think so. From a long-term historical and comparative perspective, there are two major sources of the unequal social and economic systems that arose in the Third World, as outlined in Part 1: the need for a specialized nonproducing warrior class to defend the Eurasian civilizations against nomadic predators, and the need to tie labor down to land when land was abundant and labor was scarce to secure an agrarian surplus for these warriors (and priests). Land being free, various institutional forms of coercion to tie peasants to the land and extract part of their output were needed. For free peasants would have fled to the "bush" to avoid these "taxes." Various unequal social institutions like serfdom, slavery, and the caste system can be explained in these terms.

By contrast, in Angeles's classificatory schema, his countries of "New Europe" did not face this perpetual military threat, being protected by vast oceans, and so did not need a warrior class. Moreover, the temperate agriculture they practiced allowed the free peasantry to expand their family farms without any social stratification. These countries did not need to have any coerced labor to make a living and could maintain equal societies.

Angeles's "settler colonies" in Africa and Latin America, on the other hand, while having no need for a separate military class, had another source of inequalities: their abundant natural resources, whose exploitation was labor intensive. These countries faced the same problem as the Eurasian agrarian economies of coercing scarce labor to exploit these natural resources, but not necessarily to support a military class. However, since these natural resources (unlike the abundant land in Eurasia) yielded massive natural rents, which would accrue to whoever succeeded in setting up a system of coerced labor, great inequalities were bound to be generated. Whether those acquiring the rents and using coerced labor to work their plantations and mines were indigenous or colonialists is moot. We would need to have Gini coefficients for the Aztec, Mayan, or Inca empires to show that colonialism worsened Latin America's "natural" inequalities arising from its factor endowments. It is this "bane of natural resources" that continues to perpetuate income inequality in these countries, even after throwing off the colonial yoke.

Another more telling example of the dubious conclusions of a highly influential research program is provided by a series of papers by La Porta and associates about the legal origins of differences in financial origins and their effects on economic development (La Porta, Lopez-de-Silanes, and Shleifer 2008). Relying on cross-country regressions using IV, they argue that the countries that adopted the common-law legal tradition of Britain protected finance sufficiently to allow investors to flourish, whereas the alternative continental or French system did not. Kenneth Dam, the distinguished legal scholar, has questioned this portrayal of how different legal systems work, how laws developed historically, and how government power is allocated in various legal traditions (2006). To give just one example, the "legal origins" school assumes that the British transplanted their legal system, particularly the jury system as a key anti-statist institution, to their colonies. But Dam points out that the jury system is an American institution, not a common-law one, and that the British after their unhappy experience with juries in Ireland, which were unwilling to convict Irishmen for crimes against Englishmen, did not make the mistake of transferring this to India or their African colonies. A cross-country regression cannot substitute for the hard grind required to ascertain the historical origins of the differing legal traditions in the world.

Most of this institutional econometrics pays obeisance to the work of the Nobel laureate Douglass North. But this body of research seeking empirical validation of his recent thesis (1994, 2005), that institutions are exogenous determinants of long-run economic performance, is highly dubious[8]—for in his earlier incarnation, North had rightly argued that instead of being invariant to economic factors, institutions change and adapt to changing factor prices and technology (North and Thomas 1973). Or in terms of my classification of cultural beliefs, the institutions (like property rights) that are the major concern of these new "institutionalists," and can be expected to influence long-term economic performance, are part of the material beliefs of a culture and are highly malleable.[9] There is no invariant path dependence, as the later North has argued, on long-run economic performance.[10]

Nor has the ocean of ink spilt on cross-country regressions attempting to explain the determinants of growth, or more narrowly the influence of foreign aid on development, provided any light, let alone a consensus. Using the same data sets, recent highly acclaimed popular books by William Easterly, Jeffrey Sachs, and Paul Collier come to sharply divergent views, presumably based on their prior beliefs for which their regressions are just a fig leaf.

These battles between what Srinivasan and Bhagwati have called the "RHS [right hand side] warriors engaged in mutual assured destruction" are deeply unpersuasive; a whole host of "right hand side" variables are included to explain the phenomenon purportedly being explained on the left-hand side of the regression. They rightly question the robustness of this whole cross-country regression-based empirical research program in their devastating critique of similar statistical studies that have tried to support or deny the effects of trade openness on growth. Skepticism about the purportedly "scientific" empirical nature of these studies is justified because of "their weak theoretical foundation, poor quality of their data base and inappropriate econometric methodologies."[11] They recommend the comparative study method outlined above, and on which the Lal-Myint volume was based, as providing more robust empirical evidence on various issues concerning development policy. Solow agrees (1994, 51), saying of these statistical studies:

> I do not find this a confidence inspiring project. It seems altogether too vulnerable to bias from omitted variables, to reverse causation, and above all to the recurrent suspicion that the experiences of very different national economies are not to be explained as if they represented "points" on some well-defined surface.

Meanwhile, Levine and Renelt (1992) showed the regressions are not robust, and Sala-i-Martin observes that the main message from these regression studies trying to explain growth "is that policy matters. [But] the data cannot really tell which policy is bad!"

Despite the skepticism aroused by these studies, Easterly's book on development experience in generating growth (based on cross-country regressions), *The Elusive Quest for Growth*, is misleading about what economists do now know as a result of over 50 years of experience on how growth is generated. The answer is banal. It depends on the rate of investment and its efficiency, where the latter is crucially dependent on policy (in particular, trade policy). These policies in turn are the classical-liberal policies, unfortunately entitled "the Washington Consensus."[12] What needs to be explained, if growth in so much of the world remains elusive, is why this well-known package is not universally adopted. For that, one needs to know the economic history and political economy of these different countries. Cross-country regressions will not provide the answer.

Conclusion

In summary, unlike the currently fashionable econometric methods in development studies, the method of analytical economic history involves using theoretical constructs to order whatever evidence is available to tell as plausible a story as the facts will bear, using Mill's principles of agreement and difference in a comparative analysis of different countries' historical experience. The theoretical constructs required to order the "facts" are Joan Robinson's economist's "box of tools." They are:

> economic theory in its verbal and mathematical forms, statistical theory and practice, familiarity with certain accounting conventions, statistical sources, and a background of stylized historical fact and worldly experience. The use of such tools to fashion sturdy little arguments is the metier of the economist, the economists' "method" [McCloskey 1985, 24]

Finally, the comparative studies method is essentially forensic. We need to persuade the jury of our professional peers. And because the

111

method recognizes the importance of persuading a skeptical jury, if successfully applied, it *is* persuasive!

Thus, while the inferences drawn about causality from either the theory-based econometrics or analytical economic history approaches can be persuasive, the simple-minded and atheoretical correlations being peddled in the current economic policy and development debates, on which many of the currently fashionable books on Third World poverty are based, should be looked on as statistical snake oil to be taken at one's peril.

7. Theoretical Curiosities

One of the abiding failings of "development economics" has been its fascination with theoretical curiosa and the dirigiste policy conclusions that can be drawn from them. In the early 1980s, I wrote a small book, *The Poverty of "Development Economics,"* which attempted to summarize the logical arguments and empirical evidence against this dirigiste dogma, which had done so much damage to the prospects of the Third World's poor. This book, which acquired some notoriety if not fame, marked the "neoclassical resurgence" against the dogma and the development and at least partial application in many developing countries of the classical-liberal policy package known as the Washington Consensus. (See note 12 in Chapter 6.) The reversal of those countries' past dirigisme in the 1980s and early 1990s, particularly in China and India, but also in many other parts of the Third World, led to the surge in per capita incomes, resulting in the largest reduction in structural poverty in human history. (See the documentation in the first part of this book.)

But we are now told by the "James Boswell" of "development economics," Gerald Meier, that which was his first love is alive and well.[1] The orthodox mainstream economics that had won the battle with development economics is now being trounced by the New Development Economics. And what is this new animal? Meier claims it draws from models of imperfect information, "co-ordination failures, multiple equilibria, and poverty traps" (2005, 119). "With imperfect information and incomplete markets," he writes, "the economy is constrained Pareto inefficient—that is, a set of taxes and subsidies exists that can make everyone better off" (120).

This echoes a similar claim made by Greenwald and Stiglitz (1986). But they conceded:

> It might be noted that we ignore any discussion of the political processes by which the tax-subsidy schemes described below might be effected. Critics may claim that as a result we have not really shown that a Pareto improvement is actually possible" [34n7].

About their claim of the existence of Pareto-improving government interventions, they concluded that

> we have considered relatively simple models, in which there is usually a single distortion. . . . [T]hough the basic qualitative proposition, that markets are constrained Pareto efficient, would obviously remain in a more general formulation, the simplicity of the policy prescriptions would disappear. Does this make our analysis of little policy relevance? The same objection can, of course, be raised against standard optimal tax theory. (Some critics might say, so much the worse for both)" [258].

Quite!

Meier commends Rodrik (1995) for emphasizing "co-ordination failures," and in demonstrating "how the South Korean and Taiwanese governments got interventions right" (2005, 124). He claims that this viewpoint, and the Murphy, Shleifer, and Vishny (1989) modeling of the Big Push, validate the old "development economics" of Nurkse (1953) and Rosenstein-Rodan (1943). Meier supports Krugman's (1993) belief that in its earlier incarnation development economics was not persuasive because its ideas were not formalized in mathematics. But as Stiglitz, (Krugman's discussant), rightly noted: "That we can write down a model of a phenomenon proves almost nothing. It does not make the idea right or wrong, important or unimportant." As regards Rodrik's views about smart dirigisme in Korea and Taiwan, Little (1994) convincingly showed that social rates of return to investment in these countries were inversely correlated with the degree of intervention.

I examine the basis of these "new" theoretical curiosa in greater detail, as they now form the basis of the advice given by the "new dirigistes" to alleviate Third World poverty. Fortunately, so far it has not been widely accepted by many developing countries. But it needs to be firmly countered, as it poses a threat to the continuance of the processes of poverty alleviation charted in Part One.

Poverty Traps

I have a tremendous sense of déjà vu at reading this "new" theoretical literature. The "poverty trap" view, which now has wide currency among the young, is just a resurrection of the "vicious circle of poverty" arguments of the development economics of the 1950s—except now it is attired in sophisticated mathematical garb. But Bauer's castigation of this view still stands. Bauer wrote (1987/2009, 173):

> According to this notion, stagnation and poverty are necessarily self-perpetuating: poor people generally and poor countries or societies in particular are trapped in their poverty, and cannot generate sufficient savings to escape from the trap. This notion became a cornerstone of mainstream development economics. It was the signature tune of the advocates of foreign aid throughout the 1950s. . . . Yet it is in obvious conflict with simple reality. Throughout history, innumerable individuals, families, groups, societies, and countries—both in the West and the Third World—have moved from poverty to prosperity without external donations. All developed countries began as underdeveloped. If the notion of the vicious circle were valid, mankind would still be in the Stone Age at best.

The purveyors of poverty traps have fiddled with the standard neoclassical growth model of Solow (1970). He showed that with a given per capita savings rate (as a fixed proportion of per capita income) and given rates of increase in the labor force (directly from population growth and indirectly through labor augmenting technical progress), a poor economy starting off with a low stock of capital per head and hence low per capita income will nevertheless, ceteris paribus, converge on a higher steady-state capital per head and income per capita. In the steady state, both income and the capital stock will be growing at the "natural rate of growth" given by the sum of the rate of population growth and labor-augmenting technical progress, with per capita income constant at its higher steady-state level. But during the "traverse" to this steady state from the initial position, the economy's growth rate of per capita income and capital per head will be faster than this natural rate of growth. The poorer the country, the faster will be its rate of growth of per capita income as it reaches the steady-state capital and income per head of the leaders in the world economy.

This convergence in per capita incomes, however, as Barro and Sala-i-Martin (1991, 1992) have shown, is conditional on the relevant countries having a common institutional and legal framework for economic activity. Regions within large economic units like the United States, Japan, and the European Union would meet this condition, and there is evidence of this "conditional convergence" in the growth rates there. Clearly, within this theoretical framework, there are no "poverty traps."

Savings

Now enter the "new" theoreticians. They find that many countries, particularly in Africa, although poor, don't seem to be growing faster than their richer peers, as mainstream theory predicts. So, they argue the answer must lie in there being "multiple equilibria," with some countries stuck in a steady state with a low per capita income and per capita capital stock, rather than moving smoothly on to the high per capita income steady state of the Solow framework.

So how do you theoretically generate these multiple equilibria? Simple: *Assume* that instead of the per capita savings rate being a fixed proportion of per capita income, it is a lower share at low per capita income levels, and then—after some threshold per capita income level—it suddenly jumps to a higher proportion of income. Savings per capita as a function of per capita income then becomes steeply S-shaped with respect to the capital stock per worker. Savings is low at low levels of capital per worker, increases substantially at an intermediate level, and then levels off. (See Box 7.1 for a simple diagrammatic explication of the standard Solow model and the multiple equilibria grafted on to it by the purveyors of a savings "poverty trap."[2])

So what is the evidence on the shape of the savings function for poor African countries and the likelihood they are caught in the low steady-state per capita income and capital stock "poverty trap"? Kray and Raddatz have examined the evidence and find (2007, 316):

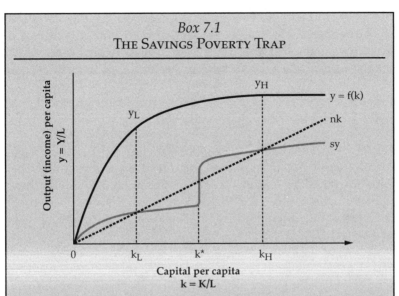

Box 7.1
THE SAVINGS POVERTY TRAP

The figure depicts the standard Solow-Swan growth model. Oy is the standard neo-classical production function showing output(income)/head ($y = Y/L$) as a function of capital per head ($k = K/L$). The ray nk shows the investment required to maintain any given capital-labor ratio constant, when the sum of the rate of population growth (p) and labor-augmenting technical progress (t) is equal to n ($n = p + t$). sy is the savings function. It is a constant at a low rate until the per capita capital stock is k_L, and then it jumps to a constant higher rate, when the capital stock per capita is k^*. There will then be two stable steady state capital-labor ratios. If the economy starts off with a per head capital stock below k_L, it will reach the low steady state capital-labor ratio k_L, and stay there. It is in a poverty trap, as its income per capita cannot rise above. If, however, it starts with a capital per head greater than k^*, it will end up in the higher steady state with capital per head of k_H and the higher steady state per capita income of y_H. For a country stuck in the poverty trap at k_L, a large gift of capital from foreign aid would push it towards the higher capital = labor ratio k_H and the higher steady state income y_H. If the threshold capital-labor ratio k^* at which the savings function jumps is to the left of k_L, then even if the country starts off with a low per capita capital stock, it will converge to the high steady state capital-labor ratio k_H and income per head of y_H.

"The actual cross-country relationship between savings rates and capital per capita observed in the data is far from meeting these conditions. If anything savings rates seem to be increasing at low levels of capital per worker, flat at intermediate levels and increasing again at high levels."[3] Once again, we have a theoretical curiosity! But, as in the past, it is being used by academics to urge the great and good in the West for massive foreign aid to save Africa.[4]

Unified Growth Theory: Technology and Population

But some theoreticians have been even more ambitious. They have sought to use growth models with multiple equilibria to explain the whole of human economic history in terms of what they call their "unified growth theory." The most prolific and ambitious in this genre is Galor (2005).[5]

Galor has a Malthusian poverty trap with a low-level per capita income that he claims dominated human history until the Industrial Revolution in the 18th century. Till then, there was slow technological progress, with output and population fluctuating around a low stable level and little improvement in average living standards. This was followed by a post-Malthusian regime, when technical progress accelerated, moving the West from its low-level equilibrium trap to the beginnings of economic growth, which accelerated with the demographic transition. Thus, the Malthusian regime ultimately "generates the necessary evolutionary pressure for the ultimate take-off" (Galor 2005). The alteration in the steady-state equilibria—from Malthusian to sustained growth—is due to masked behind-the-scenes processes of population growth and the "evolution of the distribution of genetic characteristics."

On this theory of economic history, Maddison (2008, 18), whose painstaking assembly of millennial data and their interpretation of world economic history I relied on in Part 1, comments:

> I was surprised that Galor had drawn extensively on my database to illustrate an interpretation of world economic history so different from mine. . . . Galor is an econometrician, whose theory is not derived from his own detailed measurement of change. His evidence is illustrative. In Galor (2005) it consists of 42 figures and 13 pages of algebra. He presents no tables. 21 of his graphs are attributed to Maddison, but in all except two cases, these graphs are not mine, but are derived from

118

Figure 7.1
CONFRONTATION OF MADDISON AND GALOR STYLE OF
INTERPRETING PER CAPITA GROWTH, 1000–2030 AD

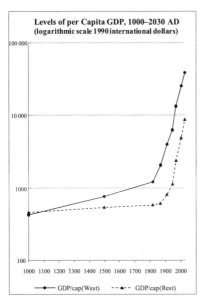

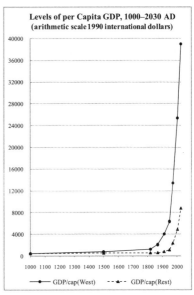

SOURCE: Maddison (2008).

tables in Maddison (2001). The trouble with these 19 graphs
is that they have an arithmetic vertical scale, and are misleading when presenting rates of change over 2000 years. I use a
vertical logarithmic scale to illustrate proportionate change
in per capita income. My graph (left of Fig. 7.1) shows a significant but slow rise in Western per capita income between
1000 and 1820 AD. His graph (right hand side of Fig 7.1) is
shaped like a half-open jackknife with a sharp and sudden
jump from flat to sharply vertical. . . . I consider the achievement of the West between 1000 and 1820 to be a long and
significant apprenticeship to modern economic growth, and
am very skeptical of sudden take-off theories. This is not my
only disagreement with Galor's ingenious theory, which
attributes too much importance to population change and
Darwinian changes in human intelligence."

So much for the empirical validity of "unified growth theory!"

The most elegant, though not persuasive, of these unified growth models, and the one that partially fits the story outlined in part one, is by the Nobel laureate Lucas (2002) in his Kuznets lectures. Lucas begins with a simple Ricardian steady-state model that has endogenous decisionmaking about family size, reflecting the Becker, Murphy, Tamura (1990) theory on the quantity-quality tradeoff in the fertility decision. He shows parsimoniously how this can be applied to obtain the steady-state equilibrium in a series of Ricardian models of what was termed "extensive" growth in Part 1. The first is that of a hunter-gatherer society, where land is abundant and free. Next, there is private appropriation of land, distributed equally over households of equal size. Now, since parents can pass on their land to their children, they have an incentive to reduce their fertility, and thus with unchanged production conditions, the steady-state consumption level is higher in this egalitarian society with private property than in the hunter-gatherer phase.

This of course does not take account of the Boserupian process discussed in Part 1, whereby the increasing population density propels a move from the low labor-intensive hunter-gatherer phase to a more intensive one, say, settled agriculture.[6] Population growth in this model, unlike in Lucas, is given exogenously. But while population is endogenous in both Lucas models of a preindustrial economy, there is no mechanics of the transition from the hunter-gatherer steady state to that in the settled agriculture stage. It merely depends on the assumed creation of property rights in land.

But what propels this move? In the Boserupian model, it is the exogenous increase in population that leads to the move to settled agriculture and the creation of property rights in land. Also in the Lucas model in its Ricardian phase, the move from the hunter-gatherer to the settled-agriculture stage leads to a smaller steady-state population in the latter than in the former, which is against the facts of historical demography (Lal 1998, 206n6).

Lucas's third model of a "class"-based agrarian economy fits the facts better for the social stratification that occurred in the sedentary riverine civilizations of Eurasia threatened by the nomads from the northern steppes and the southern Arabian deserts. In this model, the "workers" population and steady-state consumption levels are the same as in the egalitarian society. But the "landowners" will be richer since they also get land "rents." As they can pass on their land to their progeny, they will also be concerned about their children's "quality," unlike the workers. So the family size of the rich land-owners will be smaller than that of the "workers," and hence their steady-state consumption will be higher. But as Clark (2007, 225) rightly notes: "In fact in the pre-industrial world the effective family size, measured by the number of children alive at the death of their fathers, was significantly higher for higher-income parents, all the way up to very high income levels."

Lucas's final model of modern economic growth combines the earlier Ricardian fertility models with the Solow growth model, where the move from the stagnant to the perpetual growth econ-omy is entirely based on the demographic transition, which in turn is based on rising rates of return to human capital formation. I find this utterly unpersuasive.[7] Moreover, the Industrial Revolution did not accompany or follow the demographic transition, as this theory seems to imply, but preceded it. The biggest lacuna in this theory of the transition from an agrarian to an industrial economy is its failure to account for the ending of the energy constraint posed by fixed land, with the increasing substitution of land-based organic energy by the unlimited mineral energy provided by fossil fuels (Wrigley 1988). Here is another theoretical curiosity.

Malthus-cum-Darwin

An even more audacious attempt to explain the whole of human economic history based on a Malthusian poverty trap is by Clark (2007). He argues that the world had an unchanging standard of living, "with the average person in 1800 no better off than the average person of 100,000 BC" (1). The Industrial Revolution led to a sharp rise in incomes in some countries after 1800, broadly the West, but declined in others.[8] The Grim Reaper is responsible for this Clarkian Great Divergence after 1800.

Clark's evidence for the worldwide stagnation in living stan-dards before 1800 is not based (as in Galor) on a misinterpretation of Maddison's historical data, but on a denial of its relevance (19). Instead, Clark bases his conclusion on average height. He claims it is linked to diet and thus to the standard of living. Comparing the height of Stone Age survivors in modern foraging societies like the iKung and 18th-century Britons, he finds them close (57–61). Hence, he derives a flat standard of living till 1800.

As for any animal species, demography kept the Malthusian balance for *Homo sapiens*. The Grim Reaper's agents—the Four Horsemen of the Apocalypse—"were the friends of mankind before 1800. They reduced population pressures and increased material standards. In contrast, policies beloved by the World Bank and the United Nations—peace, stability, order, public health, and transfers to the poor—were the enemies of prosperity. They generated the population growth that impoverished societies" (5).

From his simple Malthusian growth model, Clark argues that societies with higher death rates have absolutely higher incomes than those with lower death rates. So the usual sources of raising per capita income—capital accumulation, increased work effort, and technical change—are of no use. The only way the average income in a society can be raised is by raising its death rate! (Box 7.2 provides Clark's simple graphic illustration of this model).

But the stagnant per capita income worldwide before the Industrial Revolution, for which Clark's stylized Malthusian model is broadly applicable, is best explained by the land constraint on the energy needs for generating Promethean intensive growth. Clark's correct assumption of diminishing returns to land captures this. But he ignores the central feature of the story in mankind's escape from structural poverty—for, it was the substitution of fossil fuels, which provided an unending supply of mineral energy, for the limited products from land in the preindustrial organic agrarian economies that was the hallmark of the Industrial Revolution. It was this that allowed, first the West and now the Rest, to escape from the age-old structural poverty of the "Malthusian economy." But Clark will not have any of this.

For instance, most economic historians attribute the rise of England, and the relative decline of the Dutch,[9] to the exhaustion of the major source of mineral energy in the Netherlands—peat—as compared with the abundant mineral energy source in England: coal (Wrigley 1988). With their stock of peat exhausted and the British Navigation Acts impeding the Dutch importation of English coal, the Dutch soon fell behind the English.[10] For Clark, however, the relative decline of the Dutch was due to demographic factors: the skewed gender ratio by 1749 (1.5:1 for women), which meant

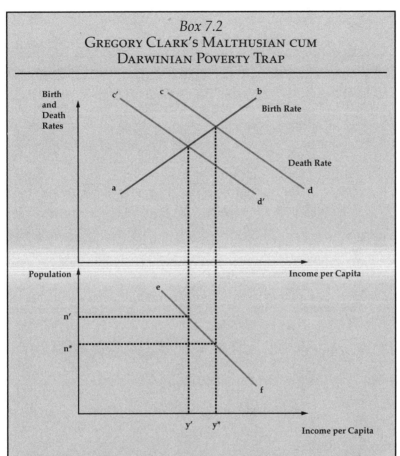

Box 7.2
GREGORY CLARK'S MALTHUSIAN CUM
DARWINIAN POVERTY TRAP

The figure depicts Gregory Clarks' Malthusian model of economic history (Clark 2007).

In Panel I, ab is the birth rate schedule with respect to per capita income, which shows rising birth rates as per capita income rises. cd is the death rate schedule, which shows death rates falling as per capita income rises. Panel II shows the population per capita income schedule, with population declining as per capita income rises.

With the initial birth and death rate schedules in Panel I, there will be an equilibrium per capita income of y*, at which the death and birth rates are equal. From Panel II, we can then read off the equilibrium population of n*.

(continued)

Box 7.2
(continued)

Suppose that the death rates decline, so the schedule shifts to c'd'. With a birth rate higher than the death rate, population will expand to n' (in Panel II), and per capita income will fall to y' in both panels. Hence his conclusion: "Anything that raised the death rate . . . increased material living standards. Anything that reduced the death rate schedule . . . reduced material living standards. (27)"

Clark then follows standard growth theory (in terms of growth accounting) and correctly argues that modern growth and the escape from the Malthusian trap depended upon innovation. But "why in the millennium before 1800 [was] there . . . in all societies . . . such limited investment in the expansion of useful knowledge. . . . and why this circumstance changed for the first time in Britain . . . around 1800?" (205). His answer: "England's advantages were not coal, nor colonies, not the Protestant revolution, not the Enlightenment, but the accidents of institutional stability and demography, in particular, the extraordinary fecundity of the rich and economically successful" (11). With urbanization, given the dirty personal habits of the British, the death rate of the poor accelerated and the children of the fecund rich and educated classes—imbued with bourgeois values—cascaded down the social scale. This Darwinian process spread bourgeois values throughout the English population. "China and Japan did not move as rapidly along the path as England because . . . their upper social strata were only modestly more fecund than the mass of the population" (11). Similarly, the current underdeveloped countries are still in the pre industrial Malthusian trap, and as they have not replicated the Darwinian selection process of England, their populations have not acquired the bourgeois virtues. So there is little hope for their poor.

Presumably, the implications for development policy is to simulate the Darwinian process that allowed the more fecund English upper classes to cascade down the social scale with their bourgeois policy and to find ways of raising the death rates of the poor (by denying them modern medicine) and encouraging the rich (through subsidies) to have larger families to escape Clark's Malthusian cum Darwinian poverty trap!

that nearly 24 percent of women in Dutch cities did not marry. The cause of this decimation of Dutch males was "colonial adventures" (Clark 2007, 102–5).

So how did England, according to Clark, escape the dismal Malthusian Trap after 1800? Clark's answer (7): natural selection. Mortality among the rich and the poor differed. As

> economic success translated powerfully into reproductive success, the richest men had twice as many surviving children at death as poorest. . . . Given the static nature of the Malthusian economy, the superabundant children of the rich had to, on average, move down the social hierarchy in order to find work.

This demographic pattern was aided and abetted by the process of urbanization, and the unhygienic personal habits of the English. Thus, the poor congregating in the English towns had a higher mortality rate than their fellows in China and Japan with much cleaner habits (108).[11] As the English rich were mainly the gentry who lived in the healthier countryside, their mortality rates were lower than those of the urban poor.

This growing surplus of rich bourgeois led, as Clark noted, to their having to move down the social order. This gradual process of the biological takeover of the jobs previously done by the feckless poor meant that the middle-class bourgeois virtues "that would ensure later economic dynamism—patience, hard work, ingenuity, innovativeness, education—were thus spreading biologically throughout the population" (8).

But income grew slowly during the Industrial Revolution, with workers gaining rather than landowners and capitalists. The Industrial Revolution did not spread to other poor countries because for biological reasons, the bourgeois virtues were lacking in what is today's Third World, and their competitive advantage in terms of low wages for industrialization was lost in over-manning in enterprise and population increases, which left them poor.

Thus, the income gap between rich and poor countries that opened up in 1800 has kept growing. For biological reasons, then, there is no hope for the world's poor bridging the gap, which opened up as a result of the superior genetic endowment of the Anglo-American world and the accompanying cultural superiority provided by the dice of natural selection. The only hope for the Third World's poor is to migrate to the rich world, or hope that the Grim Reaper differentially decimates the low-productivity workers of the Third World, while raising the fecundity of their richer more productive brethren so that the population at large acquires the bourgeois virtues.

Clark's dyspeptic vision has been ably criticized with well-known historical evidence (which I do not have the space or energy to present) by the economic historian Robert Allen and the comparative historian Jack Goldstone.[12] All the components of Clark's theses are contradicted by the evidence. Many of his predictions about how poor countries can never ascend from poverty, and his assertion that the gap between them and the rich is increasing, are contradicted by the macro evidence provided in Part 1. It is also ironic that, as part of his dismal genetic thesis, Clark should cite the iKung as having the same stature and hence standard of living as 18-century Britons. For the land of the iKung, Botswana, has had one of the highest growth rates of per capita income in the world for many decades, with a growing population of no doubt "genetically" more "inferior" inhabitants than in the West. Now that the Grim Reaper is decimating its lower class population with AIDS, the rising differential in upper- and lower-class death rates should give a further boost to the growth rate of Botswana's per capita income!

Here we have another theoretical curiosity, which fortunately has no practical application, unless it provides the misanthropic Greens (to be discussed in Chapter 10) another policy to save Spaceship Earth—by restoring the death rate to its level in the Stone Age!

Welfare States

Oddly, this desire to first expound a "new" theory and then to find facts to match it, which is the exact converse of the problems of the atheoretical statistical snake oil discussed in the last chapter, has even infected some of the saner economic historians. One is Greif (1994). His path-breaking study of the contrast between the familial (collectivist) trading networks of the Maghribi Jews and the individualist ones in the Mediterranean trading world of the 11th century showed that the very familialism of the Maghribi world, which led to their commercial success, nevertheless prevented institutional developments like contract and commercial law, which emerged as a necessity in the individualistic Genovese trading world—aided and abetted, I would add, by the legal revolution of Pope Gregory VII, which led to the rise of the West.

Greif and two coauthors have recently produced a theory to explain the Needham puzzle (Greif, Sasson, and Floetotto 2009): why England and not China had the Industrial Revolution. He has another "unified growth" model in which "society can remain trapped in low-growth equilibrium in the absence of an appropriate risk-sharing institution." In this "trap," traditional low-risk technologies are employed and per capita income remains stagnant. "If a risk sharing institution is introduced, however, a larger fraction of the agents adopt the higher risk technology [which is more productive] and the increase in wealth can reinforce the adoption of the risky technology, up to the point where every agent utilizes the HR [higher risk] technology," and sustained economic growth results.

The authors claim that the risk-sharing "technology" that put England ahead of China (despite China's having made all the discoveries required for an industrial revolution under the Sung dynasty [960–1270 AD]) was the Old Poor Law in England in the 16th and 17th centuries. This provided a "risk neutral" public safety net for the risk takers, while in China the social safety net was provided by the more communal and familial clan-based system whose economic decisions were based on the more risk-averse attitudes of the elders. The more individualist younger risk takers in England could depend on the risk-neutral Poor Law to survive if their gambles failed. Greif et al. then set up a standard overlapping-generation model with a poverty trap based on the lack of risk-taking institutions. A simulation experiment with their model convinces them that their theory is supported by the facts.

But then how do they explain the technological development under the Sung? Greif et al. claim that under the Sung (when communal families also predominated), elders had less authority than under later dynasties (26):

> Under the Song, a parent who killed an unfilial son was subject to lower punishment compared to other murders. As severe as this law may seem, it was mild compared to the law in later dynasties under which it was not a crime for a father to kill an unfilial son.

127

This is completely unpersuasive. If a welfare state is to lead to an increase in risk taking and sustained economic growth, Sweden and the United Kingdom should be the technological and industrial leaders today. However, the period since both expanded their welfare states has seen a downward slide from their past relatively stellar economic performance.[13]

The answer to the Needham problem, I have argued, is much more straightforward. China's reversal of fortune post-Sung was largely due to what I labeled the "closing of the Chinese mind" (Lal 1998, 40–48).

McNeill (1983), Jones (1988), and Lin (1995) all relate the Needham problem to the creation of the Confucian Mandarinate, which despised both soldiers and merchants. After its predatory partnership with business in the 14th century, in part to facilitate the transfer of grain by sea from the new granaries in the south to the political center in the north, the Ming dynasty restricted foreign trade and foreign contacts, and abandoned the navy its predecessors had built up. The major reason was that once the Grand Canal to Peking, linking the southern granaries to the north, had been built in 1411, the transport of grain by sea was unnecessary and was abolished in 1415. This meant that a navy was no longer needed to fend off the pirates that had threatened the sea-bound routes.

This tightening of China's traditional political constraints on soldiers and merchants was strengthened by a neo-Confucian reorientation of philosophic outlook in the 14th century. Elvin sees this as the main reason why China failed to industrialize in the Western manner after its technological lead under the Sung. This philosophical reorientation moved away from the earlier Chinese view, which emphasized conceptual mastery of external nature, toward the new view, which emphasized introspection, intuition, and subjectivity. Elvin writes (1973, 233–34):

> The consequences for Chinese science were disastrous. As the result of a highly sophisticated metaphysics there was *always* an explanation . . . for anything puzzling that turned up. . . . Given this attitude, it was unlikely that any anomaly would irritate enough for an old framework of reference to be discarded in favor of a better one. Here then was the reason why China failed to create a modern science of her own accord, and the deepest source of resistance to the assimilation of the spirit of Western science both in the 17th century and later.

A vivid illustration of this closing of the Chinese mind and its cultural divergence from England is provided by a visit to the great archeological museum in Xian. The first few rooms of the collection show the great cultural and scientific efflorescence in China from Neolithic times to the Middle Ages. Then in room after room there are the same shapes and forms in unending repetition. It is the record of a civilization that apparently thought it had reached perfection and then became frozen in aspic from about the 16th century forward. By contrast, this was the age of Shakespeare in England, followed by those of Locke and Newton, and Hume and Smith. The sheer intellectual curiosity and creativeness of these centuries preceding the Industrial Revolution are in stark contrast to what was happening in the other great Eurasian civilizations.[14]

This cultural divergence, as I argued in *Unintended Consequences* and which was summarized in Part 1, was due in part to the family revolution of Gregory the Great in the sixth century in the West. This gave rise to the individualism that led to the Renaissance and the scientific revolution, but also to the rise of nuclear families and the creation of statist safety nets for the poor, replacing the communal ones provided in the past and which continued in the other Eurasian civilizations—including China. It was not the welfare states, which were a necessary consequence of its newfound individualism, that led to the rise of the West, but the sheer escape from tradition in art and science that individualism promoted. Greif et al. have got hold of the wrong end of the stick in finding in the welfare state, rather than in the individualism that made it necessary, the springboard for the West's slow ascent from poverty.[15] Greif et al. (2009) have produced yet another theoretical curiosity.

The Big Push, "New" Trade Theory, and Industrial Policy

The 1950s' development economics had made much of concepts like the "Big Push" and "backward and forward linkages," which were based on the importance of increasing returns and pecuniary external economies. These concepts have been formalized and form the basis of a new dirigiste literature reviving the case for industrial policy. All are linked to the age-old debate about free trade and protection. The modern theory of trade and welfare has provided answers to all the questions raised in that debate. My *Reviving the*

Invisible Hand surveyed and extended these answers for the general reader, so I can be brief.

Most of the arguments for protection, going back to those of Alexander Hamilton and Friedrich List in the 18th and 19th centuries, are based on some distortion in the domestic price mechanism that keeps market prices from reflecting true opportunity costs (that is, social values). Thus a tariff, it is argued, can improve social welfare. This argument had led to the dirigiste dogma that both free trade and laissez faire are harmful. The theory of trade and welfare developed in the 1950s and 1960s disconnected the case for free trade from that for laissez faire, showing that the best way to deal with a distortion in the domestic price mechanism was to deal with it at source—by some suitable domestic tax-subsidy instruments (hence departing from laissez faire). But free trade should still be maintained. Tariffs and quantitative restrictions were often the worst possible instruments to deal with these domestic distortions and could lead to a loss of welfare.[16]

The only argument for trade intervention that survives in this modern theory is the so-called optimum-tariff argument made by J. S. Mill, according to which a country can gain in welfare by imposing an "optimal tariff" if it has monopsony power over its imports or an optimal export tax if it has monopoly power over its exports. The reason trade intervention is required is that the "distortion" is in foreign trade. But given the danger of retaliation, this argument has not had much practical relevance.

Moreover, once the political process and the ubiquitous phenomenon of rent-seeking[17] is taken into account, the case for domestic tax subsidies to "correct" a domestic distortion collapses. If producers know the government is in the "subsidy business," they are likely to lobby for a subsidy, claiming a domestic distortion in the workings of the price mechanism where none in fact exists. If successful, they stand to gain producer rents. They will be willing to spend resources—up to the limit of these rents—on seeking subsidies, which will represent a net welfare loss for the economy, since *ex hypothesi* there is no distortion to be dealt with. Because in practice it is virtually impossible to determine whether a domestic distortion exists or its size, and hence the requisite subsidy, this form of cheating will be difficult to avoid. This implies that the tax-subsidy solution for dealing with domestic distortions will not lead to a welfare improvement, and hence the best policy may be to leave well enough alone—that is, laissez faire! So even within the framework of the theory of domestic price distortions, because of these rent-seeking considerations, the wheel seems to have come full circle: free trade and laissez-faire, as the 19th-century classical liberals saw so clearly, do hang together (Lal 2003a).

While this view seems to be generally accepted regarding tariffs and quantitative restrictions, there is a growing band of "new development economists," praised by Meier (2005), who argue for government industrial policy to take account of various externalities. The successful industrialization of Japan, South Korea, and Taiwan is attributed to their use of industrial policy, which internalized these dynamic Marshallian externalities. Many countries, including South Africa, seem tempted by these arguments.[18]

The basis for this "new" dirigiste program is supposed to be the new "trade theory" that has emerged by combining various aspects of industrial organization theory, like imperfect competition and strategic trade policy. In fact, Robert Baldwin has elegantly shown much of this "new" trade theory to be mere variants of the old terms-of-trade argument, which is only valid if one's trading partners do not retaliate (1992). In the event of a trade war, the country initiating it may well be the loser. Hence, though theoretically correct, the program is not of much practical relevance.

The bases for dirigiste industrial policies are variants of the infant-industry argument based on the presumed existence of what are termed pecuniary externalities. These are to be distinguished from the technological externalities adduced by environmentalists for government intervention. The latter are like smoke from a factory that damages a nearby laundry. Government action may be needed to make the factory internalize the external costs it imposes on the laundry. These externalities exist because the relevant costs and benefits are not mediated through the price mechanism.

By contrast, pecuniary externalities reflect the interdependencies mediated through the price mechanism. So, say another whiskey producer opens a distillery that, by increasing the supply of whiskey, reduces the price. This reduces the profits of the existing whiskey distilleries but increases the welfare of whiskey drinkers—purportedly a pecuniary diseconomy for whiskey producers. But as Buchannan and Stubblebine (1962) and Viner (1931), showed ages ago, these pecuniary externalities are not Pareto-relevant, and no attempt must be made to offset them. For the loss for the producers is less or equal to the gain for the consumers. Similarly, if there is a cost-reducing innovation by a producer that reduces the price and increases his output at the expense of other producers, it is readily shown that the consumer gains (in terms of consumer surplus) offset any loss of rents of the now-inefficient producers. They represent the changes in a dynamic economy mediated through the price mechanism. No government action is required to deal with them.

So, what are the "pecuniary externalities" that, according to the proponents of industrial policy, require government action? The major one provides the argument for the Big Push developed by Rosenstein-Rodan. Suppose a new shoe factory is set up in a developing country. Not much of the domestic demand resulting from the expenditures on shoe-making will be directed to shoes, making the factory unprofitable. If, however, a large number of factories making various consumer goods are set up simultaneously, then Say's law—supply creates its own demand—will operate, and the resultant industrial complex will be viable. This idea can be called "demand complementarity." But as Little rightly noted: "The demand complementarity argument seems to require a closed economy" (1982, 38). For if the economy is open, the producer of shoes could always export his shoes if there was insufficient domestic demand, and make a profit as long as the factory was viable at "world prices."

Murphy et al. (1989) recognize this, and in their "two-good" model, the source of presumed market failure lies instead in increasing returns (economies of scale) and imperfect competition in a high-productivity "modern" good, as compared with a traditional constant-returns-to-scale low-productivity good produced under perfect competition.[19] This leads to two equilibria in the open economy: a good one, where, as a result of government intervention, the economy specializes completely in producing the modern good, and a bad one, where (without the intervention) the economy specializes completely in producing the traditional good. This model of "pecuniary externalities" is more correctly called one of increasing returns and infant-industry protection. It has been used to justify selective government intervention in industrial policy.[20]

As regards the infant-industry part, once again, as Baldwin (1969) demonstrated ages ago, a domestic tax subsidy is preferable to interventions in foreign trade. But a necessary condition for intervention is that inputs per unit of output decrease more rapidly in that industry than they do for its foreign competitors and other domestic industries. But even this condition is not sufficient. It is also necessary that the discounted net present value of the losses incurred during the high-cost phase are recouped during the post-infancy phase to earn at least the social rate of return to investment in the economy.

So what is the evidence on industrial policy based on the infant industry argument? Harrison and Rodriguez-Clare (2009) have surveyed the numerous empirical studies that have sought to answer this question.

First are the few industry studies that have attempted a correctly formulated empirical answer. These found that "protection may lead to higher growth but result in net welfare losses. . . . These case studies suggest that designing policies that increase overall welfare is very difficult" (32).

Second are cross-industry studies. From these, the authors conclude (34):

> There is no evidence to suggest that intervention for IP [industrial policy] reasons in trade even exists. If intervention were motivated by IP reasons, we would expect the pattern of protection to be skewed towards activities where positive externalities or market failures are largest. Instead existing evidence suggests that protection is motivated by optimal tariff considerations, for revenue generation, or to protect special interests.

On the evidence for Marshallian externalities (that is, the benefits of geographical concentration [agglomeration]), they find that "agglomeration maybe *necessary but not sufficient* for increased productivity. . . . To put it crudely, subsidizing the software sector may not generate a Silicon Valley in a developing country" (35–36).

Third, from the cross-country studies they find (as also reflected in Noland and Pack's survey of East Asian IP, discussed below) that "in the late 20th century, in contrast to the last century when industrial countries protected emerging industries, it appears that trade barriers are often designed to protect 'sunset' industries rather than to encourage 'sunrise' industries" (38).

Finally, on the voluminous literature, mainly econometric, on the relationship between trade openness and growth, Harrison and Rodriguez-Clare conclude (3):

> First, there was no significant relationship in the second half of the twentieth century between average protection levels and growth. Second, there is a positive association between trade volume and growth. We interpret [this] . . . to suggest that any successful IP strategy must ultimately increase the share of international trade in GDP. The fact that so many countries have been unsuccessful in offsetting the anti-trade bias of their interventions may explain why so many have failed to succeed at IP.

The model of Murphy et al., supporting a Big Push, also calls for "coordinated investment across sectors lead[ing] to the expansion of markets for all industrial goods and can thus be self-sustaining even when no firm can break even when investing alone" (Murphy, Shleifer, and Vishny 1989, 1005). This so-called coordination of investment plans is of course nothing else but the planning syndrome—the search for a centrally determined investment plan which takes into account not merely current but all future changes in the demand and supply of a myriad of goods. It is well known that no market economy can attain the intertemporal Nirvana promised by the utopian theoretical construct of Arrow and Debreu. But neither can the planners, as pointed out by Hayek and Mises in the interwar debate about the efficiency of Soviet-type central planning (Lal 1983, 1987, 2002). The collapse of this system is a conclusive empirical confirmation of the validity of the Austrian insight that, in the real world, imperfect markets are superior to imperfect planning.

So what of the purported success of industrial planning in East Asia, which is credited with the rapid industrialization of Japan, Korea, and Taiwan? The numerous studies that have tried to answer this question have been surveyed by Noland and Pack (2003). This survey's conclusions are particularly noteworthy, as one of its authors (Pack) "co-authored a paper that interprets early Korean industrial development as partly the result of clever industrial policy" (Pack and Westphal 1986). So they "do not start from the position that industrial policy cannot work" (8). And what do they conclude about the results of industrial policy in the three countries that are supposed to have successfully industrialized through selective industrial policy?

On Japan, the pioneer of industrial policy, they find that (36–37):

> the empirical estimates of many types reviewed here do not reveal robust evidence that selective intervention was welfare or growth enhancing in the period after post-War reconstruction. This could be due to the inability of policymakers to identify market failures and design appropriate interventions. However, the evidence that most resource flows went to large, politically influential "backward" sectors suggests that *political considerations may have been central* to this outcome [emphasis added].

Just as predicted by the traditional theory of trade and welfare-incorporating political economy considerations (Lal 2003a)!

In Korea, industrial policy in the mid-1970s was used for a heavy and chemical industry (HCI) drive to steer industrial output towards more capital- and technology-intensive sectors. The results were disappointing. Thus, the studies by Kim (1990) and Yoo (1990) found the policy unsuccessful. Kim found "it had the predictable result of generating excess capacity in favored sectors while starving non-favored sectors for resource, as well as contributing to inflation and the accumulation of foreign debt" (42). Yoo finds "that in macroeconomic terms the Korean economy would have been better without the HCI policy" (43). His rates-of-return analysis of HCI, light industry, and all manufacturing mirror Ian Little's (1994) finding that social rates of return in Korea were inversely correlated with the degree of dirigisme. On the role of industrial policy in promoting total factor productivity, as required by the infant industry argument, Lee (1996, 392) finds for the period 1963–83, that trade protection in the form of tariff or non-tariff barriers is negatively associated with the growth rate of labor and total factor productivity, while tax incentives and subsidized credit were uncorrelated with sectoral productivity growth, leading him to conclude that "the Korean data present evidence that less intervention in trade is linked to higher productivity growth."

On the argument for interindustry linkages and the potential welfare-enhancing coordination of investments by government, Noland and Pack conclude (2003, 46), "While government intervention might have reduced some interpersonal transactions costs, many of the potential externalities were presumably dealt with by Coasian agreements among the [chaebol] firms."

Finally, they (2003, 7–8) find no evidence to support the claim of Rodrik (1995, 1999) that Korean industrial policy was successful not by engineering an export but rather an investment boom.

On Taiwan, Noland and Pack (56) conclude, quoting the survey of evidence by Smith (2000):

> that as in the case of Japan and Korea [the empirical stud-ies] fail to find links between the [industrial policy] inter-ventions and sectoral TFP [total factor productivity] growth or trade performance in the 1980s. Rather the pattern of in-tervention appears to be driven more by political economy considerations, such as sectoral employment, the presence of large firms, or the degree of sectoral concentration, than by dynamic comparative advantage.[21]

Rosenstein-Rodan (1961) also had a second string to his bow in ar-guing for a Big Push that has been taken up by Murphy, Shleifer, and Vishny (1989). This concerned the indivisibilities in the provision of nontradable social overheads like power and transport needed by all industrial producers. This was of course the policy recommended to Africa in the 1960s. Many donors financed various public-sector infrastructure projects in anticipation of future demand but with little provision for their efficient maintenance. Africa is littered with the rusting remains of many of these grandiose monuments of the last Big Push there, of which the Tan-Zam railway remains em-blematic, particularly as the Chinese now seem to be donating large sums of money and expertise to develop African infrastructure as part of their sweeteners to acquire natural-resource mines and wells. Whether these will suffer the same fate as the Tan-Zam railway re-mains to be seen.

We also have more-detailed empirical evidence on countries that tried a Big Push in the past. Four were included in the Lal-Myint study: Ghana, Madagascar, Brazil, and Mexico. The results invari-ably were disappointing if not disastrous (as in Ghana and Madagas-car). To promote the pursuit of such bad policies just because some theorists have now been able to clothe the theoretical arguments of the older discredited "development economics" in some algebra is not only puerile but wicked—given the high costs that the poor people thus being experimented on must suffer.

So much for the efficacy of industrial policy being touted by the "new" development economics. If Third World governments choose to follow this path charted by the theorists commended by Meier (2005), it will be as disastrous for the prospects of the world's poor as was the old "development economics" of their aged peers.

Conclusion

There is no better conclusion for this and the former chapter than Bauer's (1987/2009, 175) indictment of these hoary old theories now clothed in the latest mathematical and econometric garb. In his splendid essay "The Disregard of Reality," he wrote:

> Mathematical methods often provide an effective façade or screen which covers or conceals empty formalism. They can camouflage disregard of basic propositions or simple evidence in models purporting to serve as basis for policy. Statistics, technical jargon, and sophisticated econometric techniques can also serve as a protective screen, but the use of mathematics is particularly effective because of the language barrier it provides. What we see is an inversion of the familiar Hans Andersen story of the Emperor's New Clothes. Here there "are" new clothes, and at times they are *haute couture*. But all too often there is no Emperor within.

8. Micro Everything

In the previous chapters, I have outlined how a new dirigisme is being sought to alleviate Third World poverty, despite the undoubted success of even the partial application of the classical-liberal policy package known as the Washington Consensus. This has seen a historically unprecedented decline in world poverty in the last two decades. The purported "new" "development economics" is fueled by a game that exaggerates the numbers of the world's poor, particularly in the emerging Asian giants, which have seen the largest declines in mass poverty, and by the statistical snake oil and theoretical curiosities being peddled by our best and brightest young technicians. In this chapter, I consider a third group that seeks to use more microeconomic instruments to delineate and tackle Third World poverty.

I have greater sympathy with this group, since in my misguided youth, I too was seduced by the hope that microeconomic methods embodied in social cost-benefit analysis would be able to improve the selection of investment projects in developing countries, thereby improving the lot of their poor. I began my consultancies with the World Bank in the early 1970s, helping it to adapt the existing methods of project evaluation to produce its own manual to be used in both its ex ante project selection as well as ex post evaluation. Seemingly, the pretentiously named Poverty Action Lab at MIT, which is advocating the application of its randomized-controlled-trials methodology for the selection and appraisal of World Bank and other public investments in developing countries, would fall into this fold. In the next section, I discuss this new "fix" for development policy.

Equally, since my student days in the early 1960s in Oxford, where I was befriended by an eccentric and distinguished group of social anthropologists collected around the magisterial figure of Evans Pritchard, I have had a soft spot for the anthropological approach to studying society. The microeconometrics based on the collection of detailed household and other micro data, and utilizing the theories of the new "household economics," has also appealed to me since my own first field work in rural Mahrashtra when I was writing my first book, *Wells and Welfare* (1972a). During my year-long stint at the Indian planning commission in the early 1970s, the planning unit of the Indian Statistical Institute was based there. I fondly remember the daily lunches with T. N. Srinivasan, Bagicha Minhas, Pranab Bardhan, and Suresh Tendulkar, who were based in the unit and who were collecting and analyzing various surveys of the agricultural sector and profiles of poverty in India. They were pioneering the analysis of sharecropping and interrelated factor markers well before the imperfect-information paradigm taken on by the "new" development economics commended by Meier (2005). I learned a lot from them about both the methods and results of their efforts in dealing with various questions concerning the rural economy.

This process was furthered by the two years I spent with Mark Lieserson in his employment and rural development work at the World Bank in the late 1970s, working on my books on Kenya (with Paul Collier) and *The Hindu Equilibrium*. Hans Binswanger and Mark Rosenzweig were there working on the very rich International Crops Research Institute for the Semi-Arid Tropics data they had collected in Hyderabad on dry farms in rural India. This provided very valuable lessons on Third World agriculture.

Then as the research administrator at the World Bank in the mid-1980s, I also supported its Living Standards Measurement Survey Unit, which has over the years produced invaluable microeconomic data based on state-of-the-art household surveys designed with the help of Angus Deaton and John Muellbauer. So I remain sympathetic to the field work conducted by the randomized controlled trials proponents of the Poverty Action Lab. In the second section, I note some of the more interesting findings of their surveys, as well as others based on the rural surveys conducted by the National Council of Applied Economic Research (NCAER) in New Delhi.

Finally, I examine the new fashion for microfinance and micro-insurance. Although the deservedly saintly status ascribed to the founder of Bangladesh's Grameen Bank, Mohammed Yunus, has given this movement a special aura, I take a rather cool look at this purportedly new panacea for alleviating low-end poverty.

Project Evaluation

In the 1970s, evaluation of investment projects became all the rage. This was a reaction to the growing evidence that the centralized macroplanning based on the input-output tables pioneered by Leontief and used in the form of material balances by the Soviet Gosplan, which had been adopted in many countries, was not delivering the goods. As the state had taken over much of the so-called "commanding heights" of the economy, public investment had a large share of total investment, and its choice of projects would markedly influence the growth rate. Instead of the "priceless" economics underlying the input-output table based macroplanning, it was argued that public investments should be chosen on the basis of social pricing derived from theoretical welfare economics. The resulting project evaluation method, a form of applied welfare economics, had a strong theoretical base.

Its aim was to assess the economic welfare benefits of a marginal investment in an economy with large distortions in the price mechanism, mostly due to inappropriate government interventions in the form of trade, exchange, and price controls. There were also structural distortions arising from a divergence between the cost of labor to industry and its true opportunity cost when drawn from the low-productivity agricultural sector. In addition, distributional considerations were introduced to take account of the project benefits accruing to different income groups. A social discount rate was derived to determine the social opportunity cost of capital when market interest rates were distorted through various forms of financial repression. External effects like those on the environment were also taken into account. The estimated social rate of return of an investment project under review was then compared with the social discount rate to see if it should be undertaken.

The Organization of Economic Cooperation and Development (OECD) and UN Industrial Development Organization (UNIDO) vied with each other in having manuals embodying this method written by eminent economic theorists. My UCLA colleague Al Harberger produced his own method. As part of the Nuffield College "circus" in the 1960s around Ian Little and Maurice Scott, which was spearheading the "neoclassical resurgence" against "development economics," I was involved in applying and purveying the manual written by Little and Jim Mirrlees for the OECD.

The major rival manual was written by Partha Dasgupta, Stephen Marglin, and Amartya Sen for UNIDO.

In the now incomprehensible battle for the adoption of these rival methods, which generated more heat than light, I wrote a small book comparing these alternatives for the World Bank, *Methods of Project Analysis: A Review* (1974). This was part of the bank's attempt, as the largest international financier of aid to investment projects in the Third World, to adopt more rigorous methods of appraisal. The result was the bank's own manual written by Squire and van der Tak (1975), which took over the OECD manual's "world prices" rule for estimating shadow prices for commodities and the UNIDO manual's domestic consumption numeraire (rather than foreign exchange as in the OECD manual) for estimating intertemporal shadow prices, like the social discount rate.

The bank began to pay lip service to the application of the Squire-van der Tak method in appraising its projects, in light of the impetus given to expanding lending by Robert McNamara. However, the bank staff at the coal face of its lending was not really interested in social cost-benefit analysis, but rather—as one observer commented—on social cosmetic analysis—a tendency accentuated by the fact that staff performance was judged not by the quality but the quantity of loans.

In 1973, the Indian Planning Commission decided to create a new project appraisal division (PAD). I spent a year helping Lovraj Kumar and his deputy, T. L. Shankar, set it up and provide initial estimates of shadow prices for India on the OECD (Little-Mirrlees) method. The PAD set about applying the method to some of the largest public-sector investment projects undertaken. One of these was a project to mine a huge iron-ore mountain and convert the ore into pellets for sale abroad. I was asked to evaluate this project. It turned out that at current (and projected) world prices, the project was hugely socially unprofitable. My recommendation that it be turned down was not accepted, since the steel ministry had arranged a deal with the shah of Iran, who agreed to buy the pellets at vastly inflated prices. My comment that this presumed social viability of the long-term project depended on the shah's longevity exceeding that of the project was disregarded because of an impending election in the district where the project was located and where the ruling party's prospects depended on sanctioning it. The project went ahead. The shah fell within a few years, and India was left with another white elephant. Thus, while project evaluation is undoubtedly an important tool to ensure the correct choice of public-sector investment projects, it has not had much appeal since it can undercut politicians, who often use sanctioned projects for political purposes even if they are uneconomic.[1]

In the foreign-aid ministries (like the United Kingdom's that had also adopted the Little-Mirrlees method) and the World Bank, the marginal approach underlying project evaluation came under attack because money is fungible. Although an aid agency might decide that a government investment project submitted for funding will have a positive social rate of return, this does not mean the project would *not* have been financed from the government's own resources were no aid available. A government that gets aid for a project it would have financed anyway can then releases its own funds for a project it would not have been able to finance, say, an arms factory. Thus, the aid agency is not really financing the proposed project but rather the marginal project, such as an arms factory.

This problem led the aid agencies to move from project finance to general budgetary support, but with various macro and governance conditions attached to increase the efficiency of the whole government budget. These conditional structural loans became the main instrument of foreign aid in the 1980s. But since no sanctions were imposed on governments that did not fulfill the "conditionality," in part because the donors were keen to show they were increasing foreign aid, these "structural adjustment" loans were also used for whatever purposes the recipient governments—not the donors— deemed fit. Thus, President Moi of Kenya accepted the same unmet "conditions" he had no intention of fulfilling for repeated structural adjustment loans from the international agencies!

As the dismal record of foreign aid in poverty alleviation became obvious, and as the better-governed Third World countries found that with the globalization of international capital markets they did not need foreign-aid agencies with their long drawn-out procedures and "conditions," only the "lemons"—which could not get loans from their friendly Citibank banker—were left for the aid agencies to service. With the World Bank turning from its traditional role of financing for roads, dams, and other infrastructure and later budgetary support towards the social sectors emphasizing wooly concepts like "empowerment" and other politically correct ends supported by the proponents of foreign aid in the West, the economically rigorous, but in many cases politically ineffective, use of foreign aid to change dysfunctional economy-wide policies fell by the wayside. The question became how to evaluate the effects of foreign aid on these social sectors. Having turned its back on both broad macroeconomic evaluations of foreign aid and the social cost-benefit analysis that can and has been used to evaluate projects in social sectors like health and education, some new method was needed to show the efficacy of foreign aid to alleviate poverty in these social sectors. Arise the new turn to the "micro" through randomized controlled trials!

Experiments

The economists associated with the MIT Poverty Action Lab have been at the forefront of the latest fad in *Making Aid Work* (as a book by one of its leading advocates Banerjee [2007] proclaims): random controlled evaluations. Their intellectual basis is provided by the claims made for the atheoretical randomized controlled trials discussed in Chapter 6.

Banerjee claims that "one would not want to spend a lot of money without doing at least one successful randomized trial *if one is possible*" (12). He accepts that in many cases "randomized experiments are simply not feasible, such as in the case of exchange-rate policy or central bank independence: it clearly makes no sense to assign countries exchange rates at random" (11–12). So what programs are amenable to randomized or natural experiments? Banerjee cites two trials (discussed in Chapter 6) as providing "hard evidence" for where public spending should be concentrated. The first is the Angrist and Lavy trial on the effects of smaller class size on school performance as having "proved" that "students perform better in smaller classes" (12). As shown in Chapter 6, no such conclusion is warranted.

The other is the trial on the effects of deworming on school attendance in Kenya (Miguel and Kremer 2004). This, as Deaton (2009) noted (see Chapter 6), is not based on randomization but alphabetization, which does not yield robust conclusions. In any case, why does one want to do a randomized controlled trial for deworming? Whether or not it reduces school absenteeism is beside the point because it is surely worth doing for the sake of improving the health of the children. No trial is required either to determine that a school-based rather than individual deworming program is better, because children infect each other. Even a country doctor could have pointed this out. Equally, Banerjee's (2007, 17) claim that the "cheapest strategy for getting children to spend more time in school" is deworming as compared with "a conditional cash transfer program, such as Progresa in Mexico, in which the mother gets extra welfare payments if her children go to school," is absurd. As he himself recognizes, welfare payments would be good things even if they did not promote education. And what about countries outside Africa where deworming is not a problem? Should they not promote programs to promote education like Progresa?

The trouble is that, bewitched by their randomized controlled trial method—though they are right that "we need to go back to financing projects and insist that the results be measured" (Banerjee 2007, 21)—these *randomistas* have adopted a very limited method. The far richer and theoretically grounded traditional social cost-benefit method is already available for program evaluation. Thus, the social rate of return of a deworming program would have included the direct health benefits to the children treated (distributionally weighted if preferred) as well as any indirect benefits, such as improving school attendance. This social rate of return could be compared with the social rate of return estimated for the Progresa program, and if the overall program funds are limited, all the projects ranked by their rates of return should be funded until the budget is exhausted.

Another leading study claimed to be relevant for public-investment decisions is on the effects of dams on poverty in India by Duflo and Pande (2007). This is an examination of a quasi-experiment based on the instrument variable (IV) of land gradients in an econometric study of Indian districts where large dams have been built between 1971 and 1999. The IV instrument of land gradient is used to separate

> those who live downstream from a dam [who] stand to benefit, while those in the vicinity of and upstream from a dam stand to lose. From an econometric viewpoint, this implies that we can isolate the impact of dams on two populations, and from a policy perspective, this suggests compensating losers is relatively easy [602].

They find that

> Large dams have benefited downstream populations. In contrast those living in the vicinity of the dam fail to enjoy any agricultural productivity gains and suffer from increased volatility of agricultural production. Our poverty results also suggest a worsening of living standards in the district where the dam is built, though limited data availability for the poverty outcomes limits our ability to wholly disentangle the poverty impact of dam construction from district-specific time trends in poverty, which are correlated with geographic suitability for dams [640].

This whole study is compromised by using land gradient as the IV for identifying the effects of dams on poverty, for while being external (in Deaton's [2009] sense[2]), this instrument is not exogenous. Duflo and Pande also do not provide overall distributionally weighted rates of return for the various dams, relying on the defense that implicit in the argument for their relevance "is the belief that projects with an average positive return should be undertaken, as it will be possible to compensate the losers" (460). This may be true of cost-benefit analyzes that do not use distributional weighting but not of the numerous studies that use these weights.

I can also personally contradict their confident assertion that "to the best of our knowledge there are no other systematic estimates of the impact of dams on agricultural outcomes to which we can compare our estimates." If this merely means similar cross-district econometric studies, they may be right. But this is not true of the older social cost-benefit literature that clearly no longer forms part of the knowledge base of these younger "development economists." For I spent part of my misspent youth applying the Little–Mirrlees method of the OECD manual to Indian irrigation projects. The first book I wrote, *Wells and Welfare*, was a cost-benefit study of irrigation wells in Ahmednagar district in Maharashtra for Oxfam, published by the OECD Development Centre in 1972. For this, I had to spend months in 1969 collecting the data on inputs and outputs as well as the primary weather data from the Indian Metrological office in Poona and agronomic data from the National College of Agricultural Engineering in Bedford. The major findings were that the social return to wells more than doubled with distributional weighting;

that they were negative for the use of groundwater to grow sugar-cane (as the domestic price was well above the world price of sugar because of quantitative controls on its import); and that the social returns to a hydrogeological survey (which had then not been done, but which my book helped to promote) to allow wells to be sited with greatly reduced uncertainty were massive.

My second work (Lal and Duane 1972) was a post-evaluation of a large-scale surface irrigation scheme in the Purna district in central India for the World Bank in 1972. We found that the realized social rate of return was only 5.5 percent compared with the planned 16 percent. Because of the high water table in the command area, the planned cropping pattern sought to confine water-intensive crops to well-drained areas near the canal/river beds. This was sabotaged in practice by the illegal use of irrigation water to grow water-intensive crops. This led to water logging and the destruction of a substantial part of the crop area in the command. Hence, the low social rate of return.

The engineer's mistake on the Purna project was to assume that only supplemental irrigation would be carried out in most of the command area, which would substantially raise sorghum yields, not necessitating a switch to water-intensive crops. In practice, rabi (winter/spring) yields rose but the yields for the major kharif (monsoon season crops) were almost stationary. This mistaken assumption was due to the lack of any data on the water-response function of sorghum, a lacuna that has hopefully been filled in irrigation planning in India today.

A similar lack of information on water-response functions prevented another massive and imaginative study of the large Bhakra-Nangal dam in Punjab from doing more than a cost-effectiveness analysis of the scheme. Minhas and his colleagues (1972) at the ISI Planning Unit in Delhi had devised a scheme for combining ground and surface water systems to optimize the competing uses of water at certain seasons between irrigation and power generation. But lacking water-response functions, they could not undertake this exercise.

These carefully done studies, with primary data gathered for particular projects, provide more credible policy conclusions than the cross-district regressions of Duflo and Pande, which do not take account of the differing cropping patterns, water-response functions, and other agronomic conditions of the various dams. While their study may be useful for activists in their political campaigns to stop large dam construction in India on the grounds that they damage the poor, no such conclusions can be derived from their flawed aggregate method based on IV. Once again, detailed and credible project analyzes of particular dams are needed to determine the social rates of return to building particular dams in India.

As one of Banerjee's discussants, Howard White, notes (Banerjee 2007, 87), "cost benefit analysis was introduced to do precisely what Banerjee calls for—deciding what should be financed." But he is wrong to concede that it does not do this "by examining all the possible uses of funds, as [Banerjee] suggests." In fact, there is no difficulty in estimating the "shadow" price of foreign-aid funds that can be combined with the economy-wide social rate of return to determine the rate of return ranking of projects. But White is right in stating: "Calculating the benefits requires an assumption about impact, and it is obviously best if these assumptions are based on evidence from impact evaluations. But such impact evaluations can only adopt a randomized approach in a small minority of cases."

Reading the various studies based on randomized controlled trials and IV regressions, and the claims they make for their relevance for development policy, I am struck by how limited is their scope and ambition. They remind me of the nursery rhyme:

> Little Jack Horner sat in the corner
> Eating his Christmas pie,
> He put in his thumb and pulled out a plum
> And said 'What a good boy am I!'[3]

But this may be a blessing in disguise, for since the main targets of the *randomistas* are the foreign-aid agencies they hope to persuade to adopt this limited method, it can do little harm to the prospects of the world's poor, given the growing irrelevance of aid (as discussed in Chapter 3). By contrast, the arguments based on the theoretical curiosities for Big Push industrial policies (see Chapter 7) could do real harm if adopted.

Household Surveys and the Lives of the Poor

In the early 1970s, soon after getting married to an American sociologist who had never been east of Aden, I spent a year in India with my wife. I was working as a consultant to the Indian Planning Commission. As part of my work, I had to go to Calcutta from Delhi. While I flew, my wife and another Planning Commission official took the train. My mother had packed a bagful of delicacies to keep them fed on the long trip. When they arrived at Howrah station, they still had some cheese sandwiches left, which they gave to an old female beggar on the station platform. The woman examined them, looked inside, and said, "No butter," and disdainfully threw them away. Later as we went through the slums of Calcutta, my wife remarked that she couldn't understand why all these extremely poor people seemed to be happy, smiling, and laughing.

The burgeoning household surveys are now providing empirical micro evidence that challenges these common stereotypes about the lives of the poor. The living standard measurement surveys of the World Bank, the family life surveys by RAND, and the Indian surveys of the National Council for Applied Economic Research, International Crops Research Institute for the Semi-Arid-Tropics, and National Sample Survey have provided important empirical evidence about various economic aspects of the lives of the Third World poor. Banerjee and Duflo (2007) have deftly summarized the findings of some of these surveys in 13 countries across Asia, Latin America, and Africa, providing empirical evidence on the lives of the poor, which gives the lie to the "poverty-porn" peddled by films like *Slumdog Millionaire.*

The first notable finding is that despite the popular picture of millions of wretched, starving families across the Third World, whose meager incomes do not allow them to buy enough food to eat, these surveys invariably find that the poor do not spend all their income of a $1 or less on food. Only 56–78 percent of consumption by rural households and 56–74 percent by urban ones is spent on food.

A significant portion of their budget (4–8 percent) is spent on tobacco and alcohol, and the median household spent 10 percent of its budget on festivals, including weddings, funerals, and religious festivals. These are their major source of entertainment; they spend little on movies, theater, and so on. Ownership of radios and TVs varies widely: the Indian village sample from Udaipur had the lowest ownership, with only 11 percent owning a radio (but the highest spending on festivals), while in Nicaragua half the poor households have a TV (but spend little on festivals).

Thus even those living on less than $1 a day

> do see themselves as having a significant amount of choice,
> but they choose not to exercise that choice in the direction
> of spending more on food. . . . Even the extremely poor do
> not seem to be hungry for extra calories as one might expect
> [Banerjee and Duflo 2007, 3].

They also prefer the better quality but fewer calories provided by the more expensive cereals like rice and wheat, rather than the cheaper coarser ones like *jowar* and *bajra*. They also seem to have a sweet tooth, spending almost 7 percent of their total budget on sugar, which is twice as expensive as a source of calories as grains. Thus, "even for the extremely poor, for every 1% increase in the food expenditure, about half goes into purchasing more calories, and half goes into purchasing more expensive (and presumably better tasting) calories" (5).

The chosen average intake of calories by the extremely poor in India is slightly less than 1,400 calories a day, which is half of what the Indian government recommends for a man pursuing moderate activity (Deaton and Subramanian 1996; Banerjee and Duflo 2007, 149). This low-calorie intake does lead to a lower body mass index and anemia, which in turn leads to the high level of morbidity seen by the poor as the major source of financial and psychological stress and the major cause of unhappiness. But "while the poor certainly, *feel* poor, their levels of self-reported happiness or self-reported health levels are not particularly low" (Banerjee, Deaton, and Duflo 2004; Banerjee and Duflo 2007, 150).

Most of the poor are self-employed in multiple occupations and are entrepreneurial, "in the sense of raising capital, carrying out investment, and being full residual claimants for the resulting earnings" (Banerjee and Duflo 2007, 8). Small plots of land are the major productive asset of the rural poor. But as this is insufficient to provide even a meager income, they are engaged in nonfarm businesses, often staffed with family members. They have few durable assets. The many extremely poor households operating their own businesses do so with almost no productive assets. Poor families do seek out economic opportunities, but they tend not to become too specialized. They do some agriculture but not to the point where it would afford them a full living (for example, by buying, renting, or sharecropping more land).

The poor are ill-served by the government-provided infrastructure and government provisions for health and education. The availability of electricity, tap water, and basic sanitation (latrines) to the poor varies widely across countries. None of the rural poor households in Udaipur has access to tap water, while 36 percent in Guatemala do. Only 1.3 percent of poor households have electricity in Tanzania, compared to 90 percent in Mexico. Latrine availability varies from none in Udaipur to 100 percent in Nicaragua. Generally, the urban poor have greater access to electricity and tap water than do their rural cousins.

Government provision of health and education for the poor is nearly universal across countries, but the quality is poor. The average absentee rate among teachers and health workers in Bangladesh, Ecuador, India, Indonesia, Peru, and Uganda was 19 percent among teachers and 35 percent among health workers. "Moreover, because not all teachers and health workers are actually working when in their post, even this picture maybe too favorable. Moreover absence rates are generally higher in poor regions" (15). The quality of whatever education and health that is provided is poor. Thus, even the poorest are increasingly sending their children to private schools and using private doctors (Tooley 2009).

A study of the decentralized system of local government called *panchayati raj* in India suggests a way to improve public provision of these public goods. The National Bureau of Economic Research study by Munshi and Rosenzweig (2008), based on data from a rural household survey, finds that at the ward level the "parochial (caste) politics [of *panchayati raj*] appears to simultaneously increase both the competence and commitment of elected leaders, as indicated by the characteristics of the elected representatives and their enhanced delivery of local public goods in response to constituents 'preferences' i.e., the quality and quantity of public goods preferred by the *panchayati*'s members." Reservations, except for women, are inefficient, since they "reduce the likelihood that a numerically dominant caste will emerge in a constituency, exacerbating the commitment problem." But reservations for women do not affect the probability of a caste equilibrium emerging, and the authors find that "women leaders are significantly more competent than men in that equilibrium." So the fears of those who look askance at transferring public resources to local politicians, concerned it may entrench existing power hierarchies, may have the wrong end of the stick, particularly if they are interested in maximizing the benefits from government provision of these merit goods. The best way to achieve this aim may in fact be to work through the existing hierarchies.

The Informal Sector and Microfinance

My most memorable experience on a trip to Peru in the early 1980s was the "markets tour" organized by Hernando de Soto's Institute of Liberty and Democracy in Lima. The tour showed the path that the typical poor migrant from the Andes took in the metropolis. Travelling across Lima, one got a living picture of the process: how migrants organized "invasions" of public land to build their shacks with pilfered supplies of electricity and water, and eked out a living in "informal" activities, including the creation and stocking of whole illegal covered markets the size of shopping malls. The striking thing was the enterprise of poor people (as also confirmed by the household surveys discussed in the last section) and the ubiquitousness of the trading instinct. De Soto wrote a famous book, *The Other Path* (1989,) about these informales and how they were forced into illegality because of the mercantilist system of licenses and controls, which made it impossible for them to become legal. This meant that they had to create an informal system of law often manned by moonlighting judges and lawyers from the official system. Their property rights, nevertheless, remained insecure.

In a later book, *The Mystery of Capital* (2000), de Soto extended his research to quantify the hidden capital held—mainly in the form of housing—by these informales in the Philippines, Egypt, Haiti, and Peru. His estimates are staggering. Their capital is worth many times all the foreign aid and foreign investment these countries have received since 1945. He therefore rightly concludes that it is not a shortage of capital per se or a lack of entrepreneurs that keeps these countries poor. His panacea is to unlock this hidden capital in the informal sector by making it—particularly the shanty housing—legal, by analogy with the granting of land rights to squatters in the frontier states of the United States through the Homestead Act. This would allow the informales to make their capital liquid, enabling them to use it as collateral for loans to make wider investments.

There are two problems with this idea, however. First, in the United States, with abundant land at its shifting frontier, there was no infringement of other settler rights by squatters. However, in many labor-abundant (and land-scarce) parts of the Third World, the squatters are encroaching on private land or public land designated for parks, drains, and other public goods. Why should informales be granted rights to their shacks at the expense of the rightful owners? Second, much of the illegality of informales is forced on them by the "permit raj" established in these countries in the name of planning. If these dysfunctional control systems were removed, informales could operate legally by converting some of their income into legal housing.

Apart from the legal barriers erected against the poor in eking out their low incomes and building up productive assets, they also lack access to financial markets providing insurance and credit. Financial institutions reduce the risks in specialization as well as those presented by climate variations and illness. They also provide the means to save and to smooth consumption over time. The household surveys discussed in the last section find that few of the poor have loans from a formal lending source. Most of their loans are from informal sources for which they pay on average 3.84 percent per month.

These high rates are not due to default rates, which are low (for example, just 2 percent across moneylenders in rural Pakistan [Aleem 1990]), but to delays in repayment, exacerbated by the high costs of enforcing contracts. Informal lenders also have a higher cost of capital than the formal-sector banks (32.5 percent for rural moneylenders compared with 10 percent for banks in Pakistan).

The poor also have limited access to formal insurance, the exceptions being Mexico, with half the poor having health insurance, and India, where 4–10 percent have life insurance (a form of savings).

These credit and insurance needs have historically been met through social networks. In Chapter 3, we saw how some of these networks have provided a private social safety net for the conjuncturally poor. But there have also been various forms of microfinance and collective lending that have existed for hundreds of years, going as far back as 1300. These include the "susus" of Ghana, "chit funds" in India, "tandas" in Mexico, "ansan" in Indonesia, and "tontines" in West Africa. These are mutual credit associations where members contribute their periodic savings to a common fund, which makes tiny loans to the poor. In the rotating credit (ROSCAS) version, the collective pot each period is handed sequentially to a member, the sequence determined by the members' date of entry. The contract obligating recipients to continue contributing is enforced through community sanctions.

In 1865, Friedrich Wilhelm Raiffeisen developed the concept of the credit union in Germany, and this cooperative movement spread across Europe, North America, and many developing countries. In 1895, the Bank Perkreditan Rakyat (BPR) opened in Indonesia, specializing in an early form of microfinance. It is the largest microfinance system in Indonesia today with 9,000 operations. In 1961, Accion International was founded in Venezuela with $90,000 raised from private companies to build schools and water systems. In 1973, it turned to microfinance, becoming one of the major such organizations in the world, and in 1992, it founded BancoSul of Bolivia, the first commercial bank dedicated solely to microfinance. It has more than 70,000 clients today.

In 1971, Al Whittaker and David Bussau began lending to micro entrepreneurs in Indonesia and Colombia, and in 1979, they formed Opportunity International, lending across southeast Asia and South America. In 1983, Mohammed Yunus created the Grameen Bank in Bangladesh, having discovered in 1976 that a loan of $27, which was paid back with interest, changed the lives of 43 poor families by beginning to lift them out of poverty. In 2006, Yunus he won the Nobel Peace prize as the patron saint of the microcredit movement.

In 1997, the National Microfinance Bank was created in Tanzania, and Deutsche Bank entered microfinance as part of its new drive towards social investing. In 2005, Citibank opened Citi Microfinance to broaden the reach of its financial services. In 2006, Barclays Bank launched Ghanian Microfinance, using the traditional form of "susu collection." In the same year, the World Bank's private investment arm, the IFC, invested $45 million in credit-linked notes issued by Standard Chartered Bank for microfinance lending in Africa and Asia. In 2007, JPMorgan Chase launched a microfinance unit as part of its emerging markets focus. In 2008, Sequoia Capital, a venture capital fund that backed Google, Apple, and Cisco, took an $11 million stake in SK Microfinance, a large Indian microlender. By 2006, 133 million low-income customers worldwide were receiving $4 billion of microfinance every year.

In April 2007, Mexico's Compartamos converted from a microfinance institution into a bank. It had expanded from 60,000 customers in 2000 to 800,000 in 2007, fueled by retained earnings, making it one of the largest microlenders in Latin America. It held an initial public offering (IPO) in which insiders sold 30 percent of their stock, which was oversubscribed by 13 times, and the new Banco Compartamos was soon worth $1.6 billion. This IPO was roundly denounced by Yunus, who claimed the bank's success was based on charging its poor customers 94 percent per year, with a quarter of interest revenue going to profit. Compartamos thus was a brute moneylender, Yunus asserted, the very thing his Grameen Bank was intended to destroy. Supporters of Compartamos responded that its success in tapping private investor funds makes it possible to envisage microfinance serving over one billion low-income customers in the Third World.

A number of points emerge from this condensed history.[4] First, microfinance is not new. Second, unless it is subsidized, the interest rates that have to be charged are not much lower than those of traditional moneylenders. Third, unlike the various government-run and subsidized rural credit institutions that dismally failed to meet their purported social objective of providing financial services to the Third World's poor, the new multifaceted microfinance movement seems to succeed. But is this really so, and if so, what is the secret of this private success?

Cull et al. (2009) succinctly summarize the evidence. First, there is a clear movement from socially oriented nonprofit microfinance institutions (NGOs for short) to for-profit microfinance (banks for short). Second, NGOs receive significant subsidies based on noncommercial borrowing (soft loans, which are 16 percent of their funding) and their main source, donations (39 percent). The arguments for subsidization echo the "infant industry" argument: Indeed, the most famous of these "infants," the Grameen Bank, "still takes advantage of subsidies 25 years after its start" (Armendariz de Aghion, and Morduch 2005, 19). By contrast, banks receive no subsidy, relying on commercial borrowing and deposits, which combined provide 84 percent of their funds. Third, despite these differences in financing sources, the NGOs' median interest rate of 25 percent (with the top quartile charged 37 percent or more) is substantially higher than the median 13 percent charged by microfinance banks (and 19 percent or more for the top quartile). Fourth, these differences in interest rates are due to the NGOs' higher cost per loan: 26 cents per dollar at the median versus the banks' 12 cents. This variation is not the result of scale economies (to be sure, individual bank loans are larger than NGO loans) but because the banks work the intensive margin better by providing larger loans and more services for their existing customers.

Fifth, even the median NGO earns profits (defined as revenues less costs). Their median return on equity is 3 percent, compared to 10 percent for microfinance banks. Sixth, the assumption that the "group liability" system of Grameen is the secret of its success is disproved by a randomized controlled trial in the Philippines, which found group liability was discouraging new customers and not improving repayment rates (Gine and Karlan 2008). Grameen itself has quietly dropped the "group liability" system. Lending to individuals—the banks' most common method of lending—has no higher default rates than group lending. Seventh, the effects on growth through promoting businesses of the poor are scant and ambiguous. A study of male-owned microbusinesses found high returns to capital in Mexico, but none for female micro entrepreneurs in Sri Lanka (McKenzie and Woodruff 2006). Eighth, the evidence on the effects of microfinance in reducing poverty is "inconclusive, ranging from assertions of substantial reductions in poverty in Bangladesh to zero effects in northern Thailand" (Cull et al. 2009, 188).

Although we should not object to private individuals and charities subsidizing NGO microfinance institutions, nor to private banks raising private capital for microborrowers, clearly the hope that microfinance offers some panacea to lift the "bottom billion" out of poverty is yet to be fulfilled. In fact, a correspondent with the *Financial Times*, responding to an article on microfinance by Tim Harford, wrote, "I have recently been working in Serbia. Here the foreign-owned commercial banks have massively discovered microfinance," channeling about 12 percent of GDP to microfinance loans:

> This has had two important results: first a serious shortage of funds for small and medium-sized businesses, which is deeply damaging because SMEs have by far the most sustainable growth and development potential. Second, thanks to microfinance there has been an accelerated proliferation of informal – sector microenterprises in Serbia over 2004–08, so the country is now chock-full of traders, kiosks, shops, street-traders and subsistence farms. The base of the economy is quite simply being destroyed [Bateman 2008, 10].

The author goes on to argue that the situation in Bosnia is even worse because of what "many locals call the "Africanisation (*Africanizacija*) of their economy." Clearly, microfinance is not the panacea for ending Third World poverty.

9. Saving Africa

I first went to Africa in 1970 to set up a research project funded by the United Kingdom's Overseas Development Administration, applying the Little-Mirrlees project evaluation method to foreign-investment projects in east Africa and India. Tanzania, then turning socialist under Julius Nyerere, showed no interest in this enterprise. Uganda, which was then ruled by Milton Obote, was also uninterested. (Many of the friends I made at Makerere University ended up being fed to the crocodiles when Idi Amin succeeded Obote after a military coup.) This left Kenya, which proved hospitable, particularly the Institute of Development Studies. Apart from its energetic local staff led by Dharm Ghai, it had many notable foreign visitors at the time. I got to know some of the highly qualified Kenyan civil servants, most notably Harris Mule and Philip Ndegwa, who ran a relatively efficient and corruption-free bureaucracy. The Kenyan and Indian evaluation studies appeared as a book, *Appraising Foreign investment in Developing Countries*.

But it was later in the 1970s that I really got to know Kenya well. Robert McNamara, who had become the president of the World Bank, was in his evangelical phase. He wanted to end Third World poverty and was much impressed by the socialist policies of Nyerere's Tanzania. The relatively capitalist route being taken by Jomo Kenyatta's Kenya was not to his liking. McNamara asked the East Africa department of the bank to undertake an independent study of poverty in Kenya. The department asked me and a young Oxford don, Paul Collier, to undertake this study, which had the support of the Kenyan treasury. This eventually led to our book, *Labour and Poverty in Kenya* (1986) and to Paul's becoming the world's foremost scholar of African economic development. I moved on to other parts of the world, with occasional forays into Zimbabwe and South Africa. In the Lal-Myint study, we included three African countries: Nigeria, Malawi, and Madagascar, the Nigerian case study being done by Paul and his collaborators. His numerous other books with coauthors on many aspects of African economic development and political economy have given him an unrivalled understanding of the continent. As noted, he wrote a bestseller, *The Bottom Billion* (2007), in which he uses the fashionable cross-country regression techniques discussed in Chapter 5 to bolster his arguments, rather than the vast specific multicountry knowledge he has acquired. He rightly recognizes that without growth, poverty cannot be ameliorated, but is pessimistic about the African laggards because of myriad poverty traps. So he ends up arguing for massive foreign aid as well as robust Western military intervention to address the many civil wars and poor governance that have ravaged the continent.

In this, he is joined by Sachs (2005), who advocates a Big Push based on infrastructure and medical interventions to end poverty in Africa, and Easterly (2001, 2006, 2009a), who also seems addicted to cross-country regressions using instrumental variables. He is the most pessimistic of the three regression warriors about the West being able to save Africa. Indeed, he also seems to have moved over the years from a belief in poverty traps to what may be called the Hayekian classical-liberal position.[1] I find my own views in this battle of celebrity academic poverty warriors to be most in consonance with Easterly's.[2]

This sudden flurry of popular interest in Africa is due to the growing recognition of the continuing tragedy there. In the last 40 years since independence, sub-Saharan Africa (SSA) has remained the poorest, most troubled, and tragic region in the world. It has horrendous problems that range from famines, malaria, tuberculosis, and river blindness, to the scourge of HIV/AIDS. So it is not surprising that many, including world leaders, have championed its cause and called for providing large amounts of aid. Tony Blair has called it "a scar on the conscience of the world," thus assuming a collective guilt for all. A view has emerged among some leaders, the United Nations, and rock stars that what SSA needs is a Marshall Plan (MP) like the one that contributed to the reconstruction and recovery of western Europe after the Second World War.[3] I examine the case for a Marshall Plan for Africa in the next section.

A Marshall Plan for Africa?[4]

The proposed MP for aid to sub-Saharan Africa is associated with higher amounts of aid than the already high levels received in the last 40 years. By and large, that aid has failed to achieve its avowed purposes. Worse, much of it has been squandered. Moreover, future proposals for aid proposed by the Commission for Africa and various advocates do not promise to have different results; rather, they merely create hope of improvement. Nor do the new institutional arrangements, such as the New Partnership for African Development and the African Peer Review Mechanism, provide a new optimism for better utilization of large amounts of aid.

The Marshall Plan

In the aftermath of the Second World War, Western Europe had a damaged infrastructure (particularly transport), an industrial sector geared to war production (particularly in Germany), and a neglected agricultural sector, specifically, loss of land area and fertility due to neglect of the soil, damaged irrigation facilities, and reduced livestock. The main demand for funds was for reconstruction and to address immediate food, fuel, and fertilizer shortages. Initial conditions in 1939–47 were difficult, to say the least. The condition in 1947 was described as: "production stagnating, trade collapsing, commodity hoarding, the economy teeter[ing] on the brink of disaster. Shortages pervasive and the overhang of liquid assets threatened runaway inflation" (Eichengreen 1995). The 16 countries that received aid were Austria, Belgium and Luxembourg, Denmark, France, Greece, Iceland, Ireland, Italy, Netherlands, Norway, Portugal, Sweden, Switzerland, Turkey, West Germany, and United Kingdom. (The largest recipients were United Kingdom, France, Belgium, and Germany). They received $13.2 billion, or $103 billion at 2006 prices. No country received more than the equivalent of 2.5 percent of its GDP (see Table 19.1).

Western Europe comprised countries that were among the most advanced in the world at the time. Not only were economic and social conditions superior to the rest of the world (save the United States), but before the war, the region also had mature market economies, highly advanced infrastructures, and equally advanced institutions of law and order, parliamentary democracies (until the emergence of Hitler and Mussolini), and well-established property rights. The war

159

Table 9.1
MARSHALL PLAN AID, 1948–51

Country	Funds Received (in millions of dollars)
Austria	488
Belgium and Luxembourg	777
Denmark	385
France	2,296
Greece	366
Iceland	43
Ireland	133
Italy and Trieste	1,204
Netherlands	1,128
Norway	372
Portugal	70
Sweden	347
Switzerland	250
Turkey	137
United Kingdom	3,297
West Germany	1,448

SOURCE: Martin A. Schain, ed., *The Marshall Plan: Fifty Years After* (New York: Palgrave, 2001), p. 120.

was a tremendous upheaval that challenged many institutions and political systems, indeed, the social fabric in that region.

The Basis for the Marshall Plan

The basis for aid was straightforward: to help western Europe recover from the Second World War and to help in its reconstruction. As defined in the Harvard commencement speech by Secretary of State George Marshall, the aid proposed was directed "against hunger, poverty, desperation, and chaos" (speech at Harvard University commencement, June 5, 1947).[5] This was to be a temporary enterprise to restore what had been achieved in the continent that was ravaged by war. There was no mention of the development of western Europe since it was one of the most developed regions in the world. Reconstruction was not to entail a new enterprise but a rebuilding and addition to existing infrastructure, and resurrection of some institutions that had gone into disarray or disuse during the war. To be sure, some new institutions, such as the European Coal and Steel Community and the European Payments Union, were also created, but they were not planned at the beginning of the MP.

Marshall's speech lacked details and amounts, with only a reference to a brief duration of four to five years. The important message of the speech was that Europeans were to create their own plan for rebuilding and that the United States would fund it. The work of the Economic Cooperation Administration (ECA), which administered the MP, was to boost Europe's economy, promote production, restore the currency, and facilitate international trade, especially with the United States.[6]

Private-Sector Role

Even though dollars were provided by the U.S. government and disbursed by the recipient national governments, the decisions regarding where and how to use the funds were very much in the hands of the private sector. The importance of the private sector's role is a neglected aspect in earlier accounts of the MP. That role can be seen in three respects. First, the initiative to use the funds came from private agents who made an application to the national governments, which considered requests in consultation with the ECA. The latter made sure the funds were for the purposes defined in Congress's Economic Cooperation Act, which included rebuilding privately owned firms and farms. Second, the loans were transacted through private banks, which received a deposit in local currency from the private importer to a special account that was equal to the value of the goods imported from a private American exporter. These were the so-called counterpart funds. After the food and coal emergency grants were made, the rest was all in loans to be repaid with interest on agreed repayment schedules. Third, the national governments loaned part of the counterpart funds to private industries, intermediated through private banks (Blaisdell Jr. 1950).[7] Thomas Blaisdell Jr., U.S. assistant secretary of commerce, wrote that "most of the goods sent to Europe will be ordered directly from private business firms in the United States by importers in Europe. This way, the sinews and nerves of the intricate trading organisms will grow stronger with use" (Blaisdell Jr. 1948).

In sum, the MP was designed as a flexible, mostly nonbureaucratic arrangement "owned" by the Europeans with a significant role for the private sector. It was not based on the creation of a permanent bureaucracy. Nor were the funds large for the task at hand. What "conditionality" they had related to maintaining price and exchange-rate stability. It was predominantly a promarket enterprise, given the political context in which market forces were looked at askance in light of the Great Depression and adverse socialist propaganda of the time, which infected many leading European intellectuals. It was not the funds alone that made the difference for the reconstruction of Europe, but the help the MP provided in creating an environment in which markets would work well and property rights become secure.

Aid to sub-Saharan Africa

In contrast to the MP, aid to SSA has been huge over close to 50 years with little to show for it. In fact, as aid increased, economic performance declined (Figure 9.1). A number of SSA countries still have lower per capita income today than in the 1960s, despite the rise in incomes in the late 1990s.

Official aid to SSA is estimated at more than $607 billion in current dollars over the past 30 years. The earliest aid disbursements were made when de-colonization occurred in the late 1950s. The region has received more aid than any other region in the world in the last 50 years. It remains the poorest region in the world.

The Initial Conditions

The initial conditions after independence were diametrically opposite those of western Europe, when the MP began. SSA countries were among the poorest countries in the world but not necessarily the poorest. In fact, some countries there had higher per capita GDP at that time than the fastest growing east Asian countries in the period 1965–2004, such as South Korea and Taiwan, and higher than south Asian countries, such as India, Sri Lanka, and Pakistan.

SSA countries are also among the best endowed in the world, both in land and minerals. The region has the largest oil resources after the Middle East. Angola, Cameroon, Chad, the Republic of Congo, Cote d'Ivoire, Equatorial Guinea, Gabon, Nigeria, São Tomé, and Príncipe are oil exporters. SSA has large non-oil mineral resources, from

Figure 9.1
FOREIGN AID AND GDP GROWTH IN SUB-SAHARAN AFRICA

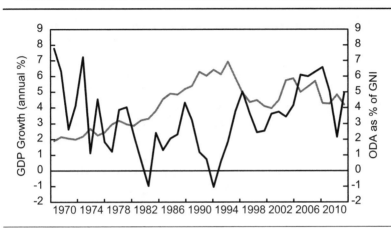

SOURCE: World Bank, World Development Indicators Online, available at www.worldbank.org/data/onlinedatabases/.

bauxite to diamonds, and enormous land resources. Its large natural endowments had attracted colonial powers during the Scramble for Africa from the late 1870s to the First World War.

Most of the 48 SSA countries became independent in the late 1950s and early 1960s. One of the earliest to become independent was Ghana (1957). It was followed by Guinea (1958), Burkina Faso, Chad, Central African Republic, Democratic Republic of Congo, Madagascar, Mali, Niger, Senegal, Somalia, Togo (all in 1960), Rwanda, Burundi (both in 1962), Malawi, Tanzania, Zambia (all in 1964), Gambia (1965), Lesotho (1966), Guinea-Bissau (1974), and Djibouti (1977). At independence, all were potential democracies, with possibilities for changing governments by electoral means. However, within a generation all became one-party states with authoritarian regimes ruled by "big men."

Poor Polity and Corruption

Africa was ill-served by the colonial impact on its traditional polities. The Scramble for Africa shattered their legitimacy, and the artificial states that were created were based on various forms of

163

paternalistic colonial rule. The artificial polities bequeathed to their nationalist successors by the colonial powers cut through the ancient configurations or amalgamated historically opposing tribes within their borders. So apart from the intertribal conflict within these states, they also have been threatened by claimants from across the new borders. With vast natural resource wealth to be grabbed and with scant sense of nationhood in these artificial tribal amalgamations, rulers found it possible to loot rents from natural resources to promote their friends and allies and coerce their enemies, with one eye always turned to the rear to prevent being overthrown in a coup. The time horizon of these predatory rulers was necessarily short, which provided an added incentive to obtain much of the God-given wealth for their own purposes and to ship much of it abroad. Thus, Africa's "big men" spent time plundering the countries' natural wealth rather than creating prosperity for their citizens. This is in contrast to those parts of the world (such as Asia) that are poor in natural resources and where the only source of wealth, even for predatory elites, lay in increasing the incomes of their prey.

But even in SSA, a number of countries have bucked the political trends arising from the bane of large natural resources. The major one is Botswana, which was among the few postcolonial states where the old political authority of the tribal chieftains was not destroyed. This was in part because their natural resource wealth (diamonds) was only discovered after gaining independence. So the colonial interest in restructuring the traditional polity was minimal.

By contrast, the traditional tribal elites in the other artificial states created by the colonial powers were marginalized or disestablished. The interwar years, after the partition of Africa was complete, saw the colonial powers undertake development as a trust for their new subjects. Development was expected to take a century, but by the 1950s "the winds of change" had led to the retreat of most of the colonial powers. Thus, the developmental and welfare phase of colonialism in Africa was relatively short. At independence, only about 3 percent of the African population of working age had secondary or higher education. This segment became the nationalist elites who inherited the artificial colonial states. Their attempts to create nation-states from this poisoned legacy through dirigiste means soon floundered. They found it easier to take what was on offer: the rents from natural resources. Consequently, corruption was rife, and it has continued (see Table 9.2).

Table 9.2

CORRUPTION IN AFRICA: GOVERNANCE RATINGS OVER TIME

Country	Year Gained Independence from Colonial Power	World Bank Governance Effectiveness Estimates, 2011[a]	Transparency International Corruption Perceptions Ratings, 2012[b]
Angola	1975	Very Bad	Very Bad
Benin	1960	Below Average	Below Average
Botswana	1966	Good	Good
Burkina Faso	1960	Bad	Below Average
Burundi	1962	Very Bad	Very Bad
Cameroon	1961	Bad	Bad
Cape Verde	1975	Average	Good
Central African Republic	1960	Very Bad	Bad
Chad	1960	Very Bad	Very Bad
Comoros	1975	Very Bad	Bad
Republic of Congo	1960	Very Bad	Bad
Democratic Republic of Congo	1960	Very Bad	Below Average
Cote d'Ivoire	1960	Very Bad	Bad
Equatorial Guinea	1968	Very Bad	Very Bad
Eritrea	1991	Very Bad	Bad
Ethiopia	N/A	Below Average	Bad
Gabon	1960	Bad	Below Average
Gambia	1965	Bad	Below Average
Ghana	1957	Below Average	Average

(continued)

Table 9.2
(continued)

Country	Year Gained Independence from Colonial Power	World Bank Governance Effectiveness Estimates, 2011[a]	Transparency International Corruption Perceptions Ratings, 2012[b]
Guinea	1958	Very Bad	Bad
Guinea Bissau	1974	Very Bad	Bad
Kenya	1963	Bad	Bad
Lesotho	1966	Below Average	Below Average
Liberia	N/A	Very Bad	Below Average
Madagascar	1960	Bad	Bad
Malawi	1964	Below Average	Below Average
Mali	1960	Bad	Bad
Mauritania	1960	Bad	Bad
Mauritius	1968	Good	Good
Mozambique	1975	Bad	Bad
Namibia	1990	Average	Above Average
Niger	1960	Bad	Bad
Nigeria	1960	Very Bad	Bad
Rwanda	1962	Average	Above Average
São Tomé and Principe	1975	Bad	Below Average
Senegal	1960	Below Average	Below Average
Seychelles	1976	Average	Above Average
Sierra Leone	1961	Very Bad	Bad

(continued)

Table 9.2
(continued)

Country	Year Gained Independence from Colonial Power	World Bank Governance Effectiveness Estimates, 2011[a]	Transparency International Corruption Perceptions Ratings, 2012[b]
Somalia	1960	Very Bad	Very Bad
South Africa	1961	Average	Below Average
Sudan	1956	Very Bad	Very Bad
Swaziland	1968	Bad	Below Average
Tanzania	1964	Bad	Below Average
Togo	1960	Very Bad	Bad
Uganda	1962	Bad	Bad
Zambia	1964	Bad	Below Average
Zimbabwe	1980	Very Bad	Very Bad

a. Zero is the mean score. Countries with scores above 1 are categorized as "very good," 0.99 to 0.49 as "good," 0.48 to 0 as "average," −0.01 to −0.50 as "below average," −0.51 to −1 as "bad," and less than −1 as "very bad."

b. In the Transparency International Corruption Perceptions Index, 2012, countries are rated on a scale from 0–100. The lowest score of any country is 8 and the highest is 90. To create a scale roughly from 1–10, each score is divided by 9.4. Eight is then the mean score. Countries with scores of 6.26 and above are categorized as "good," 6.25 to 5.01 as "above average," 3.77 to 5 as "below average," 3.76 to 2.53 as "bad," and 2.52 to 1 as "very bad."

SOURCES: World Bank Governance Indicators, http://info.worldbank.org/governance/wgi/sc_country.asp and Corruption Perceptions Index, 2012, http://cpi.transparency.org/cpi2012/.

The pervasive ethnic fractionalization, competition, and conflict, combined with the perversion of democracy, led to civil wars and regional wars, largely to capture natural resource rents. This has been particularly true of the last 40 years around the African Great Lakes.

In no other part of the world have the Four Horsemen of the Apocalypse galloped with such fury and left such devastation in their wake.[8] As mentioned above, the per capita income of the subcontinent has stagnated and in some cases fallen below its pre-independence levels. By 1998, one-third of sub-Saharan Africa's 48 countries were involved in civil wars. By 1989, there were four million officially recognized refugees and another 12 million displaced in their own countries as a result of these wars. Famine, which had disappeared with the introduction of the motor truck in the 1920s, has appeared in country after country—most recently in Zimbabwe, which used to be the breadbasket of Africa—largely because it was used as a tool of coercion in numerous civil wars or to punish ethnic rivals. Among the most affected were Angola, Chad, Central African Republic, Congo, Ethiopia, Mauritania, Rwanda, Sierra Leone, Somalia, and Uganda. Of course, many neighboring countries have been adversely affected with refugees from war-torn countries.

Changing Rationale for Aid

Foreign aid to SSA was extended for a variety of purposes. It was provided mainly for projects up to the 1980s, and later for programs as part of structural adjustment loans. These projects and programs went through many cycles and forms as the donor community kept changing its view as to what should be financed. Consequently there was little ownership by the elites of the borrowing SSA countries.

The design of aid to SSA followed the changing fashions in "development economics," for example, to overcome "poverty traps" through "big pushes" that could lead to "take-offs into self-sustained growth." These concepts have been found to be theoretically weak and empirically unfounded (see Chapter 7). This is in stark contrast to the MP, which was not based on any faulty concepts or models of growth.

Aid to SSA was the largest for any region (see Table 9.3). It averaged 6.3 percent of GDP for all SSA, but if South Africa and Nigeria (a large oil producer) are excluded, the proportion rises to double that ratio. This is in contrast to aid to Asia and Latin America. But even more important is the fact that aid was largely given

168

Table 9.3
COMPARISON OF AID WITH ECONOMIC INDICATORS ACROSS
DEVELOPING REGIONS, 2005

	Aid as a Percentage of National Income	Aid Per Capita	Aid as a Percentage of Capital Formation	Aid as a Percentage of Imports
Sub-Saharan Africa	5.54	43.9	27.35	13.41
South Asia	0.92	6.3	2.96	3.78[a]
Latin America & Caribbean	0.26	11.45	1.21	0.91

a. Figure is an estimate.

SOURCE: World Development Indicators 2006 (Washington, D.C.: World Bank, 2006), available at www.worldbank.org/data/wdi.

to the government sector and often misappropriated. Foreign aid amounted to some 60–70 percent of government budgets. Knowing that government investment had low or negative returns, it is no surprise that economic growth was low or negative and that there were huge debt repayment problems in SSA. In addition, aid to SSA perpetuated dirigiste governments that detracted from the general welfare and helped to perpetuate poverty.

Aid to SSA has not supported market reforms in any important way. Before the 1980s, the development paradigm put little emphasis on market reforms: open trade, room for private-sector initiatives, or the guarantee of property rights. Even after the 1980s, while there were attempts by the multilateral banks, particularly the World Bank, to do so, market reforms were not taken seriously in SSA. Both sides seem to have paid lip service to them. Thus, there was no shrinking of the government sector or movements towards widespread trade openness or price-based allocation of resources. This stands in contrast to western Europe after the MP, where there was a clear movement towards market reforms, even though its speed and intensity differed among different countries.

A Look to the Future

The Marshall Plan did not work as some present-day aid advocates contend. It was not the finance that was vital; rather, the support for institutions, the credibility it gave to reforms, and the movement towards democracy allowed Europe to live in peace after being the major theater of two world wars.

The advocates of a MP for sub-Saharan Africa, on the other hand, emphasize finance. For example, at Gleneagles in July 2005, leaders of the G-8 countries agreed to raise development assistance to SSA by $25 billion over the prevailing levels ($25 billion a year) until 2010 and by another $25 billion by 2015. Thus, the amounts involved would imply aid of $50 billion in the first five years and $75 billion in the next five years until 2015. In addition, in early 2005, the European Union supported the UN call for earmarking 0.7 percent of GNP, or $250 billion, for aid. Of this amount, half, or $125 billion, would go to the 48 countries in SSA (Lerrick 2005). If all this aid were to be made available, it would imply a staggering $625 billion over and above what SSA received in the last decade. The ability to use this amount without feeding corruption and creating macroeconomic problems in the absorption of resources (the Dutch Disease problems), based on the resurrection of 1950s concepts (of big pushes, poverty traps and takeoffs), all argue for a different approach from the one put forward by MP enthusiasts.

While there are claims to the contrary by some leaders and analysts (for example, Gordon Brown and Jeffrey Sachs[9]), there is little evidence that things have improved in SSA in any significant way in terms of economic management, institutional arrangements, and implementation and monitoring frameworks to sustain the view that foreign aid would lead to growth in that region. To be sure, there have been some improvements. In the last 10 years, the majority of the countries have had multiparty elections, a historical rarity in the region. But the Freedom House index for civil liberties still ranks SSA poorly, better only than the Middle East and North Africa region. There has been a recovery of growth in some of the countries in the last 10 years, due in a significant way to the recovery of commodity prices that are subject to cyclical fluctuations. But that cannot be a source for long-term growth. Without fundamental policy reforms and improvements in the institutional structures for assuring property rights in order to provide more space for the formal private sector to save and invest, SSA economic performance will remain lower than that of all other regions.

The proposed New Partnership for African Development (NEPAD) and its monitoring arm, the African Peer Review Mechanism (APRM), are good first steps to lead to policy reform and restructuring of institutions to bring about greater economic freedom. However, NEPAD and APRM's achievements to date are at best modest. They also suffer from the grand-plan approach and past obsessions such as the emphasis on regional trade for which there is little scope, and ambiguity towards private foreign capital. These new institutions also have limited ability to monitor transparently each other's performance.[10] In addition, the new approach promulgated in the Commission for Africa Report (prepared mostly by African intellectuals and politicians under the leadership of Tony Blair and Gordon Brown) argues for even more foreign aid, rather than reducing aid dependence. The Commission for Africa Report was the main document cited at Gleneagles as the source of the case for the enormous increase in aid.

A strong case can be made that instead of assuaging advanced countries' collective guilt by transferring their taxpayers' money to corrupt and ineffectual SSA governments, efforts should be made to keep markets open to African goods, allow foreign capital to flow freely, and let African citizens find their own route to development. For too long, Africa has been the theater where all the pet panaceas of western ideologues—aided and abetted by SSA predatory states—have been tried, with disastrous consequences for their long-suffering populations. There are, however, a number of shining examples, like Botswana and Lesotho, which show that SSA can produce spectacular growth despite the special factors of climate and the bane of natural resources, factors that some analysts cite for why Africa differs from the rest of the world.

The main lesson of the past is that future aid has, at best, to be modest, based on different countries' circumstances, and its employment determined by the countries themselves and different from grand plans of the past and those contemplated by some in the present. To do otherwise would be to subject the peoples of SSA to even greater disappointments than before. It would imply, as Samuel Johnson put it in another context, "a triumph of hope over experience."

Towards a Domestic Economic Renaissance

What is more, many Africans are themselves questioning the role of foreign aid in fostering development. The most vocal has been the Zambian economist and banker Dambisa Moyo, whose book *Dead Aid* (2009) is a searing indictment of the damage that past foreign aid has done to Africa by providing the means for various kleptocrats to become rich and to follow economic policies that keep their people poor. Instead of the government-to-government handouts, she recommends that Africa should access international capital markets by promoting business-friendly policies. Her prescriptions have been endorsed by Paul Kagame, the president of Rwanda ("Africa Has to Find Its Own Road to Prosperity," *Financial Times*, May 8, 2009, 13). Just as India's and China's stellar records on reducing their massive historical structural poverty had little to do with foreign aid, but rather to their moving from plan to market, many African countries will themselves realize that their continent too must find its own way to prosperity by promoting economic freedom. The last thing they need is the one great global plan run by "the UN Secretary General," as Sachs (2005, 269) has recommended.

In fact, many countries whose dirigisme had previously perpetuated poverty have learned the lesson and have changed their spots. In the 2000s, economic performance improved in many sub-Saharan countries. According to the Fraser Institute's *Economic Freedom of the World* index which measures the movement toward economic liberalism, many African countries markedly improved between 1995 and 2010, notable examples being Rwanda and Zambia. Thus Rwanda, which had a score of 3.78 in 1995, improved steadily to about 7.25 in 2010. Zambia, with a score of 3.09 in 1990, rose to 7.85 by 2010. The region's GDP grew by 35 percent from 2004 to 2010, admittedly partly on the back of rising commodity prices, with 26 of the 45 sub-Saharan economies growing at 5 percent or more in 2010. Africa is by no means doomed and does not need the West as its savior.[11]

Medical Interventions and Aid Vouchers

Though the dysfunctional nature of current foreign aid is now widely recognized even by the Lords of Poverty, and Africans themselves are increasingly speaking out against continuing aid, there remains a large political constituency in the West, particularly among the well-educated and altruistic young, for continuing the programs. Thus, in the United Kingdom, despite its deep fiscal hole in response to the Great Recession of 2008, both political parties have agreed to defend the aid budget against the deep fiscal cuts necessary to close the budgetary gap. Also, in dealing with failed states, there is still the presumption that development aid can stem the decline and restore order. I have my doubts on this. For instance, in a study of the ongoing war on terror in Afghanistan, I argued that development programs intended to get Afghan farmers to substitute other cash crops for poppies, the major source of the world's heroin supply, could not succeed. The returns on growing poppies far outstrip those to be obtained by growing the alternative crops. This means that the Taliban has now found ready recruits and funds by protecting farmers in southern Afghanistan from western attempts at eradicating the poppy, and by providing numerous illegal channels for the accompanying opium trade. The obvious solution is to declare an end to the ill-founded war on drugs and to compete with the Taliban in buying up the legalized Afghan poppy crop with aid money; the poppies could then be converted into morphine for other Third World countries (particularly in AIDS-ravaged Africa), which remain woefully short of this proven pain killer. But given the moral fervor fueled by the Christian churches behind the war on drugs,[12] it is unlikely that, despite the evidence and rational arguments against this war, it will be ended (Lal 2008a).[13]

There is more hope for some recent aid programs in the medical field. The greatest contributions that international agencies have made to alleviate poverty are, first, the Rockefeller Foundation's experimental agronomic research, which created the high-yielding varieties of maize, wheat, and rice. These have not only kept food supply rising faster than population in the Third World, but in areas where the new seeds can be adopted, they have led to large increases in the incomes of the rural poor.

The second is the immunization programs conducted over the years by the World Health Organization. The most noteworthy achievement is the worldwide elimination of small pox. The newly established Global Fund to Fight AIDS, Tuberculosis, and Malaria (GFATM), and the Global Alliance on Vaccines and Immunization (GAVI) promise to continue this work. Since the work of these agencies is subject to local performance, and has resulted in new international bureaucracies, it is too early to judge how successful they will be (see Radelet and Levine 2008).

An innovative proposal by Kremer (2008) to promote the development of new vaccines for the diseases of the poor is also noteworthy. Malaria and other tropical diseases are major killers in the Third World. However, private drug companies are reluctant to spend R&D resources on these diseases since the costs of the ultimately patented drugs would be too high to be met by payments from poor Third World consumers and governments. As a solution, Kremer suggests that aid resources be used for advance purchase commitments (APC) for vaccines. The APC would require the purchase of a large amount of the vaccine if it were developed for a given price. This would give the drug companies an incentive to do the necessary research. If they fail, the aid agencies would lose nothing. If they succeed, the aid money would have gone towards saving the life of millions.

Another fruitful idea is to create a market in foreign aid (see Easterly 2004). This has been taken up by Britain's Conservative prime Minister, David Cameron.[14] Foreign aid money from all the donors would be pooled and "vouchers [issued] to poor individuals and communities, who could exchange them for development services at any aid agency, NGO, or domestic government agency."

The Chinese Are Coming

The most notable recent event for African development is the scramble for its natural resources by the newly emerging market economies of China, India, and Russia. Of these, the recent Chinese involvement is the biggest.

With its rapid growth fueling a huge increase in the consumption of various minerals and metals,[15] China is turning to Africa as a significant supplier. More than 700 Chinese companies (large and small) have set up operations in Africa since 2000. China is now the third largest trading partner for Africa.

Chinese mining companies are shopping for platinum in Zimbabwe, copper in Zambia, iron ore in South Africa, gold in Ghana, and oil in Gabon, Angola, and Sudan. This scramble for natural resources has also drawn in companies from that other fast-growing emerging economy, India. Tata has taken over Highveld in South Africa, and NDMC (a state-owned company) is investing in Khama, Tanzania. At the same time, faced with the Islamist threat from the Middle East, the United States is turning increasingly to Africa as an alternative source for its oil needs. American officials have described the stretch from Namibia to Mauritania as the new Persian Gulf.

The Chinese involvement is usually for resources related to infrastructure deals. Chinese companies have built many of the roads that now link Cairo to Cape Town. But Chinese interest in Africa is not confined to oil and minerals. In 2007, Industrial and Commercial Bank of China, the world's biggest bank by deposits, bought 20 percent of South Africa's Standard Bank. The Chinese government recently pledged $10 billion in low-cost loans and promised to eliminate tariffs on 60 percent of African exports and to forgive the debt of many countries. Sino-African trade has increased 15 times since 2000 and in 2011 was worth $160 billion (Smith 2012).

To counter criticisms that low-wage Chinese exports are making it difficult for Africa's nascent industrialization, reports have circulated that China is planning to shift some low-wage manufacturing capacity to newly created special economic zones in Africa (Lamont and Dyer 2009).

Because Chinese involvement with Africa does not involve any political strings, there has also been criticism that it is helping to shore up dictators, for example, in Sudan and Zimbabwe. But given the West's role in shoring up the likes of Mobutu in Zaire, Abacha in Nigeria, and a host of other authoritarian rulers as part of its own involvement in Africa, this is rather like the pot calling the kettle black. There is, however, great similarity between the past western scramble for African natural resources and the current one involving China, as well as India and Russia. This scramble to invest in Africa may seem more benign than the scramble to carve it up in the 19th century, but the new scramblers are already being charged with neo-imperialism, and there has been friction between locals and Chinese workers and companies in a number of countries. How long before some nationalist African Chavez decides to nationalize some Chinese investments?

Presumably to protect their investments, the Chinese also seem to be making Africa a central part of their foreign policy—if not as yet their strategic military policy. Thus, the Chinese have increasingly become involved in UN peacekeeping operations. At the end of July 2012, there were 2,000 Chinese military and civilian personnel on 12 UN missions, the majority (made up of People's Liberation Army personnel) deployed in Africa. These numbers do not include other Chinese armed forces in Africa. For example, a report prepared for the U.S.–China Economic and Security Review Committee noted that "armed Chinese security personnel are routinely present at key oil facilities in Sudan," which host "between 5,000 and 10,000 Chinese workers, some of them decommissioned People's Liberation Army soldiers charged with protecting China's investments" (Pham 2007). These peacekeepers identify themselves as Chinese units even when they are part of a multilateral force. They are drawn from a handful of select PLA units and are recycled many times for the standard six-to-12-month deployments over their careers. They have achieved "a level of tactical and operational knowledge that is matched by only a few of the American military's foreign area officers specializing in sub-Saharan Africa" (Pham 2007). They have also forged military-to-military ties with the African countries "which are among the largest contributors to UN peacekeeping operations worldwide, not just in Africa" (Pham 2007). Thus, the Chinese do seem to be creating the instruments for military protection of their investments in Africa. Whether they will be any more successful than the Western powers that have long meddled in African affairs remains an open question.

At the moment, the Chinese engagement with Africa seems to offer an alternative to the official Western foreign-aid-based engagement, which seeks to transform the nature of African governments in the hope of spurring efficient investment and thereby growth. Without seeking to change the nature of African governance, the Chinese are providing investment and trade combined with infrastructure investments, mainly in roads. This echoes the business-oriented approach the Japanese adopted in Southeast Asia, and contrasts with the Western development effort based on government-to-government aid. African critics of foreign aid commend this: The Zambian economist Moyo, for example, states that "China's African role is wider, more sophisticated and more businesslike than any other country's at any time in the post-war period" (Pilling 2009). Perhaps like the original Marshall Plan,

China's work with private business through trade and investment will achieve more for African development and poverty alleviation than Western foreign aid has ever been able to do.

The March 2011 Libyan rebellion against Col. Muammar el-Qaddafi forced China to show its neo-imperialist hand, reminiscent of the old colonial powers' 19th-century Scramble for Africa. With 35,000 Chinese working in the oil, rail, telecommunications, and construction industries, China evacuated 32,000 of these workers with 20 civilian and four military aircraft, flying 5,900 miles from Xinjiang. A naval frigate, *Xuzhou*, provided military support for its relief operations. (It is part of the latest of six naval task forces that the Chinese have, at this writing, sent to the Gulf of Aden to protect its shipping from Somali pirates.) In addition, the Chinese supported the UN Security Council resolution to refer Qaddafi to the International Criminal Court, largely (commentators argue) to divert attention from its own suppression of the Tiananmen revolt. But these actions undermine its "noninterventionism in internal affairs" foreign-policy doctrine. With 50,000 workers in Nigeria, 20,000–50,000 in Sudan, 20,000 in Algeria, and thousands more in other parts of Africa and increasingly in South America, the Chinese have now signaled their political will and military capability to defend them with the use of force if necessary (Pilling 2011).

However, as I have argued (Lal 2005b), the recent splurge by state-owned Chinese companies in acquiring natural resource assets around the world, like the imperial powers of yore, is particularly foolish. Since these natural resources are internationally traded on deep markets such as NYMEX, no additional security is gained by owning mines and oil wells; the opportunity cost of using the resource remains its international price, whether it is owned by China or purchased in international markets. Finally, given the rise of economic nationalism and the steady erosion of any acceptance of international property rights (unlike the 19th century), these foreign acquisitions are a hostage to fortune. Even with the recent assertion of its military muscle, is it credible that the Chinese would be willing to send the equivalent of "gunboats and Gurkhas" to protect their foreign assets? This could involve not merely putting troops in the oil field but essentially taking over a country. If even the remaining superpower is incapable of doing this, it is absurd to believe that the aspiring superpowers—China and India—would be able to.

Conclusions[16]

Ultimately, there is little outsiders can do to save Africa from itself without various forms of direct and indirect imperialism (Lal 2004). Its problems relate to governance and the failure to adopt the classical-liberal economic package—for with good governance, the precious bane of natural resources can be broken, as Botswana has shown. The fact that previously, relatively well-governed and prosperous states like Zimbabwe can be ruined in a short while by bad governance shows how fragile economic freedom remains in Africa. As Gwartney and Lawson (2005) noted (13):

> Weakness in the rule of law and property rights is particularly pronounced in sub-Saharan Africa . . . The nations that rank poorly in this category also tend to score poorly in the trade and regulation categories, even though several of these nations have reasonably sized government and sound money.

But things may be turning around as countries learn from past mistakes. Crises caused by past dirigisme forces them to change course. Thus, many African countries have seen their index of economic freedom rise in the last decade. Ghana has risen from an abysmal 3.05 in 1980 to 7.09 in 2010, and Nigeria from 3.25 in 1980 to 6.01 in 2010. Apart from Zambia, Uganda remains the most economically liberal economy, with its economic freedom rating rising from 3.14 in 1980 to 7.47 in 2010.

For Africa, therefore, the greatest threat to the growing march towards economic freedom is the current campaign to throw international public money at it. The massive foreign aid Africa has received since independence has exacerbated the problems associated with natural-resource riches. Like them, much of this aid has been stolen or wasted. Also, giving countries large windfalls of foreign exchange, like natural resources, leads to an appreciation of the real exchange rate and the Dutch Disease, which makes it harder for Africa to diversify its export base.[17] Judging from past experience, the proposed concentration of new aid on infrastructure, health, and education is unlikely to be any more effective than in the past. As more money is transferred from western (and now also Chinese) taxpayers to African governments, predatory states are merely provided the means to further their own ends. It is time for Africans to eschew such foreign aid. As in Asia, the answer to Africa's economic problems must lie in beginning to set its citizens free of the shackles of the state. Africa has for too long been used by western ideologues as a laboratory for their latest dirigiste ideas. They have made Africa's problems worse. The best thing the world can do for Africa is to keep its goods and capital markets open and let the continent's entrepreneurial multitudes make their own future, beginning by learning how to hold their predatory rulers to account and ensuring that the state becomes a civil, not an enterprise, association. This is the message of classical liberalism, and it remains as valid today as in the past against the siren call of central planners who still seek to some new-fangled enterprise of their own.

10. Global Warming

The greatest threat to the alleviation of the structural poverty of the Third World is the continuing campaign by western governments, egged on by some climate scientists and green activists, to curb greenhouse emissions, primarily the CO_2 from burning fossil fuels. As we have noted, it is mankind's use of the mineral energy stored in nature's gift of fossil fuels that allowed the West and now increasingly the Rest to overcome the energy constraint imposed by the limited land-based sources of energy that formed the basis of premodern agrarian economies. This use of an unbounded energy source, accompanying the slowly rolling Industrial Revolution, allowed the ascent from structural poverty, which had scarred humankind for millennia. To put a limit on the use of fossil fuels without adequate economically viable alternatives is to condemn the Third World to perpetual structural poverty.

I have been arguing this case since 1990, when I gave the Wincott lecture on "The Limits of International Cooperation" and unwittingly stumbled onto the increasingly heated debate on global warming. Without going into the subsequent history of that debate, in this chapter I summarize how things now stand concerning the science, economics, ethics, and politics of global warming.

The Science

Sun and Stars versus CO_2

The world is being spooked by climate change. The great and the good, aided and abetted by the International Panel on Climate Change (IPCC) and the Stern Review on the Economics of Climate Change in the United Kingdom (2007), have convinced themselves and large parts of the electorates in the West that global warming is caused by human emissions of greenhouse gases, particularly CO_2.

India's and China's rapid growth, with the two largest human conglomerations arising at long last from their preindustrial slumber, will inevitably raise their emissions. Thus, even if existing concentrations of these pollutants were caused by the developed countries in their own escape from mass poverty, the future rise in emissions will come largely from the Asian giants. Hence, developed countries desire to bring India and China into some global system of mandatory curbs on carbon emissions.

There is no dispute that global warming has been occurring, although the stalling of the warming trend and the cooling observed over the last decade should give one pause. The question is: What is the cause of the rise?

The current orthodoxy accepts the theory espoused by the IPCC that greenhouse gases, in particular the mushrooming CO_2 emissions since the Industrial Revolution, are in large part responsible. A vivid popular depiction is provided by the Academy-Award-winning documentary *An Inconvenient Truth*, by that redoubtable ecowarrior Al Gore. It has successfully linked CO_2 emissions with catastrophic global climate change in the minds of the general public. Thus, one of the questions always asked by UCLA undergraduates on hearing my skeptical lecture on climate change is: "What about the ice-core evidence?" Gore makes much of the apparent correlation between temperature and CO_2 concentrations, as revealed in the Vostock ice-core data for millions of years. But, as I remind them, correlation does not imply causation. When a correct lagged regression is done for this and other ice-core data, "on long time scales variations in Vostock's CO_2 record lag behind those of its air-temperature record" (Mudelsee 2001, 587; also Fischer et al. 1999 and Callion et al. 2003). So CO_2 cannot be the cause of temperature changes. It is changes in temperature that seem to cause changes in atmospheric CO_2. But, how?

The answer lies in the oceans, which are both the primary sink for as well as emitters of CO_2. By comparison, the human contribution to global carbon emissions is negligible. When the oceans cool, they absorb CO_2; when they warm, they emit CO_2. Given the vastness of oceans, it takes a long time for the warming of the atmosphere to heat the oceans (and vice versa). Thus, the lag between the rise in global temperature and a rise in CO_2, as shown by the millennial ice-core evidence.

But what then causes global temperatures to wax and wane, as they have done for millennia? The alternative to the CO_2 theory is that changing levels in solar activity have caused changes in global climate over millennia. But it is argued that these changes in solar radiation were not large enough by themselves to explain the observed warming of the earth over the last century. Recent scientific work by Svensmark of Denmark (2007; Svensmark and Calder 2007), Shaviv of Israel and Vezier of Canada (Shaviv and Vezier 2003; Vezier 2005) has now provided a fuller alternative theory of climate change, which has been labeled "cosmoclimatology." They theorize that the climate is controlled by low cloud cover, which when widespread has a cooling effect by reflecting solar energy back into space. When there is no low cloud cover, solar energy warms the climate.

These low clouds are formed when the subatomic particles called cosmic rays, emitted by exploding stars in our galaxy, combine with water vapor rising from the oceans. The constant bombardment of the planet by cosmic rays, however, is modulated by a solar wind, which prevents the cosmic rays from reaching the earth and creating the low clouds. The solar wind is caused by varying sunspot activity. When the sun is overactive with lots of sunspots and the solar wind is blowing intensely, fewer cosmic rays get through to form the low clouds, and the planet experiences global warming, as it is doing in the current transition from the Little Ice Age of the 17th–18th centuries. Thus, with this alternative theory, global temperatures would be correlated with the intensity of the sun. When it is shining more brightly, global temperatures will rise, and when it is not, global temperatures will fall. This seems to be the case.

But there is still a missing piece in the cosmoclimatology theory, which depends on a hitherto untested hypothesis that cosmic rays influence the formation of low clouds. In 1998, Jasper Kirkby at the CERN particle physics lab proposed an experiment called CLOUD to test this theory. There were long delays in getting funding, but the experiment began in 2010, and its first results were published in 2011 (Kirkby et al. 2011) and found a 'significant' cosmic ray cloud effect. More experimentation is still required, but as Svensmark says, the CLOUD results "basically confirm our own experimental results since 2006, and do so within a larger variation of parameters. It seems to say that ions [cosmic rays] are fundamental for the nucleation of new aerosols [tiny liquids or solid particles that provide a nucleus around which droplets can form from water vapor in the air]." The media, warmist scientists, and the IPCC have denied or ignored the significance of this experiment (see Montford 2011). When the further experiments which are required to fully understand low cloud formation are finished, and the cosmic ray hypothesis is finally proved, it will be the final nail in the coffin of the CO_2 theory of climate change. The sun and the stars will have been shown to control our climate.[1]

The Continuing Scientific Wars

My wife and I saw Bertolt Brecht's play *Galileo* at the National Theatre in London. It provides interesting parallels between the last large paradigm shift in man's relationship to the stars and the current one in the new theory of cosmoclimatology.

The medieval scientific establishment was wedded to a view that conflicted with the celestial observations of the scientific skeptics, Copernicus and Galileo. The Inquisition tried to suppress the heretics by excommunication (Copernicus) or silencing them through showing them the instruments of torture (Galileo). Today, the peer-reviewed process of funding and validation of research in climatology is equally controlled—by the modern equivalent of the *Collegium Romanum* (the Vatican's Institute of Research), the IPCC.[2]

It in turn answers to the equivalent of the Inquisition, the green ideologists. Mercifully, they can only torment through derision or denying the heretics research funding, not through the frightening instruments of torture, which, on a visit to the museum in Carcassonne, will chill the bones of the most stouthearted. However, the *Collegium Romanum* was imbued with the rational scientific spirit and confirmed Galileo's discoveries in his lifetime, though it took the pope till 1993 to formally recognize the validity of his work.

Fortunately, it is much more difficult to suppress the scientific enterprise today. The IPCC—the panel of scientists that created the climate-change scare—still claims it is scientifically proven that CO_2 emissions are the cause of global warming. But this is increasingly being questioned by climatologists; since 1997, both the terrestrial and more-accurate satellite temperature readings (which are not contaminated by the "heat island" urbanization effect) seem to show global cooling, even though there has been a large increase in CO_2 emissions (Figure 10.1). This is also the period in which the sunspot activity has ceased.

Figure 10.1
A Long, Fast Decline:
Seven Years of Global Cooling at 3.6°F (2°C)/Century

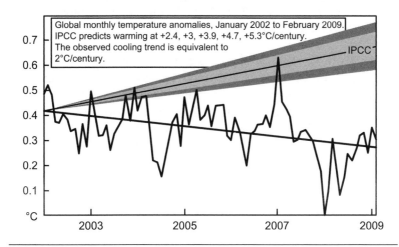

Global monthly temperature anomalies, January 2002 to February 2009.
IPCC predicts warming at +2.4, +3, +3.9, +4.7, +5.3°C/century.
The observed cooling trend is equivalent to 2°C/century.

Source: Science and Public Policy Institute.

In a remarkable March 2009 internal study on climate science suppressed by the U.S. Environmental Protection Agency (EPA), but put into the public domain by the Competitive Enterprise Institute, the scientific basis of the CO_2 theory was called into question. The study emphasizes that "global temperatures have declined—extending the current downward trend to 11 years, with a particularly rapid decline in [2007–08]. At the same time, atmospheric CO_2 levels have continued to increase, and emissions have accelerated" (U.S. EPA 2009, iii). This means that "the IPCC projections for large increases [in global temperature] are looking increasingly doubtful" (3). On the IPCC's rejection of solar variability as the *cause* of climate change, it states: "There appears to be a strong association between solar sunspots/irradiance and global temperature fluctuations" (iv).

A "paper by Scafetta and West (2008) suggests the IPCC used faulty solar data in dismissing the direct effect of solar variability on global temperatures. Their research suggests that solar variability

185

[rather than greenhouse gases] could account for up to 68 percent of the increase in earth's global temperature (www.cei.org, iv).[3]

The EPA study then provides a table by Gregory and Ken (2009, 58) that summarizes the evidence for the CO_2 and sun/cosmic ray hypotheses. This table (see Table 10.1) shows that, on a number of predictions involving observable evidence, the sun/cosmic ray explanation wins hands down. Moreover, since the sun seems to have gone to sleep over the last 12 years, there is a growing likelihood "that sunspots may vanish by 2015. Given the strong association between sunspots and global temperatures, this suggests the possibility that we may be entering a period of global cooling" (60). Perhaps another Ice Age.

When the CERN CLOUD experiment is completed, and (hopefully) vindicates Svensmark's cosmoclimatology theory, the CO_2 theory of climate change will be buried. It will be recognized that humans cannot control the climate and must adapt to its continual changes, as they have for millennia.

The Economics

It is ironic that many economists (and policymakers) base their climate-change policy recommendations on the CO_2 theory, the latest examples being the Stern Review on the Economics of Climate Change put out by the British government (2007) and the Garnaut Climate Change Review (2008) by the Australian government. But there is nothing particularly novel about the cost-benefit method used, or about the model used to incorporate the IPCC-based scientific judgments, as Nordhaus (author of the most serious study of the economics of climate change) has noted in a review (2006, also 2007). What is novel is their conclusion that without drastic immediate action to curb greenhouse emissions, the world faces economic catastrophe "on a scale similar to those associated with the great wars and the economic depression of the first half of the 20th century" Stern (2007).

This is a dramatically different conclusion from earlier models of climate change, which accepted the CO_2 theory and found that the "optimal climate change" policies involve modest reductions in emissions in the near future (Nordhaus 1994; Nordhaus and Boyer 2000). The main reason for the contrary Stern recommendations is the near-zero social rate of discount used to sum up future costs and benefits. This represents a contentious ethical judgment of the

Table 10.1
SUMMARY OF EVIDENCE FOR CO_2 AND SUN/COSMIC RAY WARMING HYPOTHESES

Issue	Prediction—CO_2 Hypothesis	Prediction—Sun/Cosmic Ray Hypothesis	Actual Data	Hypothesis Offering Best Explanation
Antarctic and Arctic Temperatures	Temperatures in the Arctic and Antarctic will rise symmetrically	Temperatures will initially move in opposite directions	Temperatures move in opposite directions	Sun/Cosmic Ray
Troposphere Temperature	Fastest warming will be in the troposphere over the tropics	The troposphere warming will be uniform	Surface warming similar or greater than tropospheric warming	Sun/Cosmic Ray
Timing of CO_2 and Temperature Changes at End of Ice Age	CO_2 increases, then temperature increases	Temperature increases, then CO_2 increases	CO_2 concentrations increase about 800 years after temperature increases	Sun/Cosmic Ray
Temperature Correlates with the Driver over Last 400 Years	NA	NA	Cosmic ray flux and Sun activity correlates with temperature, CO_2 does not	Sun/Cosmic Ray
Temperature during Ordovician Period	Very hot due to CO_2 levels > 10x Present	Very cold due to high cosmic ray flux	Very cold ice age	Sun/Cosmic Ray
Other Planets	No Change	Other planets will warm	Warming has been detected on several other planets	Sun/Cosmic Ray

SOURCE: Gregory (2009).

weight placed on the consumption of future generations relative to that of the present generation.

Any act of investment involves giving up current consumption to increase future income and consumption. If a $1 cut in consumption today raises future consumption by $1.50, we need to decide whether this extra 50 cents (because of the productivity of investment) is worth giving up the dollar today. For mortals, "a bird in hand is worth two in the bush"; they may be dead tomorrow with no hope of enjoying the extra 50 cents. So they would want to discount this future gain to make it commensurate with the dollar they are giving up today. The rate at which we discount this future income will then have two elements. One is a "pure" preference component, reflecting our uncertainty about whether we or our children and grandchildren will be alive to enjoy the extra income tomorrow. The other element depends on the fact that economic growth will raise our and our descendants' future income and consumption. By investing, we are in effect transferring a $1 from our poorer self today to add an extra 50 cents to our richer self tomorrow. So we have to make a distributional judgment of how much it is worth to make a richer future generation even richer. These two components comprise the social discount rate. Even if we accept that for society as a whole the pure time-preference element should be set at zero, since a society, unlike an individual, is in principle immortal, this still leaves the distributional weight to be placed on the intergenerational transfer. If this is set close to zero, it implies that any cut in the consumption of the current poor generation is justified to increase the consumption of the richer future generation by even an infinitesimally small amount. This is of course the policy which Stalin followed in his heavy-industry-biased forced industrialization of the Soviet Union, justifying the building of seemingly redundant steel mills at the expense of industries supplying consumer goods with the quip: "They cannot eat steel!"

The discount rate also crucially determines how far future costs and benefits need to be counted. If the discount rate is close to zero, the whole of the infinite future stream of costs and benefits becomes relevant. Hence, the highly speculative economic damage two centuries from now, which the Stern Review adduces from rising temperatures, can be valued on a par with any economic costs we currently have to incur to mitigate it. But as Nordhaus rightly notes, this low discount rate can lead to absurd results. It would imply trading off a large fraction of today's income to increase the income stream of those living two centuries from now by a tiny fraction, for with a near-zero discount rate, this tiny increase in the future generations' income stream is cumulated to near infinity.

By contrast, the estimates I made for the Planning Commission in the early 1970s, based on the same method as the Stern Review but with more plausible parameters, yielded a social discount rate of 7 percent for India (1980). At this discount rate, the present value of 1 rupee accruing 75 years from today would be worth nothing, making most of the speculative economic costs and benefits, and the apocalyptic predictions of the Stern Review, irrelevant for India.[4]

Ethics

This mathematical politics, based on increasingly questionable officially sponsored climate science, to get the Third World (particularly China and India) to curb their CO_2 emissions, is also deeply immoral. The "climate change" treaty proposed in Copenhagen in 2009 sought to put curbs on the carbon emissions of the Third World. If they did not comply, they were threatened by a draft bill, going through the U.S. Congress, to levy carbon tariffs on their exports. This is a blatant attempt to prevent these countries from industrializing and achieving Western standards of living, for until technological advances allow alternative "green" energy sources to compete with the fossil fuels, whose use is gradually eliminating poverty in the Third World, as it did in the West, large curbs on carbon emissions would condemn billions to continuing poverty.

While numerous Western economists and do-gooders shed crocodile tears about the Third World's poor, they are willing to prevent them from taking the only feasible current route out from this abject state. Nothing is more hypocritical and immoral than rich Westerners driving their gas-guzzling SUVs and emoting about the threat to Spaceship Earth from the millions of Indians who want to drive the new Tata Nanos. The salving of their consciences by buying carbon offsets (as Al Gore claims to do every time he jets around the world) is akin to the papal indulgences sold by the medieval Catholic Church, which allowed its richer adherents to assuage their guilt and "fornicate on clean sheets." For Gore to have the lights at his mansion blazing all night while arguing for restrictions on emissions from Indian power stations—when most Indians don't even have an electric light bulb—is deeply wicked.

Murthy et al. (2007) estimated that a 10 percent annual reduction in emissions over 30 years would increase the number of poor in India by 21 percent, and nearly 50 percent with a 30 percent reduction. Those development economists and sundry celebrities who on the one hand want to see the end of world poverty and on the other want to curb Third World carbon emissions should be ashamed of themselves for advocating the latter, which will make the former impossible.

This is not to downgrade the serious environmental problems caused by rapid growth in India and China. Anyone who has choked in the fetid air of Chungking, Xian, Beijing, or Delhi will know that no climate scares are needed to provide a case for dealing with their unhealthy air pollution. Similarly, India and China face a growing water crisis irrespective of what is happening to global CO_2 emissions. Subsidies to energy and water use need to be removed for efficiency reasons. Given political instability and growing political determination of supplies of fossil fuels in the countries where they are concentrated, it is sensible to diversify energy sources. Both nuclear power and coal reserves (abundant in India, China, and the United States) provide more secure alternatives. Biofuels by contrast have the disadvantage of competing for limited land with essentials like food.[5] The sun, however, offers the backstop technology that will ultimately provide unbounded energy for Third World countries in tropical climes.

Politics

On October 29, 2008, the country that had pioneered the Industrial Revolution by learning how to convert the energy stored in its vast resources of coal, was experiencing its first October snow since 1934. Inside the Palace of Westminster, the British House of Commons was passing a "climate change bill" to commit the country to an 80 percent cut in CO_2 emissions in 40 years. It received a near-unanimous vote, with only one MP, Peter Lilley, questioning its potential costs (Booker 2009b, 11). If implemented, the action would close Britain's industrial economy, make motorized transport impossible, and turn off Britain's lights, changing it into a North Korea.

190

This insanity had been preceded by the European Union's 2007 pledge to reduce its carbon emissions 20 percent below 1990 levels. In June 2009, the U.S. House of Representatives narrowly passed the Clean Energy and Security Act, which sought to cut U.S. greenhouse emissions by 17 percent off 2005 levels in 11 years. Both presidential candidates in the 2008 U.S. elections had endorsed measures to counter climate change. When the Australian government of John Howard, a climate "skeptic," was replaced by the Labor government of Ken Rudd, an attempt to introduce a climate-change bill in a country 80 percent dependent on coal was only scuppered in August in the Senate because of the resilience of one member: Stephen Fielding.

Why had this mad rush to commit economic hara kiri spread in the West, even as the Rest resolutely refused to go along? Ever since I identified this growing divide on global warming in my Wincott lecture, I have been trying to answer this question. The answer, I think, has a number of parts. The first and most important reason for the rise of eco-fundamentalism in the West[6] is that it is a secular version of a Christian narrative, which has had a tenacious hold on Western minds: St. Augustine's *City of God.* Throughout the last millennium, the West has been haunted by its cosmology. From the Enlightenment to Marxism to Freudianism to eco-fundamentalism, Augustine's vision of the Heavenly City with a Garden of Eden, a Fall leading to Original Sin, and a Day of Judgment keeps recurring. Eco-fundamentalism is the latest secular mutation. It carries the Christian notion of *contemptus mundi* to its logical conclusion: humankind is evil, and only by living in harmony with a deified nature can it be saved.[7]

The second reason is the decline of a hierarchical "center" characteristic of the nation-state and the rise of opposing "border" organizations (as Douglas and Wildavsky 1983 label them). These include the international nongovernmental organizations with specific causes, whose resonance comes from some form of moral claim, many of which concern the environment. The Vietnam War and Watergate undermined the moral authority of the "center," particularly for the young. The end of the communist threat to the West, which had provided a rationale for the "center," also aided the "border," giving greater legitimacy to the segment which emphasizes nature.[8]

The third reason is the rise of what Henderson (2001) has called "global salvationists," who are imbued with various forms of socialism, including a desire to establish a world government. They are more at home in the bureaucratic structures of international agencies, particularly the United Nations, than in the hurly-burly of domestic democratic politics. The most influential figure among those responsible for the global-warming hysteria has been the Canadian diplomat Maurice Strong. A brief account of his career is instructive.[9] Born into poverty during the Great Depression, Strong became a socialist and a firm believer in the UN as an embryo world government. He ran the Canadian government's overseas aid agency in the 1960s and saw environmentalism as a cause to further world government. In 1972, he was appointed by the UN secretary general to organize and chair the first UN conference on the human environment, which launched the UN Environment Program (UNEP), of which Strong became the first director. He retired from UNEP in 1976. Strong was also a member of the Club of Rome, which wrote the first of the alarmist reports, *Limits to Growth*, in 1972. In 1983, he became the key member of the Brundtland Commission, which coined the meaningless term "sustainable development" and endorsed Strong's growing conviction of the threat of manmade global warming, formed after he attended a conference organized by UNEP and the World Meteorological Organization (WMO). He then got UNEP and WMO to agree to an intergovernmental mechanism to provide scientific assessments of climate change. This led to the creation of the IPCC.

The high point of Strong's career was his lobbying at the UN for an Earth Summit, which took place in Rio in 1992—organized and chaired by Strong. Using the environmental NGOs to propagate his cause, which was paid for by UN agencies, he succeeded in creating the impression of worldwide popular concern about global warming. This led politicians from 172 countries to fly to Rio and sign a UN Framework Convention on Climate Change, which was to be the precursor to the Kyoto treaty in 1997. But this was to be his swansong, for in 2005 the Volcker Commission, which investigated corruption in the UN's "food-for-oil" program in Saddam Hussein's Iraq, disclosed that in 1997 Tariq Aziz, then the Iraqi foreign minister, handed a Korean contact of Strong's nearly $1 million in cash to lobby the UN for more favorable terms in this UN-run aid project. The money was passed to Strong in the form of a check, which he paid into one of his family's companies. Forced to resign from his post as a UN undersecretary, Strong retired to Beijing!

This tale underlines the fourth reason for the success of the global-warming hysteria: politicians' single-mindedness and adroit manipulation of bureaucratic structures to generate political pressure. Linked to this are various forms of corruption. The most serious has been the corruption of the science. Nothing illustrates this better than the "hockey stick" saga, what has come to be known as "Climategate," and the latest revelation of scientific fraud labeled "Glaciergate." Here are brief accounts.

The "Hockey Stick"[10]

In most climate histories, including that by Houghton (1994), a former chairman of the IPCC and an environmental adviser to Tony Blair, distinct periods of warming and cooling are recognized over recorded history.[11] Thus, around 700–400 BC, there was the "pre-Roman cold" period, followed between 200 BC and the sixth century AD by the Roman warming, when vines were planted in Britain. This warming ended abruptly in the 6th century, followed by three centuries of cooling during the Dark Ages. But from 900 AD, temperatures began to increase, giving rise to the 400-year period of the Medieval Warm Period, when temperatures were higher than in the 20th century. From 1300, temperatures began to drop, leading to four centuries of the Little Ice Age, which lasted until the slow rise in temperature during the 19th century, leading to the modern warming period. This climate history was in fact depicted graphically in Houghton and the first IPCC report in 1990 (Figure 10.2). But it posed a serious problem for proponents, like the IPCC, of manmade carbon emissions as the cause of global warming. How could the medieval and Roman warm periods be caused by human carbon emissions when these eras were clearly part of the preindustrial age and the technology to use fossil fuels to provide energy had not been invented.

In 1998, two papers by a recently qualified Ph.D. physicist-turned-climatologist, Michael Mann, appeared showing estimates from his computer models of "global" temperature extending back a 1000 years (1998, 1999). Lo and behold, the Medieval Warm Period and Little Ice Age had vanished (Figure 10.3). The graph showed a gradually declining trend in average temperatures from 1000 AD and then a sudden shooting up in the 20th century to an unprecedented level. The graph resembled a hockey stick and became the iconic

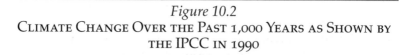

Figure 10.2
CLIMATE CHANGE OVER THE PAST 1,000 YEARS AS SHOWN BY
THE IPCC IN 1990

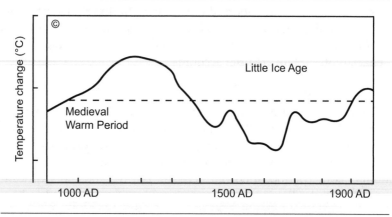

SOURCE: J. T. Houghton *et al.*, IPCC First Assessment Report, 1990.

image "proving" that manmade carbon emissions were responsible for the 20th century global warming.

Intrigued, Stephen McIntyre, a financial consultant and statistical analyst, and Ross McKitrick, an economics professor, asked Mann for the original data set. Examining this and the computer program used by Mann, they found that

> there was an error in a routine calculation step (principal component analysis) that falsely identified a hockey stick shape as the dominant pattern in the data. The flawed computer program can even pull out spurious hockey stick shapes from lists of trendless random numbers. [2003, 2005]

When they did the exercise properly, and after removing some dubious data on California pinecones used by Mann et al., the Medieval Warm Period appeared, confirming that the 15th-century warming exceeded anything in the 20th century. So damning were these flaws that despite their relative obscurity and that of the journal in which the findings were published, the issue became a *cause*

Figure 10.3
THE HOCKEY STICK GRAPH AS SHOWN BY THE IPCC IN 2001

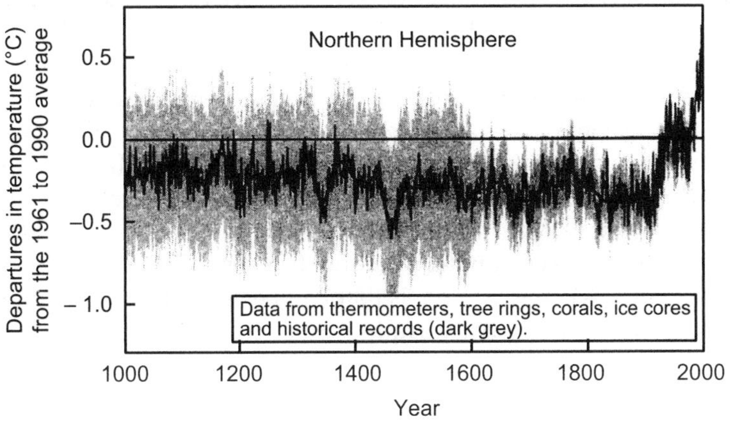

SOURCE: Mann, M. E., *et al.*, (1999).

célèbre because of the prominence the hockey stick had assumed in the public debate after it was made the center piece of the 2001 IPCC report.

Two U.S. congressional committees set up to investigate the claims and counterclaims about climate history upheld McIntyre and McKitrick. Another investigation chaired by Dr. Edward Wegman, a leading statistician, excoriated the Mann papers, as well as Mann's various highly placed supporters who had tried to whitewash them. Wegman also commissioned a "social network analysis" of Mann's defenders to find out how independent they were. It found that they "are closely connected and thus 'independent studies' may not be as independent as they might appear on the surface." Mann's supporters were "a tightly knit group of individuals who passionately believe in their thesis. However, our perception is that this group has a self-reinforcing feedback mechanism, and, moreover, the work has been sufficiently politicized that they can hardly reassess their public positions without losing credibility" (Wegman 2006; National Research Council 2006).

This self-protecting clique of climate scientists controlling peer-reviewed journals was identified in a larger study by an Australian information technology expert, John McLean, of the purported 2,500 scientists who had put together the scientific chapter in the IPCC's 2007 report (Booker 2009b, 239–242; McLean 2008). McLean found that the IPCC orthodoxy was based on the views of just 53 climate scientists who formed "a disturbingly tight network of scientists with common research interests and opinions," with "neither the papers nor opinions of the growing band of serious climatologists who doubt that humankind has an actually or potentially harmful influence on the earth's climate adequately represented." The IPCC authors relied heavily on the computer models of the Hadley Centre in the United Kingdom, models that had been programmed assuming anthropogenic global warming. Since it was "the *inputs* to the models that determined the extent of the imagined human influence on climate . . . analyzing the *outputs* to determine the extent to which they demonstrate anthropogenic influences is meaningless and futile." The clear biases observed in this chapter, McLean observed, showed it was "not science but politics elaborately dressed up" to pretend to be science." He concluded:

> Governments have naively and unwisely accepted the claims of a human influence on global temperatures made by a close-knit clique of a few dozen scientists, many of them climate modelers, as if they were representative of the opinion of the wider scientific community [McLean 2008].

Climategate

In November 2009, emails leaked from the Climate Research Unit (CRU) at the University of East Anglia, whose scientists have been at the heart of the IPCC scientific assessments, created a worldwide storm labeled "Climategate" by the British journalist James Delingpole.[12] Google soon showed that the word appeared nine million times on the Internet. These emails revealed that Professor Phil Jones, director of the CRU, the source of the most important set of terrestrial temperature data on which the IPCC relies, along with a tight network of colleagues had for years discussed various tactics to avoid releasing their data to outsiders under freedom-of-information laws. As a result, they kept coming up with excuses to conceal the data on which their findings and temperature records were based. Astonishingly, Jones even claimed in 2008 that the data were "lost." But the emails show that scientists were told to delete large chunks of data. Because this was done after receipt of a freedom-of-information request—a criminal offense—the University of East Anglia had to agree to release the data in collaboration with the Met Office's Hadley Centre after obtaining the agreement of other meteorological offices around the world.

The reason Jones and the others did not want independent appraisal of the data was that they were desperate to rescue Mann's hockey stick. The emails reveal that they were trying to manipulate the data through computer programs they did not fully understand to flatten the historical record on temperature fluctuations and to "adjust" the recent cooling temperatures upwards to show accelerating warming.

Finally, the emails reveal that the academics involved were willing ruthlessly to suppress any dissenting views by discrediting and freezing out any scientific journal that published their critics' work, ensuring that this dissenting research was not included in IPCC reports.[13]

Glaciergate

In its latest (2007) report, the IPCC claimed that the Himalayan glaciers could disappear by 2035. But in January 2010, IPCC chairman Rajendra Kumar Pachauri (a railway engineer) ignominiously had to admit that this claim had no scientific basis. This issue created a furor in India because the huge Himalayan ice sheet feeds seven of the world's major river systems on which 40 percent of the region's population depends. The EU had set up the "High Noon" project on the impact of melting Himalayan glaciers hoping that the resulting alarm would win Indian support for the climate-change treaty to be negotiated in Copenhagen in December 2009.

It appears that a little-known Indian scientist, Hosseni, had made this unsubstantiated claim in an interview with an Indian environmental magazine, *Down to Earth*, in April 1999, which was then picked up by the *New Scientist*. This was the citation in the 2007 IPCC report. Alarmed, the Indian government asked the country's most senior glaciologist, Vijaya Raina, to examine the claim. He published his report in November 2009, showing that the Himalayan glaciers had not retreated in the last 50 years, that Hosseni's claims were baseless, and that the IPCC's claims were recklessly alarmist.

Pachauri reacted fiercely, saying Raina's report was "arrogant" and "voodoo economics." A few weeks later, Pachauri had to eat crow since he and the IPCC were forced to admit that their predictions were without scientific foundation. He has been castigated by Jairam Ramesh, India's environment minister, and Raina has asked him to apologize for his "voodoo science" charge.

But he is unlikely to do so, for as *Daily Telegraph* journalists Christopher Booker and Richard North (2009) have documented, his institute TERI in Delhi has received substantial financial benefits from industry, foundations, governments, and international agencies. This financial cornucopia has also covered the numerous scientists and economists who have led the global-warming hysteria. They along with numerous "green" industries see a whole trough of subsidies coming their way, as governments, responding to the hysteria to curb carbon emissions seek to promote alternative sources of energy. Thus, the oil major BP now advertises itself as "Beyond Petroleum!" Meanwhile, if the EU targets for cutting carbon are met, the continent that ushered in the modern era could soon see a rapid decline in its standard of living.

The Copenhagen Derailment

The culmination of the climate-change movement's attempts to curb carbon emissions was to be the Copenhagen conference in December 2010, where a new treaty to save Spaceship Earth would be signed. The main purpose was to bring in the major "deniers," whose refusal to sign on to the Kyoto treaty had made it meaningless. With the new U.S. president, Barack Obama, committed to tackling climate change, and with a carbon "cap and trade" bill going through the Congress, it seemed that the world's greatest CO_2 emitter would now join the green consensus. At the same time, the objective was to bring the major emerging economies of India and China into a new agreement to curb carbon emissions. The purported scientific "consensus," the pressure of global public opinion, and threats of carbon tariffs (which the World Trade Organization had surprisingly ruled would be legal) were all to be used as means to this end. But Copenhagen turned out to be a nightmare for the climate alarmists, particularly for the EU, which had preened itself as the global leader in curbing carbon emissions and which had been expected to take the lead in negotiating a new climate change treaty.

Led by China, India, Brazil, and South Africa, the developing world made clear it was not willing to commit itself to any mandatory curb on emissions that could damage their growth prospects. Obama, unable to get his Congress to pass a climate-change bill before Copenhagen, could do no more than express his commitment to get one in the near future with defined targets to limit emissions. All countries agreed to a meaningless voluntary accord to prevent global temperatures from rising by more than 2 degrees Celsius. The developed countries were to set out their mandatory targets by the end of January 2010. That was soon shelved as unattainable by the UN agency running the conference.

But the real story at Copenhagen was provided by a small vignette at its end. Wanting to use his charm to get the recalcitrant China and India to agree to mandatory cuts in their emissions, Obama asked to sit down with Indian Prime Minister Manmohan Singh before a scheduled meeting with Chinese President Hu Jintao. Obama was told Singh was already on his way to the airport. Obama was then told that Hu was in a room nearby. When Obama entered the small room, he found the Chinese president, the Indian prime minister, and the presidents of Brazil and South Africa in a huddle. There was not even a chair for Obama, and one had to be brought in. During the next few hours, they hammered out the meaningless Copenhagen Accord. The EU, the self-proclaimed global leader on climate change, did not even get a look in, leading its commissioner ruefully to admit after the conference that it was no longer a superpower.

The Copenhagen conference marked the shifting geopolitical tectonic plates. The Third World was no longer going to be beholden to the First and was no longer willing to listen to its diktats or cajoling. It was not going to commit economic hara kiri like the West. Rather, it was determined to develop and thereby alleviate its mass poverty as the West had done: through mineral-based-energy economies.

If the West realizes that its global-warming hysteria will no longer lead to the worldwide mitigation policies it has sought, it will reverse its futile energy policies. And if it does so before the great chill, which some scientists are predicting as a result of the sun's going to sleep, it may even prevent itself from freezing. The derailment of the green agenda at Copenhagen by the Third World may have saved the world's poor and the West from ill-judged policies that would reverse the trends toward worldwide prosperity.

Conclusion

At the start of my seventh decade, as I look back over the past 50 years, during which I have studied, engaged in various debates, and traveled in the Third World, I am amazed at the transformations that have lifted billions out of poverty. One of the saddening experiences in writing this book, and of reading what younger scholars have written during the last 20 years, is the realization that many of them have little sense of this amazing achievement or its causes. Of course, the transformation is incomplete, and it would be Panglossian to say that poverty has been eliminated. But to see the glass half-empty rather than half-full betrays a lack of historical perspective. In the younger generation's proclaimed quest to end poverty, it has recycled old, discredited ideas and policies, seemingly freshened up with new theoretical and empirical bells and whistles. Perhaps the best way to conclude this book is to briefly look at the transformations (or "economic miracles" as some call them) I have personally witnessed and their causes.

Beginning in the early 1960s, as a young probationer of the Indian foreign service sent to Tokyo to learn Japanese at Waseda University, and on numerous subsequent visits to Japan, I saw the transformation of a devastated war-torn economy into the second largest economy in the world. This was based on the power of "catch up," even if done through only a partial adoption of the classical-liberal policy package. Alas, the remaining dirigiste elements in its "Asian model" of development then led to the two-decade stagnation of the economy, when the easy catch-up phase ended.

In the 1970s, I worked on various assignments in South Korea, the Philippines, and Kenya. I saw the amazing transformation of Korea, with the adoption, by and large, of the classical-liberal package, and the failure of the Philippines and Kenya to do the same because of their continuing dirigisme, or reversion to it, fueled by kleptocratic political regimes: the Marcoses in the Philippines and Moi in Kenya.

My advising Kim Jae Ik in South Korea in the early 1970s showed how a few well-trained economists at the center of power could transform economic policy and usher in a "miracle."

Meanwhile, my work in Jamaica and Sri Lanka showed the devastation that can be wrought by populist regimes in primary producing export economies as they ride the rollercoaster of the commodity price cycle. But when advising the J.R. Jayawardene government in Sri Lanka in the late 1970s and early 80s, I saw how even a partial reversal of this dirigiste populism and adoption of the classical-liberal package could reverse the decline, sadly only to be overtaken by a prolonged ethnic civil war.

In the 1980s, I had my first exposure to Latin America, which was in the midst of its debt crisis. I saw how Chile's adoption, with fits and starts, of the classical-liberal package led it out of the hole dug by dirigiste regimes in the 1960s. At the same time, the first Alan Garcia government was destroying Peru with socialist panaceas. But in Garcia's subsequent resurrection, he seemed to have changed his spots with the adoption of more conventional policies, demonstrating that politicians can learn from their mistakes.

Nowhere was this truer than in Brazil, where I worked intermittently until the early 1990s. Having seen the gyrations among various unorthodox plans to tame hyperinflation, I was heartened to see the father of the *dependencia* school, Fernando Henrique Cardoso, adopt orthodoxy with great benefit to the economy and in particular its poor. Surprisingly, this policy was carried on by his avowed socialist successor, Lula de Silva, at last allowing Brazil to fulfill what has been for so long its unfulfilled promise.

The tragedy of Argentina, which I witnessed in the 1980s, seemed to have ended on my last visit in the late 1990s thanks to its adoption of a currency board with a fixed exchange-rate to the dollar. But the tragedy in fact has continued because the architect of the plan, Domingo Cavallo, built no exit strategy towards a floating exchange-rate regime, which is needed by any country subject to large fluctuations in its term of trade (Lal 2006). With the return of traditional Peronism at the hand of the populist Kirchner duumvirate, after its repudiation by a reformed Menem in the 1990s, Argentina has returned to its bad old ways.

The Latin American story remains mixed. The continuing Chilean success and the newfound one of Brazil, based on most elements of the classical-liberal package, are ending their mass poverty and providing examples to be set against the *dirigiste* panaceas peddled in Venezuela, Bolivia, and Ecuador. As these have consistently failed in the past, time alone will tell when the inevitable crises they create will lead to economic liberalization and the emulation of their more successful neighbors.

It is the large emerging Asian giants, China and India, whose economic transformation I have witnessed and participated in, that is most notable and breathtaking. I first visited China in the mid-1980s as a guest of the Chinese Academy of Social Sciences, staying at its guesthouse in Beijing. This was an astonishing place. There were either very old but eminent economists, who had recently returned from their sojourns in the pig farms to which they had been sent during the Cultural Revolution, or very young ones. The intermediate generation had been left uneducated by the political correctness of the Cultural Revolution. Most people still wore Mao jackets, and the streets were flooded with bicycles. Pudong in Shanghai was covered with rice and vegetable farms. Plans to convert it into a business center to rival Singapore seemed a fantasy. Over the years, on frequent visits to Peking University in Beijing and Fudan University in Shanghai, I have seen these decaying cities turn into throbbing modern metropolises. I have witnessed one of the largest reductions in mass poverty, even though the movement from plan to market was incomplete, as China followed the path charted by Japan and the Asian Gang of Four.

India, which had been stuck in its low-growth path, dubbed the Hindu rate of growth, since the late 1960s, was finally prodded by an economic crisis and the example of its rival China to move from plan to market, with an equally remarkable turn in its fortunes. Like China, it has seen a reduction in its ancient poverty at a rate never seen in its history.

There is nothing miraculous about the policies that have led to these turnarounds: free trade, Gladstonian finance, and stable money. The resulting economic environment led to the unleashing of entrepreneurial drive not least amongst the poor, which transformed the high savings associated with the demographic transition into efficient investments, fostering poverty-alleviating growth. These classical-liberal economic policies were pioneered in 19th-century Britain after repeal of the Corn Laws in 1846.

The failure of young analysts in many leading Western academies to see this, and their insistence on seeking a new fix to some theoretically determined poverty trap, validated by statistical snake oil, has led to all the continuing myths about Third World poverty that I have discussed in Part 2 of this book.

But there are a number of signs that these new advocates of *dirigisme* in the West will be unable to exercise the influence their forefathers had in spreading their dogma in the 1950s and 1960s, which for so long damaged the prospects of the Third World's poor. First, in Third World countries where economic liberalization has increased the domestic opportunities of the best and brightest, the young no longer seek foreign careers. Their attitude to the West is much more instrumental, and they are unlikely to be as influenced by the intellectual fads and fashions there. For too long, the Third World has been the arena where Western intellectuals have sought to play out their intellectual and ideological battles. Africa is their last remaining battleground. But as we saw in Chapter 9, even Africa is changing, despite the Jeremiahs. If the learning process arising from mistaken policies leads the rulers of these countries to adopt economic liberalism and good governance, the best and the brightest in the African diaspora will come home. Many of them are realizing that ultimately Africa's problems can only be solved by Africans and that the West can do little to help apart from keeping its markets open and private investment flowing. Given the difficulties the West has had in foisting its "habits of the heart" on Africa through various forms of intervention, it is unlikely that a new liberal imperialism can provide any answers—particularly since Western electorates have no stomach for this course. Whether the current Chinese engagement with Africa, with echoes of the 19th-century Western colonial struggle for Africa's natural-resource spoils, will be any happier than that of its Western predecessors remains to be seen.

This leaves the international agencies as the last remaining avenue through which the various contending sects in the West hope to be able to have influence in the Third World. But, outside Africa, with the opening of global capital markets and the expansion of world trade, their influence is being eroded. They have become the main channels for assuaging Western guilt and for purveying various Western "habits of the heart" championed by myriad single-issue Western NGOs. Although they have some supporters in developing countries, these are more like what the Chinese called the "rice Christians," who were converted more by the worldly, rather than the spiritual, goods offered by missionaries of yore.

As I argued in the previous chapter, the most dangerous of these moralizing Western agents are those who have created the global-warming scare. This poses the greatest threat to the prospects of the poor in the Third World, for the great ascent from poverty, charted in the first part of the book, was based, first in the West and now increasingly in the Rest, on the transformation of "agricultural" economies deriving energy from the limited products of land to "industrial" economies deriving their energy from the (still) unlimited energy derivable from fossil fuels. The Rest are questioning the economics and ethics of the greens, and as the proclaimed scientific "consensus" behind the theory of anthropogenic global warming is increasingly undermined, the developing countries are becoming less willing to travel a path that would condemn their masses to live in continuing poverty.

Thus, the world is at a strange pass. Instead of rejoicing in what has been one of mankind's most amazing achievements over the last three decades—the spread of economic progress around the world, which is gradually eliminating the ancient scourge of mass poverty—we hear wails of doom and gloom in the West, not least from those who see this progress as threatening the very survival of Spaceship Earth. Those who charted the path to progress and the prosperity it has engendered seem determined to erode their own prosperity, which is what will happen if their politicians' commitment to savage cuts in carbon emissions is implemented. Having attempted to exorcise these imaginary (mostly Western) demons in the second part of the book, I can only end by echoing the anguished protest of Shakespeare's Isabella in *Measure for Measure* (Act ii Sc.2):

> . . . but man, proud man,
> Dress'd in a little brief authority,
> Most ignorant of what he is most assur'd,
> His glassy essence, like an angry ape,
> Plays such fantastic tricks before high heaven,
> As makes the angels weep . . .

Notes

Introduction

1. The list of the country volumes produced as part of the project, with the countries covered and their principal authors, is as follows: Malawi and Madagascar—Fredric Pryor (1990); Egypt and Turkey—Bent Hansen (1991); Sri Lanka and Malaysia—Henry Bruton (1992); Indonesia and Nigeria—David Bevan, Paul Collier, and Jan Gunning (1999); Thailand—Oey A. Meesok and associates (1987); Ghana—Douglas Rimmer (1992); Thailand and Ghana (twin study)—Gus Edgren (1990); Brazil and Mexico—Angus Maddison (1992); Costa Rica and Uruguay—Simon Rottenberg, Claudio Gonzales-Vega, and Edgardo Favaro (1993); Colombia and Peru—Antonio Urdinola, Mauricio Carrizosa Serrano, and Richard Webb (1987); Hong Kong, Singapore, Malta, Jamaica and Mauritius—Ronald Findlay and Stainslaw Wellisz (1993).

2. Lal and Myint (1996).

3. The distinction between three types of poverty—structural, conjunctural, and destitution—is attributable to Iliffe (1987) and is elaborated in Chapter 1 below.

4. Mill (1843).

5. The distinction between qualitative and quantitative induction is emphasized by J.N. Keynes (1890, 334).

6. Hayek (1952, 1994).

Chapter 1

1. "Conjunctural" poverty implies poverty which is temporary because of the "conjuncture" of various aspects of the economy, which push some people into poverty.

2. In *Unintended Consequences,* I argued that there was a change in the cosmological beliefs of the West. Cosmological beliefs concern the world view of a civilization: how people should live. They provide its moral anchor. They are transmitted through the socialization processes in childhood by harnessing the powerful emotions of shame and guilt. Most Eurasian civilizations were shame based and had similar family values, with stable settled families required for agriculture. To maintain this stability all these cultures limited the common human but ephemeral passion of love as the basis of marriage. Their values were communalist. It was the first Papal Revolution of Gregory the Great in the 6th century that changed these communalist values, which have come to characterize and distinguish the West from the Rest. For the Papal Revolution promoted love as the basis for marriage and advocated the independence of the young, which led to the rise of individualism in the West; how the independence of

the young, which led to the rise of individualism in the West; how the individual has fared since is another story. See Lal (1998, 2006).

3. Thus, the former World Bank chief economist, Joseph Stiglitz (2002), cited World Bank data and stated: "Despite repeated promises of poverty reduction made once the last decade of the twentieth century, the actual number of people living in poverty has actually *increased* by almost 100 million. This occurred at the same time that total world income actually increased by an average of 2.5 per cent annually," [p. 54].

Chapter 2

1. In Lal (1988) I show how the Boserupian theory applies to Indian agriculture over the millennia.

2. The technological advances are discussed in White (1962).

3. See McNeill (1982, 60).

4. Easterlin cites Titmus (1966, 91), who describes how among the English working class the typical mother "of the 1890s, married in her teens or early twenties and experiencing ten pregnancies, spent about 15 years in a state of pregnancy and in nursing a child for the first years of its life. She was tied, for this period of time, to the wheel of childbearing."

5. See Simon (1981) and Kremer (1993) for a formalization of this argument.

Chapter 3

1. See Iliffe (1987), to whom I owe the threefold classification of poverty.

2. This has now been converted into a national rural employment guarantee scheme. But see Bhalla (2010), who finds that, on the basis of the latest National Sample Survey data, only 14.7 percent of the amount spent reaches the targeted group.

3. See Rosenzweig (1988) for the continuing relevance of this feature in modern Indian village life.

4. See Castañeda (1992) for a detailed account of these social policy reforms and their outcome.

5. But see chapter 7 in Lal (1999).

6. Also see Arrow (1963, 55).

7. See Lal and Myint (1996, 361–66) and Lal (1999) chapter 7 for a formal argument.

8. See Sugden (1993) for a lucid account of the divergent economic traditions that flow from the technocratic and classical-liberal viewpoints.

9. See Ravallion (1992) for a full explication of this approach in the design and evaluation of poverty alleviation programs in the Third World.

10. As Platteau (2000, 156) concludes: "Even though empirical evidence is scanty (but not altogether absent), the case can reasonably be made that, barring exceptionally unfavorable circumstances (such as repeated crop failures or crop diseases affecting entire communities), traditional methods for controlling the risk of falling into distress have usually enabled the people to counter natural and other hazards in a rather effective way."

11. Also see Rempel and Lobdell (1978), Knowles and Anker (1981), Collier and Lal (1986), Oberai and Singh (1980), and Lucas and Stark (1985) on the significant size and effects of remittances within the rural and between the rural and urban sectors in Ghana, Liberia, Nigeria, Pakistan, Tanzania, Kenya, India, and Botswana.

12. See www.ifad.org/events/remittances/maps/brochure.pdf.

13. For India, see Lal and Sharma (2009). For the Philippines, see Cox, Hansen, and Jiminez (2004).

14. See Mesa-Lago (1989) for Latin America. India now seems to have begun its travel too down this primrose path. See Lal (2010b).

15. See O. Krantz (2004) for a Swedish case.

16. Granger causation is an econometric method to determine which variable (time series) is useful in forecasting another.

Chapter 4

1. See Lal (1984) and Chapter 13.2 of Lal (1988) for a model of the predatory state.

2. The classification was based on a three-factor (land, labor, and capital), multiple-good open-economy model by Krueger (1977) and its formalization in terms of a simple diagram by Leamer (1987).

3. See Lundahl and Wyzan (2005) for case studies of the political economy of reform failure in a number of countries in the second and third worlds, where "crises" did lead to some reform, but these proved unsustainable.

4. Lundahl's chapter on Haiti, in Lundhal and Wyzan (2005), and his other work on the country, for instance, strongly suggest that the continuation of the strange predatory state in Haiti is largely explicable in these terms, so that even when democracy was introduced it did not take root.

5. On this interpretation of the origins and persistence of the caste system in India, see Lal (1988). For Russia, Domar states that two facts attest to the fact that serfdom was linked to the scarcity of labor to provide a surplus for the nobility: "the first . . . [is] the replacement of the basic land tax by a household tax in the 17th century and a poll tax under Peter the Great. The second is . . . [a] cultural trait: as late as in the first half of the 19th century, the social position of a Russian landowner . . . depended less on his landholding . . . than on the number of *souls* (registered male peasants) he owned" (Domar 1970, 18–32).

6. For evidence on the substantial economies in producing certain crops on large slave plantations, see Fogel (1989), Engerman (1983), and Deer (1949).

7. But there was also a more positive aspect of the common Catholic culture of Latin America. As compared with North America, as Hugh Thomas has rightly pointed out to me, the Latins succeeded "socially" where the United States "failed." This was in part due to the planned cities, the skillful approach to racial matters enabling manumission of slaves, and of course a common Catholic culture, which left their personal and social mores closer to the "communalist" ones of the other great ancient civilizations than those based on the new-fangled "individualism" of their Protestant brethren. See Lal (1998) and Edwards (2009).

8. Veliz (1994) contrasts this universalism of Latin America with the greater tolerance of diversity in beliefs in North America, as the baroque hedgehogs of the South and the Gothic foxes of the North in the New World, reflecting Archilochus's maxim: "The fox knows many things, but the hedgehog knows only one thing" quoted in Berlin (1978).

9. See, for instance, Castaneda (1995).

10. See the critique of these regression studies of civil war and failed states in Easterly (2009a, 373–447). There is an interesting recent study by Desmet, Ortuno-Ortin,

and Wacziarg (2009) on the effects of ethnolinguistic cleavages on civil conflict, re-distribution, economic growth, and the provision of public goods. They use the data from Ethnologue (2005) to construct language trees for the whole set of 6,912 world languages and compute heterogeneity measures for ethnolinguistic fragmentation at different levels of linguistic aggregation. They find that deep linguistic cleavages originating thousands of years ago (which I have argued are the basis of differences in cosmological beliefs) and which are represented by the highest level of aggregation of the linguistic data "lead to measures of diversity that are better predictors of civil conflict and redistribution than those that account for more recent and superficial divisions." However, the finer linguistic divisions and the related measures of linguistic diversity matter for growth and public-good provision. Thus, though Chad and Zambia are both linguistically diverse at the finer levels of linguistic aggregation, Zambia is more homogenous at the coarser aggregative linguistic division with 99.5 percent of the population speaking a language from the Niger–Congo group, whereas in Chad there is three-fold division between speakers of an Afro–Asiatic language (one third), Nilo–Sharan languages (half) and the Niger–Congo family (the rest). Thus whilst Chad has had perpetual civil wars Zambia has been relatively peaceful.

11. See Przeworski and Limongi (1993) for a survey. The best of these studies is by Helliwell (1992), and the most cogent critique of the econometrics involved by Deaton and Miller (1995).

12. See Lal (2010b) for a detailed argument.

Chapter 5

1. The actual ICP procedures are more complicated. For a detailed discussion of its methods and how they have affected the World Bank's poverty numbers, see Deaton (2010).

2. But see Deaton and Heston (2008) for a lucid discussion of these problems as well as of the pitfalls in using this data in the type of cross-country econometric work that has become so popular and is discussed in greater detail in the next chapter.

3. In addition, Maddison (2008a) notes that another bias in the World Bank's Purchasing Power Parity (PPP) estimates is due to "the scrapping of the Geary-Khamis (GK) measure of PPP for the EKS (Elteto-Koves-Szulc) method favored by bureaucrats," as the method of aggregation for the five regional studies on which the PPP estimates are based. The difference between the two methods is that whereas the Geary–Khamis method of aggregation gives a weight to countries corresponding to the size of their GDP, the EKS method "gives all countries the same weight, putting Luxemburg on a par with the USA. This method systematically exaggerates the per capita income differential between rich and poor countries."

4. Pritchett 1997 argues that about $250 in 1985 PPP dollars is the minimum per capita GDP required to sustain a population; it has never been observed for more than a short period.

5. Deaton and Heston (2008) also support Bhalla's conclusion about what they call the "horror story" of the 2005 ICP, though they rather ungenerously dub him "a long time if not always reliable critic of the World Bank" (45). But they concur "it is simply not possible that *both* the current PPP estimates of Chinese GDP *and* the official growth rates of the economy can be correct," however, even Maddison's (2007a) estimates of "Chinese GDP growth since 1952 at 'only' 4.4 % a year, . . . still leads to $229 in 1985 international dollars, still below Pritchett's cutoff" (46).

6. Deaton and Heston (2008, 45).

7. Bhalla (2008).

8. In Chapter 5 of Lal (2006), I outline the politicization of the World Bank during the presidency of James Wolfensohn, while in Lal (2005a), I discuss how the international organizations set up after the Second World War to create a new liberal international economic order have now become the major purveyors of global illiberalism.

Chapter 6

1. The article by Hoover (2008) provides a succinct discussion. Also see Cartwright (2007b).

2. See Heckman (2000) for a masterly survey of the evolution of econometrics.

3. The property of orthogonality between two variables implies that there is no (zero) correlation between them.

4. This has led to a virtual flood of studies using this type of variable to explain various socioeconomic phenomena. Deaton (2009) lists "distance from the equator (as an instrument for per capita GDP in explaining religiosity, McCleary and Barro [2006]); land gradient (as an instrument for dam construction in explaining poverty, Duflo and Pande [2007]); rivers (as an instrument for the number of school districts in explaining educational outcomes, Hoxby [2000]); month of birth (as an instrument for years of schooling in an earnings regression, Angrist and Krueger [1991]); or rainfall (as an instrument for economic growth in explaining civil war, Miguel, Satyanath, and Sergenti [2004])." "The examples could be multiplied *ad infinitum*" (Deaton 2009, 2)!

5. But see the response to Deaton (2009) and Heckman (1997) by Imbens (2009).

6. Leamer's earlier paper (1983) showed how fragile were the inferences drawn from econometric evidence and how, for example, the same data set on the effects of capital punishment on the murder rates in different U.S. states generated opposing estimates based on one's priors. This led me to coin the aphorism that "all econometric evidence is equivocal"!

7. A good account and justification of this method is in Skocpol (1979).

8. Notable examples include Acemoglu et al. (2001; 2002).

9. This endogeneity of property rights was the major contribution of Demsetz's famous paper on the origins of property rights (1967). He has extended this in Demsetz (2002) to show how since the Stone Age there has been competition between private and collective ownership. It provides a succinct account within a neoclassical framework of the economic factors that have led to changing property relationships over time. It provides a rigorous, historically informed, and more persuasive theory of institutional change than provided by the new institutional economics of North and his associates. It also fits in with my historical story outlined in part one. Demsetz argues that specialization that reduces the relevance of compact settings (as in primitive agriculture) for resource-allocation problems, while increasing their complexity, leads to reliance on socio-legal systems that allow dealings with strangers. The Roman Empire provided this and thus enhanced the spread of private property. With its collapse western Europe reverted to various forms of collective ownership until, in my view, the 13th-century legal papal revolution recreated these socio-legal conditions in western Christendom, which provided the preconditions for the slow rise of the west. Also see Seabright (2004), who provides an account based on sociobiology of how a band of "shy, murderous apes" used their inherited instincts to create rules and institutions that allow strang-

ers to be treated as "honorary friends" to garner the gains from specialization. But I do not find it adds much to my discussion in Lal (1998).

10. This has also been correctly noted by Clark (2007, 210–23), who discusses many historical examples of how with changing economic circumstances institutions changed; for example, the replacement of "wager by battle" by juries for settling legal disputes in medieval England and the various means found to circumvent the Christian and Muslin bans on usury. He also provides convincing evidence to contradict North and Weingast's (1989) thesis that it was the Glorious Revolution of 1688–89 in Great Britain, with its institutional changes relating to the supremacy of parliament, that protected property rights, and the creation of the Bank of England that purportedly led to lower interest rates, which ignited British economic growth, making it the first industrial nation.

11. See Bhagwati and Srinivasan (2001) for an elaboration.

12. This policy package put together by Williamson (1989) consists mainly of macroeconomic prescriptions, not all of which are consistent with classical-liberal principles. Thus, for example, he argues for managed exchange rates, and though he emphasizes property rights, he has nothing to say about the size of government. In fact Williamson (2002), who goes some length to distance himself from the views advocated by members of the classical-liberal Mont Pelerin Society, would consider it a canard to call his policy package "classical liberal." Nevertheless, there is enough congruence that the classical-liberal policy package can be referred to as the Washington Consensus.

Chapter 7

1. See Meier (2005) and my review (Lal 2007, 459–63).

2. I am sorry to say that much of this higher nonsense has been perpetrated by my mathematical economics colleagues at UCLA. See for instance the genesis of this genre in Azariadis (1996), and Azariadis and Drazen (1990).

3. They also show how the other sources of purported theoretical "poverty traps," like low levels of technology at low levels of development or a low level of subsistence consumption, again give no empirical support to their assumptions.

4. See Sachs (2005) and the report authored by Stern for the Commission for Africa (2005). Easterly (2001) had argued for aid to break poverty traps in Africa, but in Easterly (2009a) has clearly changed his mind.

5. Galor (2005) summarizes his research, which has appeared in numerous "top" peer-reviewed journals, and hence is considered credible by the young.

6. In the appendix to Lal (1998), I provide a diagrammatic analysis of this process. This can also be put into a mathematical dynamic formulation as Pryor and Maurer (1982) have done (see Lal [1998, 248–49]), in which agriculture and output are growing at the same rate in the steady state.

7. See the discussion on differences in educational capital in explaining growth differences in Lal and Myint (1996, 70–72, 124n28).

8. See Figure 1, "World economic history in one picture" in Clark (2007).

9. Both of which saw the beginnings of Promethean growth with the rise of their mercantile economies in the 16th century and the gradual move from an organic into a mineral energy–based economy.

10. Greenfield (2001) presents another unpersuasive reason for the decline of the Dutch and the rise of the English: economic nationalism aka mercantilism.

The Dutch, she claims, were not a nation, unlike the English. A view directly countered by Maddison (2001, 75–78). While the argument that mercantilism was an engine of growth is countered in Eli Hecksher's magisterial book on mercantilism (1955). Also see Lal and Myint (1996) and my review of Greenfield's book in Lal (2003b).

11. Clark writes: "Thus the relative wealth of the English—expressed also in their comparatively greater physical stature then versus now, matched against the Chinese or Japanese in 1800—probably stemmed mostly from the relative filth in which they wallowed. For in the Malthusian economy the traditional virtues of cleanliness and hard work gave no reward to society at large, and indeed just made life harder and incomes lower."

12. Allen (2008, 969) who, in concluding his long review providing detailed evidence against Clark's various theses, writes that "he has written an economic history of the world that is a counterpart to 'the clash of civilizations.' Indeed his biological arguments for the superiority of Anglo-American culture make the differences between the West and the Rest unbridgeable and a source of perpetual conflict. Normally, it is distressing to find that the central theses of a book are contradicted by well-known evidence, but in this case it is a relief given the pessimistic prospect that *A Farewell to Alms* holds out for the future of the world." Goldstone (2007, 220) concludes: "In short, I find the thesis that Britain succeeded in concentrating a critical mass of people with the skills needed to launch the Industrial Revolution by biological selection to be unprovable, implausible, and inconsistent with much of the data and reasoning that Clark himself provides."

13. On Sweden see, for instance, Krantz (2004).

14. Thus, in the Middle East after the great intellectual and cultural efflorescence shown under the Abbasids in the Arab Empire, from the 11th century onwards there was the "closing of the Muslim mind" with the closing of the "gate of *itjihad*," which had allowed some doctrinal flexibility. This curbed the earlier curiosity and innovation in the Muslim world. See Lal (1998, 63–65). As in post-Sung China, this led to cultural and technological stagnation.

15. Another erudite attempt to explain China's reversal of fortune vis-à-vis the West in purely materialist terms, by Pomeranz (2000), is equally unconvincing. (See my review in E.H. Net Economic History Services, 2 October 2002, available at http://eh.net/bookreviews). Lal (2002) argues that the coal reserves in northwestern China, which fuelled the Sung iron and steel development in the 11th century, were not available to the Chinese economic and demographic core in the south in the 15th century. This, as I noted in my review, is unconvincing. His second reason for the great divergence is that, unlike the West, to overcome its land constraint China did not seek to expand its land frontier by exploiting the free land available to its southeast. Though "Chinese went there in significant numbers, South East Asia never became for coastal China what the New World was for Western Europe" (200). Why? Because unlike Europe's New World empires, "the Chinese merchants . . . established themselves in Southeast Asia without state backing" (200). This is the crucial point. It was the closing of the Chinese mind, and the dismantling of its navy and restriction of foreign trade and contacts, as the neo-Confucian Mandarinate took control, that explains China's great reversal of fortune.

16. Corden (1997) sets this out clearly.

17. See Krueger (1974) on rent-seeking.

18. I dealt with these arguments and those of the so-called "new" trade theory for government industrial policies in detail in Lal (1992, reprinted in Lal [1993]).

19. But they continue the muddle created by Scitovsky's (1954) definition of "pecuniary externalities," which were not those as defined by Buchanan and Stubblebine (1962) and Viner (1931), but which concerned increasing returns and imperfections of markets (particularly those for futures). Thus, Murphy, Shleifer, and Vishny (1989, 1004), write: "In all the models described in this paper, the source of multiplicity of equilibria is pecuniary externalities generated by imperfect competition with large fixed costs"!

20. See Pack and Westphal (1986) for the most cogent statement.

21. A conclusion also supported by Little (1994) and Thorbecke and Wan (1999).

Chapter 8

1. Ironically, while the applications of the OECD and UNIDO manuals are now minimal, the Harberger method is being widely used in Latin America. This is largely because over the years Harberger and his Chilean students have trained a large number of Latin American economists in the method, and since many of Harberger's students are in important economic ministries all over the continent, they have ensured that these methods are applied (at least rhetorically!) in evaluating public-sector projects.

2. Discussed in Chapter 6.

3. Until one recalls the meaning one of Jack Horner story. When Henry VIII was dissolving the monasteries (in Tudor England) after his break with Rome in order to seize their gold and lands, the bishop of the richest Benedictine monastery, at Glastonbury, sent his steward Richard Whiting (Jack Horner) with 12 title deeds to various manorial estates to bribe the king, hoping thereby to spare Glastonbury. Realizing the plan would not work, Whiting (Horner) stole the deeds to the manor of Mells (the "plum" of the 12 manors) and then served on the jury that convicted the old bishop—his former master—of treason. The Glastonbury abbey was destroyed, its lands and assets seized, and the bishop hung, drawn, and quartered. Horner moved into the Manor of Wells, and his family lived there till the 20th century. Perhaps the *randomistas* are hoping for a similar plum!

4. This is based on Harford (2008) and Cull, Demirguc-Kunt, and Morduch (2009). Also see de Aghion and Murdoch (2005).

Chapter 9

1. This conversion is explicit in Easterly (2009b).

2. Readers might be interested in a discussion on foreign aid among Easterly, Steven Radelet (another regression warrior), Branko Milanovic (of the World Bank), and me at Cato Unbound, April 2006 (www.cato-unbound.org/archives/april-2006/). Most revealing was my exchange with Milanovic, whose contributions were breathtaking in their unworldliness. He advocated a global welfare agency financed by a global Tobin tax (on financial transactions), which would "identify a group that is largely poor, and would give them a one or two time cash grant of, say $100 per person or per family." These cash doles could be "applied in many countries from Angola to Zimbabwe." I replied that "as regards his proposal to hand cash grants to the deserving poor from Angola to Zimbabwe, who would get these cash grants to the intended beneficiaries? Humanitarian activists and NGOs? If they can't get food and medicines

to the hungry and sick because of local government impediments, does he seriously believe these foreign agents carrying their sacks of dollars will be able to hand out their $100 to each targeted family without it being 'misappropriated' by local government agents?"

3. The official title for the Marshall Plan was The Economic Recovery Program. Although it was undertaken during the Truman administration, Secretary of State George Marshall's name was attached to it because of his outstanding leadership and his national popularity.

4. This section is based on Lal and Rajapatirana (2007).

5. On April 2, 1948, the U.S. Congress passed the Economic Cooperation Act, implementing the Marshall Plan. The bill outlined $17 billion in grants and loans to European nations for the purpose of buying U.S. products. The Economic Cooperation Administration was formed to administer the program.

6. The ECA was headed by Paul Hoffman, a leading automobile industry executive, not a government bureaucrat. (Republicans insisted on private-sector leadership.) Similarly, the ECA representatives in European capitals who acted as advisers were also prominent businessmen, not bureaucrats.

7. The extent of private-sector involvement can be gauged by the writings of Blaisdell (1950): "From the beginning, private trade provided the mechanism for moving goods and services which were involved in the program."

8. Although Easterly (2009a, 381), is right to state that "whilst many of these disasters may be more likely in Africa than elsewhere, they are inherently rare occurrences. [His] Table 2 shows that the Four Horsemen are the experience of a small minority of Africans—still far too many, but less than what seems to be implied by the stereotypes."

9. See Sachs et al. (2004), which provides the formal argument and evidence behind the UN Millennium Projects' call for a new Marshall Plan. In the discussion of the paper, "Richard Cooper disagreed sharply with the authors' proposals for greatly expanding aid to sub-Saharan Africa at this time, unless one could ensure that the aid could be used effectively . . . because they lacked the elementary functions of law and order that would be needed to deliver aid effectively. Cooper also questioned some of the paper's analysis of Africa's economic plight. He noted "that over the last 50 years per capita income had grown by 60%, longevity has increased before adjusting for the impact of AIDS, infant mortality has fallen and population growth has been rapid. Nor was Cooper persuaded that geography makes Africa a special case: other countries, such as Switzerland, are landlocked and have fewer resources than Africa. . .Cooper suggested that drastic measures may be needed in some parts of African countries, such as a twenty-first century version of the British colonial office (for example, a UN trusteeship, with forces to back stop it), to provide minimal law and order so that economies could begin meaningful development and make use of expanded aid" (230–31). On the last point, see Lal (2004) and Collier (2009).

10. This is clearly demonstrated by the reluctance on the part of the African leadership to censure Robert Mugabe, the president of Zimbabwe, who has brought the country to rack and ruin and sullied the image of Africa. He has been so emboldened by the public silence of African leaders at the March 2007 Southern African Development Community Summit that he stood for election again in 2008. Although he demonstrably lost the election, he has still clung on to power with the acquiescence of most African leaders, not least those in South Africa.

11. In fact, the recent turnaround has left many to see Africa as the next region to have its own growth miracle. See Mallaby (2013).

12. The international war on drugs goes back to the Shanghai Opium Commission of 1909 and the U.S. involvement of the war on drugs by President Theodore Roosevelt, under pressure from the powerful missionary lobby, the International Reform Lobby, even though Roosevelt wanted to maintain a licensed opium trade and legal consumption. See Lal (2008a) for details.

13. Recently, Aiyar (2011) argued in the *Times of India* that instead of purchasing the Afghan poppy crop, which by raising the price would induce other areas also to take up poppy cultivation, the aid agencies should purchase opium from Australia and dump it in Afghanistan, driving the price to zero, thereby decimating the Taliban and the Afghan warlords financially! Unfortunately this is even less likely to be accepted by the advocates of the war on drugs, as lowering the price of heroin on Western streets could lead to higher consumption.

14. In a speech at Oxford Town Hall, June 29, 2006, Cameron said: "One idea we will investigate, based on our belief in trusting people—and our instinctive dislike of top down solutions – is aid vouchers. Aid vouchers, put directly in the hands of poor communities, would be redeemable for development services of any kind with an aid agency or supplier of their choice. The vouchers could be converted into cash by the aid agencies. Such an innovation would help show us what the poor really want – and who is most effective in meeting their needs" (Easterly 2008, 37).

15. World Mining Stocks 2005 estimated that China accounts for "20% of total world aluminum flow, 23% of alumina; over 20% of copper; 10% of nickel; around 22% of zinc: nearly 30% of crude steel; and one third of world's iron ore" (Dairimani 2008).

16. This is based on Lal (2005, 74–6).

17. "Dutch Disease" is the term referring to a country's deindustrialization associated with one, some, or all of the following: a considerable natural resource discovery; a substantial increase in natural-resource prices on world markets; any large increase in foreign currency, including foreign direct investment; and foreign aid. The two main signs of a country suffering from the disease are a decrease in the price competitiveness and thus the exports of its manufactured goods, and an increase in imports.

Chapter 10

1. In CERN's press release on the CLOUD experiment, Kirby stated, "We've found that cosmic rays significantly enhance the formation of aerosol particles in the mid troposphere and above. These aerosols can eventually grow into the seeds for clouds. However , we've found that the vapours previously thought to account for all aerosol formation in the lower atmosphere can only account for a small fraction of the observations—even with the enhancement of cosmic rays. . . Additional vapors must therefore be involved."

2. For a lucid account of the formation of the IPCC and its takeover by scientists with an a priori belief in anthropogenic global warming see Booker (2009b).

3. Also see Scafetta and West (2008), who show how the short-term fluctuations in the sun's irradiance are also linked to the earth's average surface temperature along with the longer term solar cycles. They show that the IPCC erroneously ignores these fluctuations as noise, assuming its distribution is Gaussian, when in fact it is not.

They then show how fluctuations in solar irradiance are linked to those in earth's surface temperature in addition to the longer term solar cycles.

4. For a more wide-ranging critique of economists' shortcomings in their treatment of climate change see Henderson (2009).

5. The diversion of cereals to biofuel, particularly in the United States, has led to the secular rise in food prices since 2000 (Lal 2008b). The proximate cause of the 2022 "revolutions" in the Middle East was the spike in food prices caused in part by the diversion of cereal production to ethanol rather than food consumption (Lal 2011).

6. Here the "West" is not synonymous with industrial countries since it excludes Japan. See Lal (1995a) on eco-fundamentalism

7. As Bramwell (1989, 23), the historian of the ecological movement, states, "When science took over the religion in the nineteenth century, the belief that God made the world with a purpose in which Man was paramount declined. If there was no purpose, how was man to live on the earth? The hedonistic answer, to enjoy it as long as possible, was not acceptable. If Man had become God, then he had become the shepherd of the earth, the guardian, responsible for the oekonomie of the earth." Also, "There is no God the Shepherd; so man becomes the shepherd. There is a conflict between the desire to accept nature's harmonious order, and a need to avert catastrophe because ecologists are apocalyptical, but know that man has caused the impending apocalypse by his actions. Ecologists are the saved" (16).

8. Thus, Douglas and Wildavsky (1983, 123), state: "The border is worried about God or Nature, two arbiters external to the large scale social systems of the center. Either God will punish or nature will punish; the jeremiad is the same and the sins are the same: worldly ambition, lust after material things. Large organization."

9. This is based on Booker (2009a).

10. A forensic account of this saga and how a "hockey team" is still active in global-warmist scientific circles to resurrect this statistical artifact is provided in Montford (2010).

11. In Lal (2004, 216), I had used a diagram from Houghton 1994 to show this well-known pattern (Figure 8.1).

12. This account is based on Booker (2009a). Also see Singer (2010).

13. In related developments, Steve McIntyre had formal errors made by James Hansen, director of the NASA's Goddard Institute of Space Science, in 2008, forcing a revision of this other major source for global surface temperatures. Meanwhile in Australia and New Zealand, when local scientists compared the official temperature record with the original data on which it was based, they found that a flat temperature chart had been manipulated to show temperatures steadily rising.

Bibliography

Acemoglu, Daron, Simon Johnson, and James A. Robinson. 2001. "The Colonial Origins of Comparative Development: An Empirical Investigation." *American Economic Review* 91 (5): 1369–1401.

———. 2002. "Reversal of Fortune, Geography and Institutions in the Making of the Modern World Income Distribution." *Quarterly Journal of Economics* 117 (4): 1231–94.

Adams, Richard H., and John Page. 2005. "Do International Migration and Remittances Reduce Poverty in Developing Countries?" *World Development* 33 (10): 1645–69.

Ahmad, Ehtisham, Jean Dreze, John Hills, and Amarya Sen, eds. 1991. *Social Security in Developing Countries*. Oxford, UK: Clarendon Press.

Aiyar, S. A. 2011. "Dump Opium in Afghanistan, Bankrupt Taliban." *Times of India,* February 20, http://blogs.timesofindia.indiatimes.com/Swaminomics/entry/dump-opium-in-afghanistan-bankrupt-taliban.

Aleem, Irfan. 1990. "Imperfect Information, Screening and the Costs of Informal Lending: A Study of a Rural Credit Market in Pakistan." *World Bank Economic Review* 4 (3): 329–49.

Allen, Robert C. 2008. "A Review of Gregory Clark's *A Farewell to Alms: A Brief Economic History of the World.*" *Journal of Economic Literature* 46 (4): 946–73.

Angeles, Luis. 2007. "Income Inequality and Colonialism." *European Economic Review* 51 (5): 1155–76.

Angrist, Joshua D. 1990. "Lifetime Earnings and the Vietnam Era Draft Lottery." *American Economic Review* 91 (5): 1369–1401.

Angrist, Joshua D., and Alan Krueger. 1991. "Does Compulsory School Attendance Affect Schooling and Earnings?" *Quarterly Journal of Economics* 106 (4): 979–1014.

Angrist, Joshua D., and Victor Lavy. 1999. "Using Maimonides' Rule to Estimate the Effect of Class Size on Scholastic Achievement." *Quarterly Journal of Economics* 1 (2): 533–75.

Armendariz de Aghion, Beatriz, and Jonathan Morduch. 2005. *The Economics of Microfinance*. Cambridge, MA: MIT Press.

Arrow, Kenneth, J. 1963. "Uncertainty and the Welfare Economics of Medical Care." *American Economic Review* 52 (5): 941–73.

———. 1965. "A Reply." *American Economic Review* 55 (1/2): 154–58.

Azariadis, Costas. 1996. "The Economics of Poverty Traps." *Journal of Economic Growth* 1 (4): 449–96.

Azariadis, Costas, and Allan Drazen. 1990. "Threshold Externalities in Economic Development." *Quarterly Journal of Economics* 105 (2): 501–26.

Bairoch, P. 1988. *Cities and Economic Development: From the Dawn of History to the Present*. Chicago: University of Chicago Press.

Baldwin, Robert E. 1969. "The Case against Infant Industry Protection." *Journal of Political Economy* 77 (3): 295–305.

———. 1992. "Are Economist's Traditional Policy Views Still Valid?" *Journal of Economic Literature* 30 (2): 804–29.

Banerjee, Abhijit V., ed. 2007. *Making Aid Work.* Cambridge, MA: MIT Press.

Banerjee, Abhijit V., Angus Deaton, and Esther Duflo. 2004. "Wealth, Health, and Health Services in Rural Rajasthan." *American Economic Review* 94 (2): 326–30.

Banerjee, Abhijit V., and Esther Duflo. 2007. "The Economic Lives of the Poor." *Journal of Economic Perspectives* 21 (1): 141–67.

Bardhan, Pranab. 1980. "Interlocking Factor Markets and Agrarian Development: A Review of Issues." *Oxford Economic Papers* 32 (1): 82–98.

———. 1989. *Land, Labour and Rural Poverty.* New York: Columbia University Press.

Barr, Nicholas. 1992. "Economic Theory and the Welfare State: A Survey and Interpretation." *Journal of Economic Literature* 30 (2): 741–803.

Barro, Robert J. 1998. *Determinants of Economic Growth: A Cross-Country Empirical Study.* Cambridge, MA: MIT Press.

Barro, Robert J., and X. Sala-i-Martin. 1991. "Convergence across States and Regions." *Brookings Papers on Economic Activity* 22 (1): 107–58.

———. 1992. "Convergence." *Journal of Political Economy* 100 (2): 22–51.

Bateman, Milford. 2008. "Microfinance's 'Iron Law'—Local Economies Reduced to Poverty." *Financial Times,* December 20/21, 10.

Bauer, Peter. (1971) 1976. *Dissent on Development.* Cambridge, MA: Harvard University Press.

———. 1987. "The Disregard of Reality." *Cato Journal* 7 (1): 29–42. Reprinted in *Peter Bauer and the Economics of Prosperity,* edited by James A. Dorn and Barun S. Mitra. New Delhi: Academic Foundation, 2009.

Becker, Gary. 1983. "A Theory of Competition among Pressure Groups for Political Influence." *Quarterly Journal of Economics* 18 (3): 371–400.

———. 1985. "Public Policies, Pressure Groups and Deadweight Costs." *Journal of Public Economics* 28 (3): 329–48.

Becker, Gary S., Kevin M. Murphy, and Robert Tamura. 1990. "Human Capital, Fertility, and Economic Growth." *Journal of Political Economy* 98 (5): S12–S37.

Becker, Gary S., Tomas J. Philipson, and Rodrigo R. Soares. 2005. "The Quantity and Quality of Life and the Evolution of World Inequality." *American Economic Review* 95 (1): 277–91.

Berlin, Isaiah. 1978. *Russian Thinkers.* London: Hogarth Press.

Berman, Harold J. 1983. *Law and Revolution.* Cambridge, MA: Harvard University Press.

Bevan, David, Paul Collier, and Jan Gunning. 1999. *The Political Economy of Poverty, Equity and Growth: Indonesia and Nigeria.* New York: Oxford University Press.

Bhagwati, Jagdish N., and T. N. Srinivasan. 2001. "Outward-orientation and Development: Are Revisionists Right?" In *Trade, Development and Political Economy: Essays in Honor of Anne Krueger,* edited by Deepak Lal and Richard H. Snape. Basingstoke, UK: Palgrave Macmillan.

Bhalla, Surjit. 2002. *Imagine There Is No Country: Poverty, Inequality and Growth in the Age of Globalization.* Washington, DC: Institute of International Economics.

———. 2008. "Most Asians Dead in 1950." *Business Standard,* August, 23.

———. 2010. "Does NREGA Really Work?" *Business Standard,* March 27.

Blaisdell, Thomas C., Jr. 1948. "The European Recovery Program—Phase Two." *International Organization* 2 (3): 443–54.

———. 1950. "The Foreign Aid Program and the United States Commercial Policy." *Proceedings of the Academy of Political Science* 23 (4): 53–63.

Bloch, Marc. 1965. *Feudal Society.* 2 vols. London: Routledge.

Bogue, Donald J. 1969. *Principles of Demography.* New York: Wiley.

Booker, Christopher. 2009a. "Climate Change: This Is the Worst Scientific Scandal of Our Generation." *Daily Telegraph*, November 28.

———. 2009b. The *Real Global Warming Disaster.* London: Continuum.

Booker, Christopher, and Richard North. 2009. "Climate Change Guru and a Question over Business Deals." Special Report. *Sunday Telegraph*, December 20.

Boone, Peter. 1994. "The Impact of Foreign Aid on Savings and Growth." Mimeo. London School of Economics.

Boserup, Ester. 1965. *The Conditions of Agricultural Growth.* London: Allen and Unwin.

Boyd, Robert, and Joan B. Silk. 2003. *How Humans Evolved.* 3rd ed. New York: W. W. Norton & Co.

Bramwell, Anna. 1989. *Ecology in the 20th Century: A History.* New Haven, CT: Yale University Press.

Brennan, Geoffrey, and James M. Buchanan. 1980. *The Power to Tax: Analytical Foundations of the Fiscal Constitution.* Cambridge, UK: Cambridge University Press.

Brockerhoff, Martin, and Ellen Brennan. 1997. *The Poverty of Cities in the Developing World.* New York: Population Council.

Bruno, Michael, and William Easterly. 1996. "Inflation's Children: Tales of Crises That Beget Reform." NBER Working Paper No. 5452, National Bureau of Economic Research, Cambridge, MA.

Bruton, Henry J. 1992. *The Political Economy of Poverty, Equity and Growth: Sri Lanka and Malaysia.* New York: Oxford University Press.

Buchanan, James M., and Craig Stubblebine. 1962. "Externality." *Economica* 29, (116): 371–84. Reprinted in K. J. Arrow and T. Scitovsky's *Readings in Welfare Economics.* London: Allen and Unwin, 1969.

Cain, Peter J. and Tony Hopkins. 2002. *British Imperialism 1638–2000.* London: Longmans.

Callion, Nicolas, Jeffrey P. Severinghaus, Jean Jouzel, Jean-Marc Barnola, Jiancheng Kang, and Volodya Y. Lipenko. 2003. "Timing of Atmospheric CO_2 and Antarctic Temperature Changes Across Termination III." *Science* 299 (5613): 1728–31.

Cartwright, Nancy. 2007a. "Are Rcts the Gold Standard?" *BioSocieties* 2 (1): 11–20.

———. 2007b. *Hunting Causes and Using Them: Approaches to Philosophy and Economics.* Cambridge, UK: Cambridge University Press.

Castañeda, Jorge G. 1995. *The Mexican Shock.* New York: New Press.

Castañeda, Tarsicio. 1992. *Combating Poverty.* San Francisco: ICS Press.

Central Intelligence Agency. 2007. *The World Factbook.* Washington, DC: CIA. http://www.cia.gov/library/publications/the-world-factbook.

Chen, Shaohua, and Martin Ravallion. 2008. "The Developing World Is Poorer Than We Thought, But No Less Successful in the Fight Against Poverty." Policy Research Working Paper WPS 4703, World Bank, Washington, DC.

Clark, Gregory. 2007. *A Farewell To Alms: A Brief Economic History of the World.* Princeton, NJ: Princeton University Press.

Collier, Paul. 2007. *The Bottom Billion: Why the Poorest Countries Are Failing and What Can Be Done about It*. New York: Oxford University Press.

———. 2009. *War, Guns, and Votes*. London: The Bodley Head.

Collier, Paul, and Jan Willem Gunning. 1999. "The IMF's Role in Structural Adjustment." *Economic Journal* 109 (459): F634–F651.

Collier, Paul, and Anne Hoeffler. 1998. "On the Economic Causes of Civil War." *Oxford Economic Papers* 50 (4): 563–73.

Collier, Paul, and Deepak Lal. 1986. *Labour and Poverty in Kenya, 1900–1980*. Oxford, UK: Clarendon Press.

Collier, Paul, and Nicholas Sambanis. 2003. *Africa* and *Europe, Central Asia and Other Regions*. Vols. 1 and 2 of *Understanding Civil War: Evidence and Analysis*. Washington, DC: World Bank.

Commission for Africa. 2005. *Our Common Interest*. London: Penguin.

Corden, Warner Max. 1997. *Trade Policy and Economic Welfare*. 2d ed. New York: Oxford University Press.

Cox, Donald, and Emmanuel Jimenez. 1990. "Achieving Social Objectives through Private Transfers: A Review." *World Bank Research Observer* 5 (2): 205–18.

———. 1992. "Social Security and Private Transfers in Developing Countries: The Case of Peru." *World Bank Economic Review*, World Bank Group, 6 (1): 155–69.

———.1993. "Private Transfers And The Effectiveness Of Public Income Redistribution In The Philippines," *Boston College Working Papers in Economics* 236, Boston College Department of Economics, Boston, MA.

Cox, Donald, Bruce E. Hansen, and Emmanuel Jiminez. 2004. "How Responsive Are Private Transfers to Income? Evidence from A Laissez Faire Economy." *Journal of Public Economics* 88 (9/10): 2193–219.

Cull, Robert, Asli Demirgüç-Kunt, and Jonathan Morduch. 2009. "Microfinance Meets the Market." *Journal of Economic Perspectives* 23 (1): 167–92.

Dahrendoff, Ralf. 1990. *Reflections on the Revolution in Europe*. London: Chattto and Windus.

Dam, Kenneth. 2006. *The Law-Growth Nexus: The Rule of Law and Economic Development*. Washington, DC: Brookings Institution Press.

Darimani, Abdulai. 2008. "Minerals Resource Extraction in Africa: Continuity and Shifts." Paper presented at Africa-Canada Forum Symposium, Harrington, Quebec, September 28, http://www.ccic.ca/_files/en/working_groups/003_acf_2008_acf_darimani_canada_paper.pdf.

Dasgupta, Partha. 1993. *An Enquiry Into Well-Being and Destitution*. Oxford: Clarendon Press.

De Soto, Hernando. 1989. *The Other Path: The Invisible Revolution in the Third World*. New York: Harper and Row.

———. 2000. The *Mystery of Capital: Why Capitalism Triumphs in the West and Fails Everywhere Else*. New York: Basic Books.

Deaton, Angus. 2009. "Instruments of Development: Randomization in the Tropics, and the Search for the Elusive Keys to Economic Development." NBER Working Paper No. 14690, National Bureau of Economic Research, Cambridge, MA.

———. 2010. "Price Indexes, Inequality, and the Measurement of Poverty." *American Economic Review* 100 (1): 1, 5–34.

Deaton, Angus, and Alan Heston. 2008. "Understanding Ppps and PPP-Based National Accounts." NBER Working Paper No. 14499, National Bureau of Economic Research, Cambridge, MA.

Deaton, Angus, and Ron Miller. 1995. *International Commodity Prices, Macroeconomic Performance, and Politics in Sub-Saharan Africa*. Princeton Essays in International Finance No. 79. Princeton, NJ: Princeton University Printing Services.

Deaton, Angus, and S. Subramanian. 1996. "The Demand for Food and Calories." *Journal of Political Economy* 104 (1): 133–62.

Deerr, Noel. 1949. *The History of Sugar*. London: Chapman and Hall.

Derringer, K., and L. Squire. 1996. "A New Data Set for Measuring Income Inequality." *World Bank Economic Review* 10 (3): 565–92.

Delumeau, Jean. 1990. *Sin and Fear: The Emergence of A Western Guilt Culture, 13th–18th Centuries*. New York: St. Martin's Press.

Demsetz, Harold. 1967. "Toward a Theory of Property Rights." *American Economic Review* 57 (2): 347–59.

———. 1989. *Efficiency, Competition, and Policy*. Oxford: Blackwell.

———. 2002. "Toward a Theory of Property Rights II: The Competition between Private and Collective Ownership." *Journal of Legal Studies* 31 (2): S653–S672.

Desmet, Klaus, Ignacio Ortuno-Ortin, and Romain Wacziarg. 2009. "The Political Economy of Ethnolinguistic Cleavages." NBER Working Paper No. 15360, National Bureau of Economic Research, Cambridge, MA.

Dixit, Avinash. 2007. "Evaluating Recipes for Development Success." *World Bank Research Observer* 22 (2): 131–57.

Domar, Evesy. 1970. "The Causes of Slavery or Serfdom: A Hypothesis." *Journal of Economic History* 30 (1): 18–32.

Douglas, Mary, and Aaron Wildavsky. 1983. *Risk and Culture*. Berkeley, CA: University of California Press.

Drèze, Jean, and P. V. Srinivasan. 1995. "Widowhood and Poverty in India: Some Inferences from Household Survey Data." Development Economics Research Program Paper No. 62, London School of Economics, London.

Duflo, Esther, and Rohini Pande. 2007. "Dams." *Quarterly Journal of Economics* 122 (2): 601–46.

Dumont, Louis. 1970. *Homo Hierarchicus*. London: Widenfeld and Nicholson.

Elvin, Mark. 1973. *The Pattern of the Chinese Past*. Stanford, CA: Stanford University Press.

Easterlin, Richard A. 2000. "The Worldwide Standard of Living Since 1800." *Journal of Economic Perspectives* 14 (1): 7–26.

Easterly, William R. 2001. *The Elusive Quest for Growth*. Cambridge, MA: MIT Press.

———. 2002. "Cartel of Good Intentions: The Problem of Bureaucracy in Foreign Aid." *Journal of Policy Reform*, 5(4):223–50.

———. 2004. "Does Foreign Aid Reach the Poor?" SAIS Lecture, Johns Hopkins School of Advanced International Studies, Washington, DC, December, www.sais-jhu.edu/programs/i-dev/easterly%20presentation.pdf.

———. 2006. *The White Man's Burden*. New York: Penguin.

Easterly, William R., ed. 2008. *Reinventing Foreign Aid*. Cambridge, MA: MIT Press.

———. 2009a. "Can the West Save Africa?" *Journal of Economic Literature* 47 (2): 373–447.

———. 2009b. "Trust the Development Experts—All 7bn of Them." *Financial Times*. May 29.

Edgren, Gus. 1990. *The Political Economy of Poverty, Equity, and Growth: Twin Study of Ghana and Thailand*. ARTEP Working Papers Series. New Delhi: ILO-ARTEP.

Edwards, Sebastian. 2009. "Latin America's Decline: A Long Historical View." NBER Working Paper No. 15171, National Bureau of Economic Research, Cambridge, MA.

Eichengreen, Barry. 1995. "Mainsprings of Economic Recovery in Post War Europe." In *Europe's Post-War Recovery*, edited by Barry Eichengreen. Cambridge, UK: Cambridge University Press.

Elbadawi, Ibrahim, and Francis Mwega. 2000. "Can Africa's Savings Collapse Be Reversed? *World Bank Economic Review* 14 (3): 415–43.

Engerman, Stanley M. 1983. "Contract Labor, Sugar, and Technology in the Nineteenth Century." *Journal of Economic History* 43 (3): 635–59.

Engerman, Stanley M., and Kenneth L. Sokoloff. 1994. "Factor Endowments, Institutions, and Differential Paths of Growth Among the New World Economies: A View From Economic Historians of the United States." NBER Working Paper, Historical Paper No. 66, National Bureau of Economic Research, Cambridge, MA.

Ethnologue. 2005. *Ethnologue: Languages of the World*. 15th ed. Dallas, TX: SIL International, www.ethnologue.com.

Fields, Gary. 1991. "Growth and Income Distribution." In *Essays on Poverty, Equity and Growth*, edited by G. Psacharopoulos. Oxford, UK: Pergamon Press.

Findlay, Ronald, and Stanislaw Wellisz, eds. 1993. *The Political Economy of Poverty, Equity, and Growth: Five Small Open Economies*. New York: Oxford University Press.

Fischer, H., Martin Wahlen, Jesse Smith, Derek Mastroianni, and Bruce Deck. 1999. "Ice Core Record of Atmospheric CO_2 around the Last Three Glacial Terminations." *Science* 283 (5408): 1712–14.

Fogel, Robert W. 1989. *Without Consent or Contract*. New York: Norton.

———. 1999. "Catching Up With the Economy." *American Economic Review* 89 (1): 1–21.

———. 2005. *The Escape from Hunger and Premature Death, 1720–2100: Europe, America, and the Third World*. Cambridge, UK: Cambridge University Press.

Galor, Oded. 2005. "From Stagnation to Growth: Unified Growth Theory." In *Handbook of Economic Growth*, edited by P. Aghion and N. Durlaf. Amsterdam: Elsevier.

Garnaut, Ross. 2008. *The Garnaut Climate Change Review: Final Report*. Cambridge, UK: Cambridge University Press.

Garraty, John A. 1978. *Unemployment in History*. New York: Harper and Row.

Gilbert, Christopher, Andrew Powell, and David Vines. 1999. "Positioning the World Bank." *Economic Journal* 109 (459): F598–F633.

Giné, Xavier, and Dean Karlan. 2008. "Peer Monitoring and Enforcement: Long Term Evidence from Microcredit Lending Groups with and without Group Liability," http://siteresources.worldbank.org/DEC/Resources/LTPeerLendingPhilippines.pdf.

Goldsmith, Raymond W. 1984. "An Estimate of the Size and Structure of the National Product of the Early Roman Empire." *Review of Income and Wealth* 30 (3): 263–88.

Goldstone, Jack A. 2007. "Unraveling the Mystery of Economic Growth." *World Economics* 8 (3): 207–25.

Goodin, Robert, and Julian Le Grand. 1987. *Not Only the Poor*. London: Allen and Unwin.

Goody, Jack. 1983. *The Development of the Family and Marriage in Europe*. Cambridge, UK: Cambridge University Press.

Greenfield, Liah. 2001. *The Spirit of Capitalism: Nationalism and Economic Growth* Cambridge, MA: Harvard University Press.

Greenwald, Bruce C., and Joseph E. Stiglitz. 1986. "Externalities in Economies with Imperfect Information and Incomplete Markets." *Quarterly Journal of Economics* 101 (2): 229–64.

Gregory, Ken. 2009. "Climate Change Science." Friends of Science, www.friendsof science.org/assets/documents/fos%20essay/climate_change_science.html.

Greif, Avner. 1994. "Cultural Beliefs and the Organization of Society: A Historical and Theoretical Reflection on Collectivist and Individualist Societies." *Journal of Political Economy* 102 (5): 912–50.

Greif, Avner, Diego Sasson, and Max Floetotto. 2009. "Risk, Institutions, and Growth: Why England and Not China?" Mimeo. Stanford University, Stanford, CA.

Gwartney, James, and Robert Lawson. 2005. *Economic Freedom of the World: 2005 Annual Report*. Vancouver, BC: Fraser Institute.

Gwartney, James, Robert Lawson, and Joshua Hall. 2012. *Economic Freedom of the World: 2012 Annual Report*. Vancouver, BC: Fraser Institute.

Hancock, G. 1989. *Lords of Poverty: The Power, Prestige, and Corruption of the International Aid Business*. London: Macmillan.

Hansen, Bent. 1991. *The Political Economy of Poverty, Equity and Growth: Egypt and Turkey*. New York: Oxford University Press.

Harberger, Arnold C. 1984. "Weights in Social Cost-Benefit Analysis." *Economic Development and Cultural Change* 32 (3): 455–74.

Harford, Tim. 2008. "The Battle for the Soul of Microfinance." *FT Magazine*, December 6.

Harrison, Ann, and Andres Rodriguez-Clare. 2009. "Trade, Foreign Investment, and Industrial Policy for Developing Countries." NBER Working Paper No. 15261, National Bureau of Economic Research, Cambridge, MA.

Hayek, Fredrich A. (1952) 1979. *The Counter-Revolution of Science*. Indianapolis: Liberty Press.

———. 1974. "The Pretence of Knowledge." Nobel Lecture. Reprinted in *Eight Prizes That Changed the World*, edited by N. Karlson. Stockholm: Ratio Institute, 2009.

———. 1994. *Hayek on Hayek*, London: Routledge.

Heckman, James J. 1997. "Instrumental Variables: A Study of Implicit Behavioral Assumptions Made in Making Program Evaluations." *Journal of Human Resources* 32 (3): 441–62.

———. 2000. "Causal Parameters and Policy Analysis in Economics: A Twentieth Century Retrospective." *Quarterly Journal of Economics* 115 (1): 45–97.

Heckman, James J., and Sergio Urzua. 2009. "Comparing IV With Structural Models: What Simple IV Can and Cannot Identify." NBER Working Paper No. 14706, National Bureau of Economic Research, Cambridge, MA.

Hecksher, Eli. 1955. *Mercantilism*. 2 vols. London: Allen and Unwin.

Helliwell, John F. 1992. "Empirical Linkages between Democracy and Economic Growth." NBER Working Paper No. 66, National Bureau of Economic Research, Cambridge, MA.

Henderson, David. 2001. *Misguided Virtue*. London: Institute of Economic Affairs.

———. 2009. "Economists and Climate Science: A Critique." *World Economics* 10 (1): 59–90.

Hoover, Kevin D. 2008. "Causality in Economics and Econometrics." In vol. 1, *The New Palgrave Dictionary of Economics*. 2d ed. New York: Palgrave Macmillan.

Houghton, John. 1994. *Global Warming: The Complete Briefing*. Oxford, UK: Lion Hudson.

Hoxby, Caroline M. 2000. "Does Competition among Public Schools Benefit Students and Taxpayers?" *American Economic Review* 90 (5): 1209–38.

Hudson Institute. 2009. *The Index of Global Philanthropy and Remittances*. Washington, DC: Hudson Institute.

————. 2012. *The Index of Global Philanthropy and Remittances*: Washington, DC: Hudson Institute.

Iliffe, John. 1987. *The African Poor*. Cambridge, UK: Cambridge University Press.

Imbens, Guido W. 2009. "Better Late Than Nothing: Some Comments on Deaton (2009) and Heckman and Urzua (2009)." NBER Working Paper No. 14896, National Bureau of Economic Research, Cambridge, MA.

Jimenez, Emmanuel. 1989. "Social Sector Pricing Revisited: A Survey of Some Recent Contributions." In *Proceedings of the World Bank Annual Conference on Development Economics*, 109–38. Washington, DC: World Bank.

Johnson, D. Gale. 2000. "Population, Food, and Knowledge." *American Economic Review* 90 (1): 1–14.

Jones, Eric. 1988. *Growth Recurring*. Oxford, UK: Oxford University Press.

Kagame, Paul. 2009. "Africa Has To Find Its Own Road To Prosperity." *Financial Times*, May 8.

Karlan, Dean, and Jonathan Zinman. 2006. "Expanding Credit Access: Using Randomized Credit Supply Decisions to Estimate the Impacts." Yale University and Dartmouth College. Draft.

Kenny, Charles. 2005. "Why Are We Worried about Income? Everything That Matters Is Converging." *World Development* 33 (1): 1–19.

Keynes, John Neville. 1890. *The Scope and Method of Political Economy*. London: Macmillan.

Kirkby, Jasper, et al. 2011. "Role of Sulphuric Acid, Ammonia and Galactic Cosmic Rays in Atmospheric Aerosol Nucleation," *Nature* 476 (7361): 42–433.

Klitgard, Robert. 1990. *Tropical Gangsters*. New York: Basic Books.

Kim, Ji Hong. 1990. "Korean Industrial Policy in the 1970s: The Heavy and Chemical Industry Drive." KDI Working Paper 9015, Korea Development Institute, Seoul.

Knowles, James C., and Richard Anker. 1981. "An Analysis of Income Transfers in a Developing Country." *Journal of Development Economics* 8 (2): 205–26.

Kraay, Aart, and Claudio Raddatz. 2007. "Poverty Traps, Aid, and Growth." *Journal of Development Economics* 82 (2): 315–47.

Krantz, Olle. 2004. *Economic Growth and Economic Policy in Sweden in the 20th Century: A Comparative Perspective*. Ratio Working Paper No. 32, Ratio Institute, Stockholm.

Kremer, Michael. 1993. "Population Growth and Technological Change: One Million B.C. to 1990." *Quarterly Journal of Economics* 108 (3): 681–716.

————. 2008. "Making Vaccines Pay." In *Reinventing Foreign Aid*, edited by William R. Easterly. Cambridge, MA: MIT Press.

Krueger, Anne O. 1974. "The Political Economy of the Rent-Seeking Society." *American Economic Review* 64 (3): 481–87.

————. 1977. *Growth, Distortions and Patterns of Trade among Many Countries*. Princeton Studies in International Finance No. 40. Princeton, NJ: Princeton University.

————. 1998. "Whither the World Bank?" *Journal of Economic Literature* 36 (4): 1983–2020.

Krugman, Paul R. 1993. "Toward a Counter-Counterrevolution in Development Theory." In *Proceedings of the World Bank Annual Conference on Development Economics 1992: Supplement to the World Bank Economic Review and the World Bank Research Observer*, edited by L. H. Summers and S. Shah, 15–38. Washington, DC: World Bank.

Kupperman, Karen O. 1993. *Providence Island 1630–1641: The Other Puritan Colony*. Cambridge, UK: Cambridge University Press.

La Porta, Rafael, Florencio Lopez-De-Silanes, and Andrei Shleifer. 2008. "The Economic Consequences of Legal Origins." *Journal of Economic Literature* 46 (2): 285–332.

Laffont, Jean-Jacques. 1989. *The Economics of Uncertainty and Information.* Cambridge, MA: MIT Press.

Lal, Deepak. 1972a. "The Foreign Exchange Bottleneck Revisited: A Geometric Note." *Economic Development and Cultural Change* 20 (4): 720–30. Reprinted in *Development Economics*, vol. 3 of *The International Library of Critical Writings in Economics No. 18*, edited by Deepak Lal. Aldershot, UK: Edward Elgar, 1992.

———. 1972b. *Wells and Welfare: An Exploratory Cost-Benefit Study of the Economics of Small Scale Irrigation in Maharashtra.* Paris: OECD Development Centre.

———. 1974. "Methods of Project Analysis: A Review." World Bank Staff Occasional Paper No.16, Johns Hopkins University Press, Baltimore, MD.

———. 1978. *Poverty, Power and Prejudice.* London: Fabian Society. Reprinted in *Against Dirigisme*, edited by Deepak Lal. San Francisco: ICS Press, 1994.

———. 1980. *Prices for Planning: Toward the Reform of Indian Planning.* London: Heinemann Educational Books.

———. 1983. *The Poverty of Development Economics.* London: Institute of Economic Affairs. U.S. editions: Cambridge, MA: Harvard University Press, 1985; 2d Revised and Expanded U.S. Ed., Cambridge, MA: MIT Press, 2000.

———. 1984. "The Political Economy of the Predatory State." DED Discussion Paper No. 105, World Bank, Washington, DC.

———. 1987. "The Political Economy of Economic Liberalization." *World Bank Economic Review* 1 (2): 273–99. Reprinted in *The Repressed Economy: Causes, Consequences, Reform*, edited by Deepak Lal. Economists of the Twentieth Century Series. Aldershot, UK: Edward Elgar, 1993.

———. 1988. *The Hindu Equilibrium.* 2 vols. Oxford: Clarendon Press.

———. 1990. "Fighting Fiscal Privilege: Towards A Fiscal Constitution." Social Market Foundation Paper. London. Reprinted in *Against Dirigisme*, edited by Deepak Lal. San Francisco: ICS Press, 1994.

———. 1992. "Industrialization Strategies and Long-Term Resource Allocation." In *Development Strategies for the 21st Century*, edited by Teruyuki Iwasaki, Takeshi Mori, and Hiroichi Yamaguchi. Tokyo: Institute of Developing Economies. Reprinted in *The Repressed Economy: Causes, Consequences Reform*, edited by Deepak Lal. Economists of the Twentieth Century Series, Aldershot, UK: Edward Elgar, 1993, 241–68.

———. 1993. *The Repressed Economy: Causes, Consequences, Reform.* Economists of the Twentieth Century Series. Aldershot, UK: Edward Elgar.

———. 1994. *Against Dirigisme.* San Francisco: ICS Press.

———. 1995. "India and China: Contrasts in Economic Liberalization." *World Development* 23 (9): 1475–94. Reprinted in *Unfinished Business*, edited by Deepak Lal. New Delhi: Oxford University Press, 1999.

———. 1996. "Participation, Markets, and Democracy." In *New Directions in Development Economics*, edited by M. Lundahl and B. J. Nudulu. London: Routledge. Reprinted in Deepak Lal, *Unfinished Business.* New Delhi: Oxford University Press, 1999.

———. 1998. *Unintended Consequences: the Impact of Factor Endowments, Culture, and Politics On Long-Run Economic Development.* Cambridge, MA: MIT Press.

———. 1999. *Unfinished Business.* New Delhi: Oxford University Press.

———. 2000. "Review of Kenneth Pomeranz's 'The Great Divergence: China, Europe, and the Making of the Modern World Economy.'" EH.Net, October, http://eh.net

/book_reviews/great-divergence-china-europe-and-making-modern-world
-economy.

———. 2003a. "Free Trade Laissez Faire: Has the Wheel Come Full Circle?" *World Economy* 26 (4): 471–82.

———. 2003b. "Review of Liah Greenfield's 'The Spirit of Capitalism: Nationalism and Economic Growth.'" EH.Net, February, http://eh.net/book_reviews/spirit-capitalism-nationalism-and-economic-growth.

———. 2004. *In Praise of Empires: Globalization and Order.* New York: Palgrave Macmillan.

———. 2005a. *The Hindu Equilibrium.* Revised and abridged ed. Oxford, UK: Oxford University Press.

———. 2005b. "The Race for Oil." *Business Standard,* November 15, http://www.business-standard.com/article/Opinion/Deepak-Lal-The-race-for-oil-105111501092_1.html.

———. 2005c. "The Threat to Economic Liberty from International Organizations." *Cato Journal* 25 (3): 503–20.

———. 2006. *Reviving the Invisible Hand: The Case for Classical Liberalism in the Twenty-First Century.* Princeton: Princeton University Press.

———. 2007. "Review of Gerald Meier's 'Biography of a Subject: An Evolution of Development Economics.'" *Journal of Economic Literature* 45 (2): 459–63.

———. 2008a. "An Indian Economic Miracle?" *Cato Journal* 28 (1): 11–34.

———. 2008b. "Biofuels: An Assault on the World's Poor." *Business Standard,* February 19, http://www.business-standard.com/article/opinion/deepak-lal-biofuels-an-assault-on-the-world-s-poor-108021901086_1.html.

———. 2010a. "The Entitlement Economies." *Business Standard,* May 15, http://www.business-standard.com/article/opinion/deepak-lal-the-entitlement-economies-110051500010_1.html.

———. 2010b. "The Great Crash of 2008: Causes and Consequences." *Cato Journal* 30 (2): 265–77.

———. 2011. "On Revolutions." *Business Standard,* February. http://www.econ.ucla.edu/lal/busta/busta0211.pdf.

Lal, Deepak, and Paul Duane. 1972. "A Reappraisal of the Purna Irrigation Project in Maharashtra, India." World Bank, Washington, DC.

Lal, Deepak, and Hla Myint. 1996. *The Political Economy of Poverty, Equity and Growth.* Oxford, UK: Clarendon Press.

Lal, Deepak, and Sarath Rajapatirana. 2007. "The Triumph of Hope over Experience: A Marshall Plan for Sub-Saharan Africa." *Development Policy Outlook* No. 2, American Enterprise Institute, Washington, DC.

Lal, Deepak, and A. Sharma. 2009. "Private Household Transfers and Poverty Alleviation in Rural India: 1998–99." *Margin* 3 (2): 97–112.

Lal, Deepak, and Martin Wolf, eds. 1986. *Stagflation, Savings, and the State.* New York: Oxford University Press.

Lamont, James, and Geoff Dyer. 2009. "China Eyes Industrial Bases in Africa." *Financial Times,* FT.Ccom, December 3, http://www.ft.com/cms/s/0/040beac2-e041-11de-8494-00144feab49a.html#axzz2Lf18FFGn.

Lane-Fox, Robin. 1988. *Pagans and Christians.* London: Penguin.

Leamer, Edward. 1983. "Let's Take the Con Out of Econometrics." *American Economic Review* 73 (1): 31–43.

———. 1984. *Sources of International Comparative Advantage.* Cambridge, MA: MIT Press.

———. 1987. "Patterns of Development in the Three Factor, N-Good General Equilibrium Model." *Journal of Political Economy* 95 (5): 961–99.

———. 2009. *Macroeconomic Patterns and Stories: A Guide for MBAs.* Berlin: Springer.

Lee, Jong-Wha. 1966. "Government Interventions and Productivity Growth in Korean Manufacturing Industries." *Journal of Economic Growth* 1 (3): 391–414.

Lee, Ronald. 1988. "Induced Population Growth and Induced Technological Progress: Their Interaction in the Accelerating Stage." *Mathematical Population Studies* 1 (3): 265–88.

Lerrick, Adam. 2005. "Forgiving the World Bank: But Should We Forget that Lending Failed?" American Enterprise Institute, Washington, DC.

Levine, Ross, and David Renelt. 1992. "A Sensitivity Analysis of Cross-Country Growth Regressions. *American Economic Review* 82 (4): 942–63.

Lewis, W. Arthur. 1955. *The Theory of Economic Growth.* London: Allen and Unwin.

Lin, Justin Y. 1995. "The Needham Puzzle: Why the Industrial Revolution Did Not Originate in China." *Economic Development and Cultural Change* 41 (2): 269–92.

Little, Ian M. D. 1982. *Economic Development Theory, Policy, and International Relations.* New York: Basic Books.

Little, Ian M. D. 1994. "Trade and Industrialization Revisited." *Pakistan Development Review* 33 (4): 359–89.

Little, Ian M. D., and Juliet Clifford. 1965. *International Aid.* London: Allen and Unwin.

Little, Ian M. D., and James A. Mirrlees. 1974. *Project Appraisal and Planning for Developing Countries.* London: Heinemann Educational Books.

Little, Ian M. D., R. N. Cooper, W. M. Corden, and S. Rajapatirana. 1993. *Boom, Crisis, and Adjustment: the Macroeconomic Experience of Developing Countries.* New York: Oxford University Press.

Lluch, Constantino. 1986. "ICOR's, Savings Rates and the Determinants of Public Expenditure in Developing Countries." In *Stagflation, Savings, and the State*, edited by Deepak Lal and Martin Wolf. New York: Oxford University Press.

Loayza, Norman, Klaus Schmidt-Hebbel, and Luis Serven. 2000. "Saving in Developing Countries: An Overview." *World Bank Economic Review* 14 (3): 393–414.

Lucas, Robert E., Jr. 2002. *Lectures on Economic Growth.* Cambridge, MA: Harvard University Press.

Lucas, Robert E., Jr., and Oded Stark. 1985. "Motivations to Remit: Evidence from Botswana." *Journal of Political Economy* 93 (5): 901–18.

Lundahl, Mats, and Michael L. Wyzan, eds. 2005. *The Political Economy of Reform Failure.* London: Routledge.

Maddison, Angus, and Associates. 1992. *The Political Economy of Poverty, Equity, and Growth: Brazil and Mexico.* New York: Oxford University Press.

Maddison, Angus. 2001. *The World Economy: A Millennial Perspective.* Paris: OECD.

———. 2007a. *Chinese Economic Performance in the Long Run—Second Edition Revised and Updated: 960–2030 AD.* Development Centre Studies, Paris: OECD.

———. 2007b. *Contours of the World Economy, 1–2030 AD.* Oxford, UK: Oxford University Press.

———. 2009. "Measuring the Economic Performance of Transition Economies: Some Lessons from Chinese Experience." *Review of Income and Wealth* 55 (s1):423–41.

———. 2008. "The West and the Rest in the World Economy: 1000–2030: Madisonian and Malthusian Interpretations." *World Economics* 9 (4): 75–99.

Mallaby, Sebastian. 2013. "Africa Is Hooked in Growth after 12 Years of Progress," *Financial Times*, January 2.

Mann, Michael E., Raymond S. Bradley, and Malcolm Hughes. 1998. "Global Scale Temperature Patterns and Climate Forcing Over the Past Six Centuries." *Nature* 392: 779–87.

———. 1999. "Northern Hemisphere Temperatures during the Past Millennium: Inferences, Uncertainties and Limitations." *Geophysical Research Letters* 26 (6): 759–62.

Matthews, R. C. O. 1986. "The Economics of Institutions and the Sources of Growth." *Economic Journal* 96 (384): 903–18.

McCleary, Rachel M., and Robert J. Barro. 2006. "Religion and Economy." *Journal of Economic Perspectives* 20 (2): 49–72.

McCloskey, D. M. 1985. *The Rhetoric of Economics*. Madison, WI: University of Wisconsin Press.

McEvedy, Colin, and Richard Jones. 1978. *Atlas of World Population History*. London: Penguin Books.

McIntyre, Stephen, and Ross McKitrick. 2003. "Corrections to the Mann et al. (1998) Proxy Database and Northern Hemispheric Average Temperature Series." *Energy and Environment* 14 (6): 752–71.

McIntyre, Stephen, and Ross McKitrick. 2005. "The M & M Critique of the MBH98 Northern Hemisphere Climate Index, Update and Applications." *Energy and Environment*, 16 (1): 69–99.

McKenzie, David, and Christopher Woodruff. 2006. "Do Entry Costs Provide an Empirical Basis for Poverty Traps? Evidence from Mexican Microenterprises." *Economic Development and Cultural Change* 55 (1): 3–42.

McLean, John. 2008. *Prejudiced Authors, Prejudiced Findings*. Haymarket, VA: Science and Public Policy Institute.

McNeill, William H. 1982. *The Pursuit of Power*. Chicago: University of Chicago Press.

Meerman, J. 1979. *Public Expenditure in Malaysia: Who Benefits and Why?* New York: Oxford University Press.

Meier, Gerald. 2005. *Biography of a Subject: An Evolution of Development Economics*. New York: Oxford University Press.

Meltzer, A., and S. F. Richard. 1981. "Test of a Rational Theory of the Size of Government." *Journal of Political Economy*, 89 (5): 914–27.

Mesa-Lago, Carmelo. 1989. *Ascent to Bankruptcy: Financing Social Security in Latin America*. Pittsburgh, PA: University of Pittsburgh Press.

Miguel, Edward, and Michael Kremer. 2004. "Worms: Identifying Impacts on Education and Health in the Presence of Treatment Externalities." *Econometrica* 72 (1): 159–217.

Miguel, Edward, Shanker Satyanath, and Ernest Sergenti. 2004. "Economic Shocks and Civil Conflict: An Instrumental Variables Approach." *Journal of Political Economy* 112 (4): 725–53.

Mill, John Stuart. 1843. *A System of Logic*. London: J. W. Parker.

Minhas, Bagicha S., K. S. Parikh, and T. N. Srinvisan, with S. A. Marglin and T. E. Weisskopf. 1972. *Scheduling the Operations of the Hjakra System*. Calcutta: Indian Statistical Institute.

Mohan, C. Raja. 2010. "Chinese Takeaway." *Indian Express*, March 11, http://www.indianexpress.com/news/chinese-take-away/709394/.

Montford, Andrew W. 2010. *"The Hockey Stick Illusion: Climategate and the Corruption of Science."* London: Stacey International.

———. 2011. "Cloud Experiment Links." http://www.bishop-hill.net/blog/2011/8/24/cloud-experiment-links.html.

Morduch, Jonathan. 1999. "The Role of Subsidies in Microfinance: Evidence from the Grameen Bank." *Journal of Development Economics* 60 (1): 229–48.

Morse, Richard M. 1964. "The Heritage of Latin America." In *The Founding of New Societies*, edited by L. Hartz. New York: Harcourt, Brace and World.

Mosley, Paul. 1987. *Overseas Aid*. Brighton, UK: Wheatsheaf, 1987.

Moyo, Dambisa. 2009. *Dead Aid: Why Aid Is Not Working and How There Is Another Way for Africa*. London: Allen Lane.

Mudelsee, Manfred. 2001. "The Phase Relations among Atmospheric CO_2 Content, Temperature and Global Ice Volume over the Past 420ka." *Quaternary Science Reviews* 20 (4): 583–89.

Munshi, Kaivan, and Mark Rosenzweig. 2008. "The Efficacy of Parochial Politics." NBER Working Paper No. 14335, National Bureau of Economic Research, Cambridge, MA.

Murphy, Kevin M., Andrei Shleifer, and Robert W. Vishny. 1989. "Industrialization and the Big Push." *Journal of Political Economy* 97 (5): 1003–26.

Murthy, N. Satyanarayana, Manoj Panda, and Krit Parikh. 2007. "CO_2 Emission Reduction Strategies and Economic Development of India." *Margin* 1 (1): 85–118.

Needham, Joseph. 1978. *The Shorter Science and Civilization in China*. 3 vols. Cambridge, UK: Cambridge University Press.

Noland, Marcus, and Howard Pack. 2003. *Industrial Policy in an Era of Globalization: Lessons From Asia*. Washington, DC: Institute for International Economics.

Nordhaus, William D. 1994. *Managing the Global Commons*. Cambridge, MA: MIT Press.

———. 2006. "The 'Stern Review' of the Economics of Climate Change." NBER Working Paper No. 12741, National Bureau of Economic Research, Cambridge, MA.

———. 2007. *The Challenge of Global Warming: Economic Models and Environmental Policy*. New Haven, CT: Yale University Press.

Nordhaus, William D., and Joseph Boyer. 2000. *Warming the World*. Cambridge, MA: MIT Press.

North, Douglass C. 1994. "Economic Performance through Time." *American Economic Review* 84 (3): 359–68.

———. 2005. *Understanding the Process of Economic Change*. Princeton, NJ: Princeton University Press.

North, Douglass C., and Robert P. Thomas. 1973. *The Rise of the Western World*. Cambridge, UK: Cambridge University Press.

North, Douglass C., and Barry R. Weingast. 1989. "Constitutions and Commitments: the Evolution of Institutions Governing Public Choice in Seventeenth Century England." *Journal of Economic History* 49 (4): 803–32.

National Research Council. 2006. *Surface Temperature Reconstructions for the Last 2,000 Years*. Washington, DC: National Academic Press.

Nurkse, Ragnar. 1953. *Problems of Capital formation in Underdeveloped Countries*, Oxford, UK: Basil Blackwell.

Oakeshott, Michael. 1993. *Morality and Politics in Modern Europe*. New Haven, CT: Yale University Press.

Oberai, A. S., and H. K. M. Singh. 1980. "Migration, Remittances and Rural Development." *International Labor Review* 119 (2): 229–41 .

Organisation for Economic Co-operation and Development (OECD). 2007. *Policy Coherence for Development: Migration and Developing Countries 2007*. Paris: OECD Development Centre.

Pack, Howard, and Larry E. Westphal. 1986. "Industrial Strategy and Technological Change." *Journal of Development Economics* 22 (1): 87–128.

Paz, Octavio. 1988. *Sor Juana*. Cambridge, MA: Harvard University Press.

Peltzman, S. 1980. "The Growth of Government." *Journal of Law and Economics* 23 (2): 209–87.

Pham, J. Peter. 2007. "Pandas in the Heart of Darkness: Chinese Peacekeepers in Africa." *World Defense Review* 25, October 25, http://worlddefensereview.com/pham102507.shtml.

Philipson, Tomas J., and Rodrigo R. Soares. 2002. "World Inequality and the Rise in Longevity." In *Annual World Bank Conference on Development Economics 2001/2002*, edited by Boris Pleskovic and Nicholas Stern. Washington, DC: World Bank.

Pilling, David. 2009. "Africa Builds As Beijing Scrambles To Invest." *Financial Times*, December 10.

———. 2011. "Libya Gives Beijing A Lesson in Intervention." *Financial Times*, March 3.

Pinker, Stephen. 2002. *The Blank Slate*. New York: Viking, Penguin.

Platteau, J.-P. 2000. "Traditional Systems of Social Security and Hunger Insurance: Some Lessons from the Evidence Pertaining to Third World Village Societies." In Pomeranz, Kenneth E., *The Great Divergence: China, Europe and the Making of the Modern World Economy*. Princeton, NJ: Princeton University Press, 2001.

Pomeranz, Kenneth E. 2001. *The Great Divergence: China, Europe and the Making of the Modern World Economy*. Princeton, NJ: Princeton University Press.

Przeworski, Adam, and Fernando Limongi. 1993. "Political Regimes and Economic Growth." *Journal of Economic Literature* 7 (3): 51–69.

Pritchett, Lant. 1997. "Divergence, Big Time." *Journal of Economic Perspectives* 11 (3): 3–17.

Pryor, Frederic L. 1990. *The Political Economy of Poverty Equity and Growth: Malawi and Madagascar*. New York: Oxford University Press.

Pryor, Frederic L., and S. B. Maurer. 1982. "On Induced Economic Change in Pre-Capitalist Societies." *Journal of Development Economics* 10 (3): 325–53.

Radelet, Steven, and Ruth Levine. 2008. "Can We Build A Better Mousetrap? Three New Institutions To Improve Aid Effectiveness." In *Reinventing Foreign Aid*, edited by William Easterly 431–60, Cambridge, MA: MIT Press.

Ratha, Dilip. 2007. "Leveraging Remittances for Development." World Bank Development Prospect Group. Paper Presented at the Second Plenary Meeting of the Leading Group on Solidarity Levies to Fund Development, February 6–7, Oslo, Norway.

Ratha, D. and W. Shaw. 2006. *Global Economic Prospects 2006: Implications of Remittances and Migration*. Washington, DC: World Bank.

Ravallion, Martin. 1991. "Reaching the Poor through Public Employment: Arguments, Evidence and Lessons from South Asia." *World Bank Research Observer* 6 (2): 153–76.

———. 1992. "Poverty Comparisons: A Guide to Concepts and Methods." Living Standards Measurement Study, Working Paper No. 88, World Bank, Washington, DC.

Rempel, H., and R. Lobdell. 1978. "The Role of Urban-to-Rural Remittances in Rural Development." *Journal of Development Studies* 14 (2): 324–41.

Reynolds, Lloyd, G. 1985. *Economic Growth in the Third World*. New Haven, CT: Yale University Press.

Rimmer, Douglas. 1992. *Staying Poor: Ghana's Political Economy, 1950–1990*. Oxford, UK: Pergamon Press.

Rodrik, Dani. 1994. "Getting Interventions Right: How South Korea and Taiwan Grew Rich." NBER Working Paper No. 4964, National Bureau of Economic Research, Cambridge, MA.

———. 1995. "Trade Strategy, Investment, and Exports: Another Look at East Asia." CEPR Discussion Paper No. 1305, Centre for Economic Policy Research, London.

———. 1999. *The New Global Economy and Developing Countries: Making Openness Work.* Policy Essay 24, Overseas Development Council, Washington, DC.

Rosenstein-Rodan, Paul N. 1943. "Problems of Industrialisation of Eastern and South-Eastern Europe." *Economic Journal* 53 (2010/2011): 202–11.

———. 1961. "Notes on the Theory of the 'Big Push.'" In *Economic Development for Latin America,* edited by Howard S. Ellis and Henry C. Wallich. New York: St. Martin's.

Rosenzweig, Mark. 1988. "Risk, Implicit Contracts and the Family in Rural Areas of Low-Income Countries." *Economic Journal* 98 (393): 1148–70.

Rottenberg, Simon, Claudio Gonzales-Vega, and Edgardo Favaro. 1993. *The Political Economy of Poverty, Equity, and Growth: Costa Rica and Uruguay.* New York: Oxford University Press.

Sachs, Jeffrey D., John W. McArthur, Guido Schmidt-Traub, Margaret Kruk, Chandra Bahadur, Michael Faye, and Gordon McCord. 2004. "Ending Africa's Poverty Trap." In *Brookings Papers on Economic Activity,* 1, 117–240, Brookings Institution, Washington, DC.

Sachs, Jeffrey. 2005. *The End of Poverty: Economic Possibilities for Our Time.* New York: Penguin Press.

Sala-i-Martin, Xavier. 2006. "The World Distribution of Income: Falling Poverty and . . . Convergence, Period." *Quarterly Journal of Economics* 121 (2): 351–97.

Scafetta, Nicola, and Bruce J. West. 2008. "Is Climate Sensitive to Solar Variability?" *Physics Today* 61 (3): 50–51.

Scafetta, Nicola, and Richard C. Willson. 2009. "ACRIM-Gap and TSI Trend Issue Resolved Using a Surface Magnetic Flux TSI Proxy Model." *Geophysical Research Letters* 36 (5): 1–5.

Schain, Martin A., ed. 2001. *The Marshall Plan: Fifty Years After.* New York: Palgrave.

Schumpeter, J. A. 1950. *Capitalism, Socialism, and Democracy.* New York: Harper and Row.

Scitovsky, Tibor. 1954. "Two Concepts of External Economies." *Journal of Political Economy* 62 (2): 143–51.

Seabright, Paul. 2004. *The Company of Strangers: A Natural History of Economic Life.* Princeton, NJ: Princeton University Press.

Selowsky, Marcello. 1979. *Who Benefits From Public Expenditure? A Case Study of Colombia.* New York: Oxford University Press.

Sen, Amartya K. 1982. *Poverty and Famines.* New York: Clarendon Press.

Shaviv, Nir, and Jan Veizer. 2003. "Celestial Driver of Phanerozoic Climate?" *Geological Society of America Today* 13 (7): 4–10.

Simon, Julian. 1981. *The Ultimate Resource.* Princeton: Princeton University Press.

Singer, S. Fred. 2010. "Junkscience: Climategate Distortion of Temperature Data." SEPP Science Editorial, http://www.sepp.org/science-editorials.cfm?whichcat=Global%20Warming&whichsubcat=Junkscience#A25.

Skocpol, Theda. 1979. *States and Social Revolutions.* Cambridge, UK: Cambridge University Press.

Smith, David. 2012. "China's Booming Trade with Africa Helps Tone Its Diplomatic Muscle." *The Guardian,* March 22.

Smith, Heather. 2000. *Industry Policy in Taiwan and Korea in the 1980s.* Cheltenham: Edward Elgar.

Solow, Barbara I. 1991. "Slavery and Colonization." In *Slavery and the Rise of the Atlantic System,* edited by B. I. Solow. Cambridge, UK: Cambridge University Press.

Solow, Robert M. 1970. *Growth Theory: An Exposition.* Oxford: Clarendon Press.

———. 1985. "Economic History and Economics" *American Economic Review* 75 (2): 328–31.

———. 1994. "Perspectives on Growth Theory." *Journal of Economic Perspectives* 8 (1): 45–54.

Squire, Lyn. 1993. "Fighting Poverty." *American Economic Review* 83 (2): 377–82.

Squire, Lyn, and Herman van der Tak. 1975. *Economic Analysis of Projects.* Washington, DC: International Bank for Reconstruction and Development.

Srinivasan, T. N. 1994. "Data Base for Development Analysis: An Overview." *Journal of Development Economics* 44 (1): 3–27.

Stern, Nicholas. 2007. *The Economics of Climate Change: The Stern Review.* Cambridge, UK: Cambridge University Press.

Stigler, George, ed. 1988. *Chicago Studies in Political Economy.* Chicago: Chicago University Press.

Stiglitz, Joseph. 2002. *Globalization and Its Discontents.* London: Allen Lane.

Sugden, R. 1993. "Welfare, Resources, and Capabilities: A Review of Inequality Reexamined by Amartya Sen." *Journal of Economic Literature* 31 (4): 1947–86.

Svensmark, Henrik. 2007. "Cosmoclimatology." *Astronomy and Geophysics* 48 (1): 1.18–1.24.

———. 2011. "The Cosmic Ray/CLOUD Seeding Hypothesis is Converging with Reality." The Blogosphere, ICECAP, http://icecap.us/index.php/go/joes-blog/ henrik_svensmark_the_cosmic_ray_cloud_seeding_hypothesis_is_converging_ with/.

Svensmark, Henrik, and Nigel Calder. 2007. *The Chilling Stars: A New Theory of Climate Change.* London: Icon Books.

Swamy, G. 1981. "International Migrant Workers Remittances: Issues and Prospects." World Bank Staff Working Paper No. 481, World Bank, Washington, DC.

Tocqueville, A. de. (1835) 1966. *Democracy in America.* London: Collins.

Thomas, Hugh. 1979. *A History of the World.* New York: Harper and Row.

Titmus, Richard M. 1966. *Essays On the Welfare State.* London: Unwin University Press.

Thorbecke, Eric, and Henry Wan. 1999. *Taiwan's Development Experience: Lessons on Roles of Government and Market.* Boston: Kluwer Academic Publishers.

Tooley, James. 2009. *The Beautiful Tree: A Personal Journey into How the World's Poorest People Are Educating Themselves.* Washington, DC: Cato Institute.

Transparency International. 2012. *Corruption Perceptions Index 2006,* www.transparency .org/policy_research/surveys_indices/cpi.

United Nations Development Program. 1998. *Human Development Report.* New York: Oxford University Press.

Urquiola, Miguel, and Eric Verhoogen. 2009. "Class-Size Caps, Sorting, and the Regression-Discontinuity Design." *American Economic Review* 99(1): 179–215.

———. 2009. "Class-Size Caps, Sorting, and the Regression Discontinuity Design." *American Economic Review* 99 (1): 179–215.

U.S. Environmental Protection Agency. 2009. "Proposed NCEE Comments on Draft-Technical Support Document for Endangered Analysis for Greenhouse Gas Emissionsunder the Clean Air Act," available at http://cei.org/sites/default/files/ DOC062509-004.pdf.

Veizer, Jan. 2005. "Celestial Climate Driver." *Geoscience Canada* 32 (1).

Veliz, Claudio. 1994. *The New World of the Gothic Fox*. Berkeley: University of California Press.

Viner, Jacob. 1931. "Cost and Supply Curves." *Zeitschrift für Nationaükonomie* 3: 23–46. Reprinted in *Readings in Price Theory*, edited by G. J. Stigler and K. E. Boulding. London: Allen and Unwin.

Wegman, Edward J., David Scott, and Yasmin Said. 2006. "Ad Hoc Committee Report on the 'Hockey Stick.'" Global Climatic Reconstruction, http://www.uoguelph .ca/~rmckitri/research/WegmanReport.pdf .

White, Lynn. 1962. *Medieval Technology and Social Change*. Oxford: Clarendon Press.

Williamson, John. 1989. "What Washington Means By Policy Reform." In *Latin American Readjustment: How Much Has Happened?* edited by J. Williamson. Washington, DC: Institute for International Economics.

———. 2002. "Did the Washington Consensus Fail?" Speech at the Center for Strategic and International Studies, Washington, DC, November 6.

World Bank. 1992. *Poverty Reduction Handbook*. Washington, DC: World Bank.

———. 2004. *World Development Report*. New York: Oxford University Press.

———. 2006. *World Development Indicators 2006*. World Bank, Washington, DC, http:// data.worldbank.org/products/data-books/WDI-2006.

———. 2007. *Worldwide Governance Indicators: 1996–2006* and *Worldwide Governance Indicators 2007*, www.govindicators.org.

———. 2009. *World Development Indicators 2009*. World Bank, Washington, DC, http:// data.worldbank.org/products/data-books/WDI-2009

———. 2012. "An Update to the World Bank's Estimates of Consumption Poverty in the Developing World." World Bank, Washington, DC, http://siteresources.worldbank .org/INTPOVCALNET/Resources/Global_Poverty_Update_2012_02-29-12.pdf.

Worrall, John. 2002. "What Evidence in Evidence-Based Medicine? *Philosophy of Science* 69, (S3): S316–S330.

Wrigley, Edward A. 1988. *Continuity, Chance, and Change: the Character of the Industrial Revolution in England*. Cambridge, UK: Cambridge University Press.

Wynia, Gary W. 1990. *The Politics of Latin American Development*. 3rd ed. Cambridge, UK: Cambridge University Press.

Yoo, Jung-Ho. 1990. "The Industrial Policy of the 1970s and the Evolution of the Manufacturing Sector." KDI Working Paper 9017, Korea Development Institute, Seoul.

Xinhua. 2012. "UN Official Praises Chinese Peacekeepers' Performance." *Xinhua*, July 7.

Index

About the Author

Deepak Lal is the James S. Coleman Professor Emeritus of International Development Studies at the University of California at Los Angeles, professor emeritus of political economy at University College London, and a senior fellow at the Cato Institute. He was a member of the Indian Foreign Service (1963-66) and has served as a consultant to the Indian Planning Commission, the World Bank, the Organization for Economic Cooperation and Development, various UN agencies, South Korea, and Sri Lanka. From 1984 to 1987, he was research administrator at the World Bank. Lal is the author of a number of books, including *The Poverty of Development Economics; The Hindu Equilibrium; Against Dirigisme; The Political Economy of Poverty, Equity and Growth; Unintended Consequences: The Impact of Factor Endowments, Culture, and Politics on Long-Run Economic Performance;* and *Reviving the Invisible Hand: The Case for Classical Liberalism in the 21st Century.*

Cato Institute

Founded in 1977, the Cato Institute is a public policy research foundation dedicated to broadening the parameters of policy debate to allow consideration of more options that are consistent with the principles of limited government, individual liberty, and peace. To that end, the Institute strives to achieve greater involvement of the intelligent, concerned lay public in questions of policy and the proper role of government.

The Institute is named for Cato's Letters, libertarian pamphlets that were widely read in the American Colonies in the early 18th century and played a major role in laying the philosophical foundation for the American Revolution.

Despite the achievement of the nation's Founders, today virtually no aspect of life is free from government encroachment. A pervasive intolerance for individual rights is shown by government's arbitrary intrusions into private economic transactions and its disregard for civil liberties. And while freedom around the globe has notably increased in the past several decades, many countries have moved in the opposite direction, and most governments still do not respect or safeguard the wide range of civil and economic liberties.

To address those issues, the Cato Institute undertakes an extensive publications program on the complete spectrum of policy issues. Books, monographs, and shorter studies are commissioned to examine the federal budget, Social Security, regulation, military spending, international trade, and myriad other issues. Major policy conferences are held throughout the year, from which papers are published thrice yearly in the Cato Journal. The Institute also publishes the quarterly magazine Regulation.

In order to maintain its independence, the Cato Institute accepts no government funding. Contributions are received from foundations, corporations, and individuals, and other revenue is generated from the sale of publications. The Institute is a nonprofit, tax-exempt, educational foundation under Section 501(c)3 of the Internal Revenue Code.

CATO INSTITUTE
1000 Massachusetts Ave., N.W.
Washington, D.C. 20001
www.cato.org